Bomber County

DANIEL SWIFT

D1647379

PENGUIN BOOKS

PENGUIN BOOKS

Published by the Penguin Group
Penguin Books Ltd, 80 Strand, London WC2R 0RL, England
Penguin Group (USA) Inc., 375 Hudson Street, New York, New York 10014, USA
Penguin Group (Canada), 90 Eglinton Avenue East, Suite 700, Toronto, Ontario, Canada M4P 2Y3
(a division of Pearson Penguin Canada Inc.)
Penguin Ireland, 25 St Stephen's Green, Dublin 2, Ireland (a division of Penguin Books Ltd)
Penguin Group (Australia), 250 Camberwell Road,
Camberwell, Victoria 3124, Australia (a division of Pearson Australia Group Pty Ltd)
Penguin Books India Pvt Ltd, 11 Community Centre,
Panchsheel Park, New Delhi – 110 017, India
Penguin Group (NZ), 67 Apollo Drive, Rosedale, Auckland 0632, New Zealand
(a division of Pearson New Zealand Ltd)
Penguin Books (South Africa) (Pty) Ltd, 24 Sturdee Avenue,
Rosebank, Johannesburg 2196, South Africa

Penguin Books Ltd, Registered Offices: 80 Strand, London WC2R 0RL, England

www.penguin.com

First published in the United States of America by Farrar, Straus and Giroux 2010
First published in Great Britain by Hamish Hamilton 2010
Published in Penguin Books 2011

1

Printed in Great Britain by Clays Ltd, St Ives plc

A CIP catalogue record for this book is available from the British Library

ISBN: 978-0-141-03699-1

www.greenpenguin.co.uk

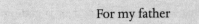

For my father

Can you read all this – my writing my dear is getting worse and worse. Doing too much ~~writing~~ flying I expect.

James Eric Swift, 16 June 1941

No war poetry can be expected from the Royal Air Force.

Robert Graves, 23 October 1941

Contents

Prologue: A Refusal to Mourn

The beach where the body washed up is wide and white, with cafés raised on stilts and couples drinking beer in the sand. There are windsurfers; children smacking the waves. He came to land in the middle of a summer holiday, and the mismatch is startling after the calm of the cemeteries where my father and I have spent the day. We buy ice creams in Callantsoog, the mall of a town that leads from the beach, and climb the high dunes.

Ice creams are 'ijscoupes' in Dutch. My father and I keep on our shoes as we walk on the sand, although we are surrounded by swimming costumes. There are promisingly sombre and warlike defences, great lines of black granite stretching out into the sea, and we marvel at them for a moment. What we are doing on the beach is looking for the memory of a corpse. But there is no sense of him here for there is no sense of debt. These are happy holidaymakers, and they are turning leisurely away.

The cemeteries scattered along the strange curve of land that is Noord-Holland are rich with duty. 'He died that we may live,' read so many of the gravestones, and the visitors' books are a chorus of insistent remembrance. 'We will not forget you,' the visitors write. On these hot days in June we are alone in the cemeteries.

In the first week of June 2007, my father and I took a trip. We went to Holland for an imperfectly marked anniversary, for on 12 June sixty-four years earlier my grandfather, my father's father, was killed. He was the pilot of a Lancaster bomber on a raid on Münster, and his plane never returned. Rather, his body washed up on a beach in Holland, and is buried there today.

Of the fall, little is known. The letter from the Air Ministry to my grandmother explains that his body was found at Callantsoog on 17 June 1943, and two days later buried at Huisduinen cemetery. In 1946, the corpse was disinterred and moved a hundred miles south, to Bergen op Zoom. There were six other men on the plane. On 14 August 1943, the body of Sergeant J. J. Anderton washed ashore twelve miles south, at Bergen aan Zee. Anderton was the rear gunner on the Lancaster; the bodies of the five remaining crew members were never found. All we had was a date and a place, so we went to look and to work out what these words meant, the strange Dutch names with too many vowels.

We start in Brussels and drive north. The landscape is washed out; there is not very much of it, here. Holland is so flat that it looks like an airfield, and this effect is deepened by its most striking characteristic, the great new windmills, each a hundred feet high with huge white propellers. The plain of reclaimed land, sea-flat, round the archipelago of Zeeland leads to the spike of Noord-Holland, stretching north of Rotterdam. On one side is the North Sea, and the other is the IJsselmeer, the inland sea.

Holland is so flat that you might land a plane on it, if you had to; Holland is so flat you might attempt a crash landing. But Holland is also so close to England that you might think you could make it home to one of the emergency airstrips in Norfolk, just across the North Sea. These skies were full of planes on the night of 11 June 1943. There were 783 British bombers raiding Düsseldorf, and a further seventy-two on Münster, and all of them, in the hours before dawn, were trying to get home. Two Lancasters crashed in the IJsselmeer; another Lancaster and a Halifax downed in the Oosterschelde, one of the narrow channels in the Zeeland archipelago. Two more Lancasters and two Wellingtons fell to the sea off Noord-Holland. Further north, in the Waddenzee off Fryslân, a Stirling on its return from Düsseldorf was lost, and a Halifax from 51 Squadron survived all the way across the North Sea only to be shot down by a British anti-aircraft convoy just shy of the coast of Norfolk.

These are only the bombers we know were lost at sea that night. Two further Lancasters, two Wellingtons, a Halifax and a Stirling were lost without trace, and a further thirty-three planes crashed on land. They rained down in northern Belgium and near the target zones; they were shot down by Luftwaffe night-fighters at Eindhoven and Rotterdam or by the flak line at Amsterdam. Thirteen bombers fell on the Netherlands that night – five Lancasters, five Halifaxes and three Wellingtons – and this was the way home.

Flying west over the sea-flat landscape of Holland, before you reach the coast, a range of dunes a hundred feet high rises up, dividing the beaches from the fields. At Wijk aan Zee, sometime on that same morning of 12 June 1943, a Lancaster on its way back from Düsseldorf crashed on the dunes, and the crew are buried together in the civilian cemetery at Beverwijk; the seven are boxed around in stone and their graves are covered by the same creeping plant. Behind them is a single grave: Flying Officer H. C. Treherne of the Royal Canadian Air Force, who died on 29 June 1943. His body was found on the same beach on 14 August of that year. He was from Truro, in Nova Scotia, and he was twenty-two years old.

At the tip of Noord-Holland, where the dunes reach and finally fall into the sea, there is a bright red lighthouse. My grandfather was first buried here, on 19 June 1943, in a grave numbered 189 at Huisduinen cemetery. Huisduinen means 'House of the Dunes': it is a seaside resort, full of rows of brick houses and plump Dutch and German holidaymakers. In a café overlooking the sea and the lighthouse there are faded sepia photographs of people on the beach in the 1930s, before the war, and this sunny day in early June there are tables of schoolchildren raising their hands and eating plates of chips, drinking Coke.

The cemetery is shambolic, rambling. There is a Jewish corner, a children's section, a little field of Islamic graves. The dunes are creeping in. The paths are sandy, and the people buried often have a connection to the sea. In the 1950s, a boatful of Greek sailors drowned off the coast, and they are here, as are twenty Dutch soldiers killed in 1940 or 1944, at the fall or the liberation of Holland.

At the cemetery, a groundsman on a tractor tells us in broken English about the flying monument at Den Helder, the tough little port round the bay. In the town, an ancient man walks us through the hot grid of streets to find it. It is a memorial for the North Coates Strike Wing. North Coates is an airbase in Lincolnshire, for the Bristol Beaufighters that attacked shipping along the Dutch coast. 241 airmen from North Coates were lost, and on the memorial two officers are named. Pilot Officer Ernest Kidd was twenty-four, and Pilot Officer Harold Stevenson was twenty-two, and both were lost in a raid of 18 July 1943.

Kidd and Stevenson, the pilot and the navigator from Lincoln-shire, are not buried here. Their bodies are down the coast, where they today lie three rows from my grandfather. This curious busi-ness with the body, when I first read of it, struck me as undignified and somehow lonely, and it was a comfort to see, here, that he was not alone. Crews from at least eleven other planes were first buried at Huisduinen, and then at Bergen op Zoom: a Lancaster from 156 Squadron raiding Essen was shot down over the sea on 3 April 1943; the crew of a Halifax, raiding Leipzig, lost on 4 December of that same year; as were a Lancaster raiding Brunswick and a Whitley raiding Bremen. These bodies were recovered from the water or from the beach. His fate was common.

Squadron Leader James Eric Swift is buried in row 32B of Bergen op Zoom cemetery. '12 June 1943,' it says on his gravestone, below his name: 'The peace of God which passeth all understanding'. To his right is Flying Officer M. W. P. Clarke, the pilot of a Halifax crashed into the sea on 22 June 1943; behind him is Sergeant F. A. J. Edwards, the wireless operator on another Halifax, again lost at sea on 26 July 1943. He is surrounded by men who shared his end in different planes and on different raids. To his left are four Polish air-men, their graves tucked closely together, whose Wellington was shot down by a night-fighter on 6 June 1942. One row in front of him are the crew of a Stirling lost just south of Den Helder on 4 June 1942.

The cemeteries daydream of order. They are administered by the Commonwealth War Graves Commission, which was founded in May 1917 to discipline the tombs of First World War dead. As Sir Frederic Kenyon, the director of the British Museum who was in 1918 hired by the Commission to justify the design of cemeteries, wrote: 'The rows of headstones in their ordered ranks carry on the military idea, giving the appearance as of a battalion on parade, and suggesting the spirit of discipline and order which is the soul of an army.' Wherever possible, a crew or unit who died together are buried together, with no precedence given to higher ranks. The white headstones stand in regular lines, and the design is common to each cemetery, whether in Holland, North Africa or Malaysia. Each headstone is two feet six inches high, and one foot three inches wide; the inscription gives rank, name, regiment number and date of death. In any cemetery with more than forty graves there is a Cross of Sacrifice, a tall white crucifix, and where there are more than a thousand the cemetery will also include a Stone of Remembrance, a wide flat slab with three shallow steps leading up to it.

'It is clearly undesirable,' wrote Kenyon, 'to allow free scope for the effusions of the mortuary mason, the sentimental versifier, or the crank', and while he does not mention them here, he has in mind the families of the dead. For these rigorously uniform cemeteries, the same and the same and the same, were greeted with horror when the designs were first made public in 1919. There were debates in Parliament, and letters to the newspapers. As Lady Florence Cecil, wife of the Bishop of Exeter and mother of three sons lost in the First World War, wrote to *The Times* on 23 December 1919: 'these memorials to the dead do not as a rule appeal to mourners either collectively or as individuals. The bereaved desire consolation from personal tributes to their dead, not from well-drilled patterned uniformity.' Not only do we mourn for individuals, Lady Cecil is saying: we mourn also as individuals, and how we act at the grave may be as much about our own desires as it is about the body in the ground before us.

Against such objections, however, the cemeteries stand today in strict and perfect lines, empty in the Dutch afternoons. Kenyon wrote: 'Each cemetery, it is hoped, will be beautiful, or at least satisfying in itself; but their effect becomes cumulative if all, under whatever circumstances, have the same main features and express the same ideas', and my father and I continue to visit cemeteries along the curve of the coast even after we have found my grandfather's grave. On the morning he fell there were six others with him: a young engineer named Norman Greenwood and the navigator, Cornelius Geary; the gunners, Charles Nash and James Anderton; the bomb aimer, Daniel Thomas, and the wireless operator, Christian Miller. Anderton spent two months in the water and is buried at a different cemetery, called Bergen General, and as if to distribute our tentative mourning, my father and I drive up to see him too.

The force of the cemeteries lies in their repetition of a boast: an ideal of what Kenyon called 'the whole sense of comradeship and of common service', where officers are buried by their men, pilots with their gunners. As Calvin wrote in 1574: 'death sheweth what we bee, and what is our nature.' Here, these men are shown to be soldiers and airmen, and the other traces of their lives – the whirls of experience and oddity that made them individuals – are irrelevant. In civilian cemeteries, gravestones will list a date of birth as well as of death, the moment of entry into as well as the point of departure from the little story of a life. The war graves list only the date of death, as if to say: when their lives began and what they did before, that is not of our concern.

But the graves are not wholly mute, for Kenyon allowed one element of variation. 'Leave should be given,' he wrote:

> for a short inscription of not more than three lines, to be added on the application of the next-of-kin, or other person or organisation

(such as a regiment or religious community) whose claim is approved by the Commission, and at the cost of the applicant; but that the inscription must be of the nature of a text or prayer, and that the Commission shall have absolute power of rejection or acceptance.

Anything you write at a grave takes upon itself the nature of a prayer, but the humble verses on the stones at Bergen op Zoom are simple rhymes. 'We would give the world and more / To see the face we loved / come smiling at the door,' reads one marker, and another speaks of 'A loving husband / Always ready to aid / One that was better / God never made'. They rhyme because rhyme is orderly, and because it is easy to remember.

Sometimes an unexpected poetry appears. On the grave of T. McCluskey, a flight engineer who died on 1 June 1944, is the claim: 'Cut is the branch that might have grown full straight', taken without attribution from Christopher Marlowe's savage morality play about an over-ambitious scholar, *Dr Faustus*. Elsewhere in Bergen op Zoom, the gravestone of A. R. E. Grayburn describes the missing soldier as 'a verray parfit gentle knight', which is from Chaucer's *Canterbury Tales*, and A. E. Housman is quoted. 'The lads that will die in their glory / And never be old' is from *A Shropshire Lad*, Housman's wistful telling of the losses of nineteenth-century England. Rereading the poem later, I came across the phrase I might choose as the marker for a missing airman: 'Comrade, if to turn and fly / Made a soldier never die / Fly I would, for who would not?'

But more often, the cemetery verses offer call-and-response in misquotation, with minor variations, on the theme of mortality. 'Into the mosaic of victory / Went a precious jewel – our son,' runs one, and a couple of rows later: 'In the mosaic of victory / Lies this, our precious part'. Like the children's game of Chinese Whispers, repeating an almost-copy of what you heard, these graves were playing with each other, hiding and seeking along the narrow rows. One marker mourned 'A smiling face / A heart of gold', and another recalled 'Beautiful memories / A smiling face'. Rupert Brooke, the beautiful boy poet of the First World War, is everywhere here. Gunner A. J. Farthing of the Royal Artillery asks:

> Think this of me
> There's some corner
> Of a foreign field
> That is for ever England

and Pilot Officer A. F. Buck, lost at twenty-two, promises:

> Some corner
> Of a foreign field
> That is for ever England
> Thy will be done.

The family of M. Hinksman, a driver with the Royal Army Service Corps, hoped that:

> Because of him
> This corner
> In this foreign land
> Will be for ever England

and these three stand now within two rows of each other.

This was not a failure of the imagination but a testament to the repetitive formality of grief. In the cemeteries, it came to seem to me that the graves were quoting one another; that they were carrying on a conversation in verse, and they were little interested in our needy presence in the elegant houses of the dead.

At some point in the cemeteries, as I read the gravestones and wandered, their individual identities began to melt. I had been noting the names on the graves, their dates and regiments and honours, but it was a hot afternoon, and many graves to read, so I soon gave up on all this detail and instead wrote only the lines of poetry. The cemetery verses began to replace the soldiers and airmen they were once chosen to commemorate.

> He is not dead
> He doth not sleep
> He hath awakened
> From the dream of life

I noted, without pausing to take also the name; elsewhere, 'Rest peacefully, darling' caught my eye, shocking in its intimacy. 'His life a beautiful memory / His death a silent grief', I saw, but since the memory of the life wasn't mine, I left it silent also on the name. The graves share this impulse: they are most moving when most obscure, when the pure white stone of mourning is encumbered with as little fact as possible. 'In memory of dear George / Killed in western Europe,' ran one inscription, too lazy or proud to note more. He was called George, he was loved, and he died somewhere.

These clean stones, mean on detail but rich in dignity, allow a little space for the play of the imagination. At a grave marked 'A soldier of the 1939–1945 war', I spent time wondering who he might have been, and my father and I were momentarily excited by this:

> An airman of the 1939–1945 war.
> A Sergeant in the Royal Canadian Air Force.
> 12 June 1943.
> Known Unto God.

There was a Canadian sergeant on my grandfather's plane, and this could have been him. The date of the death and its means, the nationality and the rank all fit that which we knew of the mid-upper gunner, Charles Nash. In the absence of any other limiting detail, any note to falsify our fantasy, we were free to believe for a moment that we had found something here, something previously unseen.

What faded for me in Holland was the particularity of my grandfather's death. We began with a story so striking in its obscure places and its detail – a story of flying, falling, a body found and buried, moved and reburied – and came to see that there were many like this, many others. These other men of the missing are doubles, whose lives shadowed each other. The second corpse recovered from my grandfather's plane was that of the oldest man on the raid, a gunner called Sergeant James Joseph Anderton, and he is buried at a cemetery fifty miles up the coast, and his death is dated 12 June 1943. Yet at Bergen op Zoom is buried Sergeant James John Anderson, who died also on 12 June 1943. Change one letter, and you have a different airman who died on the same day. Anderson was from 51 Squadron, where Anderton was from 83 Squadron; Anderson was pilot of a Halifax, in a raid on Düsseldorf, and Anderton was gunner in a Lancaster raiding Münster: both flew and fell and died and were buried, and for a moment, they are two halves of the same story of bombing and loss.

The war cemeteries are memorials to quantity: they mourn in numbers, offer a consolation of scale, and this is how they resist the chaotic particularities of war death. 'And death shall have no dominion,' wrote Dylan Thomas:

> Dead men naked they shall be one
> With the man in the wind and the west moon;
> When their bones are picked clean and the clean bones gone,
> They shall have stars at elbow and foot;
> Though they go mad they shall be sane,
> Though they sink through the sea they shall rise again;
> Though lovers be lost love shall not;
> And death shall have no dominion.

Those who fly with the wind and the west moon, and those who sink into the sea, are not separate from one another but further iterations of the same. The final line of the stanza repeats the first, and to compound the effect of ongoing process, of the same happening again and again, the poem opens with a conjunction: '*And death shall have no dominion*'.

The point of poetic repetition is that the second utterance of a phrase borrows the weight of the first. Repetition is quotation, and each death is a quotation of one previous. If memorials are quotations, then perhaps mourning may be too. Neither my father nor I had ever mourned this man. In the cemeteries, I wanted to learn how to mourn, and since this was a bomber, I needed to see how others had traced the loss of other bombers. In the war cemeteries of Noord-Holland, at the foot of the quiet grave, I needed Dylan Thomas.

Dylan Thomas is an unexpected war poet, and his letters suggest that he himself would have expected it least of all. For Thomas, the war kept getting in the way. He was terrified of being called up, and equally afraid that the outbreak of hostilities would prevent the irregular flow of cheques from his publishers upon which he survived. 'This bloody war won't stop the Dent monthly allowance, will it?' he wrote to his agent on 1 September 1939, the day that Germany invaded Poland. As E. M. Forster wrote: '1939 was not a year in which to start a literary career.' Thomas's third book, *The Map of Love*, was published a fortnight before Britain declared war on Germany. When after a couple of months of poor sales, his publisher wrote to describe the unfavourable news, Thomas replied: 'I blame the war.'

Blaming the war was useful. On 29 August 1939, he told his father: 'if I could pray, I'd pray for peace', and in other letters to friends and contemporary poets he unpacked why this might be. 'The Armed forces are not conducive to the creation of contemplative verse,' he announced to a friend on 14 September 1939, and continued in a curious image borrowed from the First World War: 'all my few sources of income are drying up as quickly as blood on the Western Front.' That same day, he grumbled to another acquaintance: 'Soon there will not be a single paper paying inadequately for serious stories & poems.' On 13 December 1939, he wrote to his old friend the poet and airman Vernon Watkins: 'What do I want for Christmas? Oh, that's nice. I want a war-escaper – a sort of ladder, I think, attached to a balloon, – or a portable ivory tower or a new plush womb to escape back into.'

When success eluded him, he blamed the war, for he hated its distraction. 'All I want is time to write poems,' he wrote in September 1939, and the notion that war could prompt poetry seems never to have occurred to him. Thomas quarantined his poetry from the war with an almost maniacal intensity. He longed to flee to America, and told the American poet Kenneth Patchen on 27 November 1939:

> To call me an escapist is no insult. As far as a country at war goes, I'm hermetic. I want, among other things, to go on working, and I know I can work only in peace; I can't do a Brooke in a trench; mud shells shit and glory will make me swear & vomit, not write. So I want to be where there still is peace, peace at least from the propagating of hate, the enforcements of military discipline, the extraordinarily rapid growth of dictatorship all around me, and the immediate prospect of a noble death ha ha or ignoble detention ho ho as an antisocial shirker and – worse still – unrepentant individualist.

Recalling both the name and vocabulary of the famous Great War poets, Thomas turns against their example: his vision of poetry is founded on perfect isolation from the actual matters of combat.

As he told it, the Second World War was a personal affront to the poetic career and day-to-day life of Dylan Thomas. On V-J Day, which marked victory over Japan and the end to all hostilities, he wrote to his wife Caitlin to complain about the crowds at the festivities. 'London was terrible, terrible, terrible,' he reported, and they caused him to miss his train. Not long after the end of the war, the poet and anthologist Oscar Williams sent Thomas two copies of a collection of poems he had recently assembled. Called simply *War Poetry*, the anthology for obvious reasons excludes Thomas's own verse, and there must have been some trace of a provocation hidden in Williams's apparently generous gift of two copies to the most famous anti-war poet in Britain. 'Thank you for the two copies: one for each eye,' replied Thomas, and went on to restate his earlier position:

> War can't produce poetry, only poets can, and war can't produce poets either because they bring themselves up in such a way that this outward bang bang of men against men is something they have passed a long time ago on their poems' way towards peace. A poet writing a poem is at peace with everything except words, which are eternal actions; only in the lulls between the warring work on words can he be at war with men.

Poetry, he insists, is a thing of peacetime; or rather, a war of its own, apart from the wars of men. Thomas continues: 'I think capital-letter War can only in subject matter affect poetry. Violence and suffering are all the time, & it does not matter how you are brought up against them.'

'It does not matter how you are brought up against them': perhaps Dylan Thomas tried so hard to separate himself from the war because he was a poet already at war. His most famous poems give again and again in rolling phrases the war of the heart, of man against nature, of the emotions locked in terrible struggle against the natural world. Here, for example, are the opening lines of one of his best-known early poems:

> The force that through the green fuse drives the flower
> Drives my green age; that blasts the roots of trees
> Is my destroyer.

And here, written less than a year before his death, is one of the most often quoted exhortations in English poetry:

> Do not go gentle into that good night,
> Old age should burn and rave at close of day;
> Rage, rage against the dying of the light.

Forcing, raging, blasting, burning: these are his central metaphors, and they are also the language of an emotional vision of warfare. Long before the German invasion of Poland, Thomas had militarized man's engagement with the world.

This fierce attention to the inner life at the expense of the daily modern world gives Thomas's poetry its resonance. He cares for things being the same, same as they ever were, not things being different, as they are now. As his biographer Paul Ferris notes: 'He was an answer to the machine; his poems contain few images from the twentieth century.' But to see Thomas solely as the chronicler of the raging inner life is to obscure an extraordinary cluster of war poems amongst his works. The mechanisms of modern war did ultimately matter to Thomas, and he was brought up against them in the autumn of 1940 and the spring of 1941. Dylan Thomas avoided participation in combat but he could not avoid the German bombing of England, and in time he wrote three haunting poems about the particular grief of aerial bombardment.

From September 1940, the bombs crept into Thomas's fears and dreams. On the night of 1 September, Thomas's hometown of Swansea was bombed. A week later, the Blitz began in London, and Thomas was in town for a meeting at the BBC. As he wrote to Vernon Watkins:

I can't imagine Gower bombed. High explosives at Pennard. Flaming onions over Pwlldn. And Union Street ashen. This is all too near. I had to go to London last week to see about a BBC job, &

left at the beginning of the big Saturday raid. The Hyde Park Guns were booming. Guns on the top of Selfridges. A 'plane brought down in Tottenham Court Road. White-faced taxis still trembling through the streets, though, & buses going, & even people being shaved.

Swansea sits on the Gower Peninsula; Pennard is an area to the west of the city, famous for its golf course, and Union Street is a shopping strip. Thomas names the landmarks under the bombs, and goes on:

Are you frightened these nights? When I wake up out of burning birdman dreams – they were frying aviators one night in a huge frying pan: it sounds whimsical now, it was appalling then – and hear the sound of bombs & gunfire only a little way away, I'm so relieved I could laugh or cry.

When Thomas wrote this letter, during the first days of the Blitz, he was visiting friends in Gloucestershire, but could hear the planes a hundred miles away over London. Later, in February 1941, he and Caitlin were staying with his parents in Bishopston just outside Swansea, and after one night of particularly severe air raids he went into the city to see the damage. 'Our Swansea is dead,' he said to the friend who accompanied him on the tour of the rubble.

These experiences took time to filter through to verse. In the summer of 1941, when he was working in London, Thomas wrote a strange sonnet about a victim of the Blitz, 'Among Those Killed in the Dawn Raid was a Man Aged a Hundred'. It begins with the explosion, but the bomb itself is curiously unmentioned:

When the morning was waking over the war
He put on his clothes and stepped out and he died,
The locks yawned loose and a blast blew them wide,

> He dropped where he loved on the burst pavement stone
> And the funeral grains of the slaughtered floor.

In dying, the old man becomes one with his surroundings: like the slaughtered floor and the funeral grains, his experience is shared by all at the scene. 'The craters of his eyes grew springshoots and fire,' continues Thomas, as the modern machinery of planes and bombs are tied into a natural cycle of an old man dying. What interests Thomas in death as in life is the collapse of personal variation, the moment at which particularity ceases and all things become the same.

The force of Thomas's poetry arises from its dirge-like dignity. Repetitive, running on, alliterative, everything he writes sounds a little like liturgy, and in the spring of 1944 he returned to bombing and wrote a poem that may best be read as a requiem mass for the air raid dead. 'Ceremony after a Fire Raid' begins with the same metamorphosis of individual mourning into an abstract ceremonial pattern. 'Myselves,' he writes:

> The grievers
> Grieve
> Among the street burned to tireless death
> A child of a few hours.

The newborn child is both one death and many, just as the single mourning poet is also all who will grieve, and he goes on to instruct how the service should proceed:

> Begin
> With singing
> Sing
> Darkness kindled back into beginning.

This is a collective form of grief, where 'by the fire-dwarfed / Street we chant the flying sea / In the body bereft.'

The final stanza of the poem offers a vision of a burning city filled with 'luminous cathedrals' and 'the weathercocks' molten mouths', where the poet sees:

> the dead clock burning the hour
> Over the urn of sabbaths
> Over the whirling ditch of daybreak
> Over the sun's hovel and the slum of fire
> And the golden pavements laid in requiems.

The burning cities and the falling bombs haunted Dylan Thomas, and he described the scenes as an almost biblical landscape of violent transformation. But they are for him above all cycles rather than moments: the circling sun, and burning clocks, and the requiems they sing are all repetitions. The poet's duty, here in the slum of fire, is to find a vocabulary proper to mark these elements of an ongoing saga of life and death, of birth and resurrection, of destruction and the cycles of verse.

In his most famous poem of the Second World War, written at New Quay in Wales in early 1945, Thomas returns once more to the question of how to mark those killed in the air raids. The title of the poem, 'A Refusal to Mourn the Death, by Fire, of a Child in London', is deceptive, for the poem does offer a version of mourning. Faced with 'The majesty and burning of the child's death,' Thomas writes:

> I shall not murder
> The mankind of her going with a grave truth
> Nor blaspheme down the stations of the breath
> With any further
> Elegy of innocence and youth.

He will not sing, that is, in the elegiac mode: he will not detail this child, nor her specific passing. But the poem itself is an act of mourning for all who have been lost, and this one little girl – he notes that she is a girl, though gives no other detail of character – here carries a larger pattern of remembrance. In long lovely lines, he goes on:

> Deep with the first dead lies London's daughter,
> Robed in the long friends,
> The grains beyond age, the dark veins of her mother,
> Secret by the unmourning water
> Of the riding Thames.

This one death will be as many, and the poem speaks in the voice of a gravestone inscription: here lies one from London. 'After the first death, there is no other,' it ends. All other deaths are as quotations of this one, repetitions of the single experience, and the duty of the poet is to mark the death but to keep the secret of the passing.

This is what it means, then, to refuse to mourn. It does not mean a refusal to mark. It is a diffuse kind of passion, one that creeps like the sand of the dunes at Huisduinen over the other graves too, one that can encompass both James Eric Swift and J. J. Anderton, Kidd and Stevenson, a nameless Canadian. The war graves of northern Holland stand secret by the unmourning water of the North Sea, and in their long rows they tell us that mourning must be a collective act, not for one alone but for other men lost in the flames.

On our last day in Holland, in another identical cemetery, some-thing occurs to my father. We buy a couple of plants – *Alchemilla mollis*, known as ladies' mantle, which is hardy, my father says, and will probably survive the summer without too much attention – and drive back to Bergen op Zoom. There is no trowel at the ceme-tery, so my father digs with his hands while I carry water from the tap in the small plastic orange juice bottles we had bought for lunch in the car. The cemetery is empty as before, but we pause to check that other graves have this same plant – a sign, perhaps, that it will live here – and drive to Brussels.

The rules for the behaviour of mourners at Commonwealth War Graves are clearly stated on their website. 'If you are visiting a cemetery or memorial we are delighted for you to lay a floral tribute,' they instruct: 'We ask that this is not permanent; it will be removed from the grave by our staff once it has faded.' We went to Holland and we didn't find him, exactly. But we were cheating a little, as we already knew where he was buried. I'm not sure that we wanted to find him, in the end; I think we probably wanted to invent him for ourselves. I think I wanted to tell a story, and he was available.

Chapter 1. Five Minutes after the Air Raid

12 June 1943

After the air raid, Virginia Woolf went for a walk. 'The greatest pleasure of town life in winter – rambling the streets of London,' she had written, a decade before. She called it 'street haunting', and in the essay of that title she gives instructions on how this should be done. 'The hour should be the evening and the season winter, for in winter the champagne brightness of the air and the sociability of the streets are grateful,' she wrote: 'The evening hour, too, gives us the irresponsibility which darkness and lamplight bestow. We are no longer quite ourselves.' Picture her, then, stepping out into the bombed city. It is perhaps a little earlier in the day than she might have liked, this afternoon in the middle of January 1941, and in less than three months she will be dead, but today she is here to take a quiet pleasure in the ruins.

'I went to London Bridge,' she notes in her diary:

I looked at the river; very misty; some tufts of smoke, perhaps from burning houses. There was another fire on Saturday. Then I saw a cliff of wall, eaten out, at one corner; a great corner all smashed; a Bank; the Monument erect; tried to get a Bus; but such a block I dismounted; & the second Bus advised me to walk. A complete jam of traffic; for streets were being blown up. So by tube to the Temple; & there wandered in the desolate ruins of my old squares; gashed; dismantled; the old red bricks all white powder, something like a builders yard. Grey dirt & broken windows; sightseers; all that completeness ravished & demolished.

She is watching carefully, making her way north and then west, through traffic jams and rubble, and she pauses for a while in 'my old squares', the wide and orderly spaces of Bloomsbury where she used to live. But then, quite simply, life interrupts: 'So to Buzsards where, for almost the first time, I decided to eat gluttonously. Turkey &

pancakes. How rich, how solid. 4/- they cost. And so to the L.L. where I collected specimens of Eng. litre [English literature].' From Bloomsbury, she walked past the Air Ministry on Oxford Street on her way to Buzsards, a café known for its wedding cakes and before the war its tables out on the street. After lunch, she goes on to the London Library in St James's Square. The fastest route is straight down Regent Street, and she had work to do on a new book.

Woolf's diaries, as the war begins, tell of a growing fascination. On the Sunday that Britain declared war, she was sewing black-out curtains at Monk's House, the cottage in Sussex she shared with her husband Leonard, and she wrote: 'I suppose the bombs are falling on rooms like this in Warsaw.' Three days later: 'Our first air raid at 8.30 this morning. A warbling that gradually insinuates itself as I lay in bed. So dressed & walked on the terrace with L. Sky clear. All cottages shut. All clear.' The bombs did not come that morning, but she waits and she watches. 'No raids yet,' she recorded on Monday, 11 September, but saw 'Over London a light spotted veil' of the silver barrage balloons on steel ropes, to defend the city from low-flying planes. The winter comes, and then the spring; a German bomber flies over Monk's House; Holland falls, and Belgium, and Chamberlain resigns. She is always looking at the skies. 'The bomb terror,' she writes in her diary: 'Going to London to be bombed.' In May 1940 there are rumours of invasion, and at the end of the month: 'A great thunderstorm. I was walking on the marsh & thought it was the guns on the channel ports. Then, as they swerved, I conceived a raid on London; turned on the wireless; heard some prattler; & then the guns began to lighten.' Transformed by her poised imagination, the rain becomes a raid, and then the falling bombs return to rain. 'I conceived a raid,' writes Virginia Woolf, the great novelist, thinking bombers where there were none.

Of course, in these fixated times she was at work on a novel. She called it 'Poyntz Hall' but it was published after her death as *Between the Acts*, and it too imagines bombers. After the country-house pageant which is the centre of the novel, the Reverend Streatfield stands on a soap box to address the audience on the subject of funds for 'the illumination of our dear old church', and as he begins to speak:

> Mr Streatfield paused. He listened. Did he hear some distant music?
>
> He continued: 'But there is still a deficit' (he consulted his paper) 'of one hundred and seventy-five pounds odd. So that each of us who has enjoyed this pageant has still an opp . . .' The word was cut in two. A zoom severed it. Twelve aeroplanes in perfect formation like a flight of wild duck came overhead. *That* was the music. The audience gaped; the audience gazed. The zoom became drone. The planes had passed.
>
> '. . . portunity,' Mr Streatfield continued, 'to make a contribution.'

The duck-like passing planes gently, ironically interrupt the platitudes of village life, but they are not wholly fictional. Throughout the spring and summer of 1940, Woolf had been watching the fighters scrambling over the downs, to the Battle of Britain, and hearing the distant music as the bombers came and went. Some days that summer, her diary is little more than a war report: 'Nightly raids on the east & south coast. 6, 3, 12 people killed nightly.' And even on the nights when there are no bombers – 'Listened for another; none came' – she begins to imagine them, to transform them into something useful. On the last Thursday of May 1940 she went out for a walk and 'Instantly wild duck flights of aeroplanes came over head; manoeuvred; took up positions & passed over.'

So much of Woolf's diaries reads as the roughs for so much of her published writing, and the notes on bombing from 1940 find their way into an essay, 'Thoughts on Peace in an Air Raid'. She wrote it in August for an American symposium on women in the war and here she returns to the moment when the bombers are above. As she narrates: 'The sound of sawing overhead has increased. All the searchlights are erect. They point at a spot exactly above this roof. At any moment a bomb may fall on this very room. One, two, three, four, five, six . . . the seconds pass.' Here we are, waiting and watching, as so often she was, and this time, as always before, the bombs do not fall, and she goes on:

> But during those seconds of suspense all thinking stopped. All feel-ing, save one dull dread, ceased. A nail fixed the whole being to one hard board. The emotion of fear and of hate is therefore sterile, unfertile. Directly that fear passes, the mind reaches out and instinct-ively revives itself by trying to create. Since the room is dark it can only create from memory. It reaches out to the memory of other Augusts – in Bayreuth, listening to Wagner; in Rome, walking over the Campagna; in London. Friends' voices come back. Scraps of poetry return.

In the moments after the air raid, the frozen imagination – nailed to one hard board – awakes again, and it does so by remembering, and creating; by making something new from fragments of the past, a memory of music, a line of poetry.

In the last week of August 1940, the weather was hot, and every day in Woolf's diary there are air raid warnings. On the afternoon of Saturday, 7 September, the Blitz begins, and two days later she and Leonard go to London. 'Left the car & saw Holborn,' she writes:

> A vast gap at the top of Chancery Lane. Smoking still. Some great shop entirely destroyed: the hotel opposite like a shell. In a wine shop there were no windows left. People standing at the tables – I think drink being served. Heaps of blue green glass in the road at Chancery Lane. Men breaking off fragments left in the frames.

The bombs continue to fall on the city. In the middle of October, she and Leonard return to London once more. They pass their old flat, in Tavistock Square, now open to the sky – 'I cd just see a piece of my studio wall standing: otherwise rubble where I wrote so many books,' she notes – and go on to their apartment at Mecklenburgh Square. Here, the windows had been blown out by a near bomb – 'All again litter, glass, black soft dust, plaster powder' – and they retrieve a few of their possessions. Some diaries and notebooks; 'Darwin, & the Silver, & some glass & china'; her fur coat, now dusty: at half past two they climb back into their little car and drive out to Sussex. She had long been ready to leave the city. In September, she had written to her old friend Ethyl Smith: 'When I see a great smash like a crushed match box where an old house stood I wave my hand to London.' Now, 'Exhilaration at losing possessions', she writes, and 'I shd like to start life, in peace, almost bare – free to go anywhere.'

Virginia Woolf was haunted by air raids, and after she killed herself at the end of March 1941, some were quick to blame the bombers. Violet Dickinson wrote to Virginia's sister Vanessa: 'I think she was dreadfully bothered by the noise and aeroplanes and headaches', and Malcolm Cowley, reviewing the posthumously published *Between the Acts* in the *New Republic*, called her 'a war casualty'. The raids for her were a dark fascination, and in a long diary entry written on Wednesday, 2 October 1940, she is sitting at Monk's House watching the sunset and thinking of her death in an air raid. 'Oh I try to imagine how one's killed by a bomb,' she writes, and furnishes the scene:

> I've got it fairly vivid – the sensation: but cant see anything but suffocating nonentity following after. I shall think – oh I wanted another 10 years – not this – & shant, for once, be able to describe it. It – I mean death; no, the scrunching & scrambling, the crushing of my bone shade in on my very active eye & brain: the process of putting out the light, – painful? Yes. Terrifying. I suppose so – Then a swoon; a drum; two or three gulps attempting consciousness – & then, dot dot dot

Yet there is no full stop, and if there is a death-wish here it is overwhelmed by an opposite desire: to imagine the moment and to tell what comes after the air raid. She calls it 'the process of putting out the light', the last moments of consciousness, but she is not quite willing to let go of her deep literariness, for she is quoting Othello's words before he strangles Desdemona. 'Put out the light,' he curses her, and 'then put out the light.' It is a scene impossible to render, but 'I've got it fairly vivid': here is a trace of writerly pride.

After the air raid, a scrap of poetry returns, and a memory of August in Rome. There are sightseers in the rubble, picking at the fragments of blue green glass, and perhaps a taste of wine from the blown-out wine shop. Later in the afternoon, perhaps, a plate of turkey and pancakes at a café on Oxford Street.

This is not to say that the things we recover from the ruins are easy, or even necessarily good for us. On the day of her death, Virginia Woolf walked out to the river that runs near her house in Sussex and collected a stone from the bank. Putting the stone into the pocket of the fur coat she had retrieved from the flat at Mecklenburgh Square five months earlier, she drowned herself.

But it is to say that we do not only find death in the ruins. That day in Mecklenburgh Square Woolf took her books and china too, and the stationer's ring-bound journal in which she wrote her final diary entries. In the last months of her life, Woolf was planning an ambitious new book, a study that was to be about all of literature and all of her reading.

This was her grandest bid to bring something back from the ruins. She was not reading despite the bombs; she was reading with them, and the two – reading and bombs – are jumbled together in one of her last letters. 'Did I tell you I'm reading the whole of English literature through?' she wrote to Ethyl Smith on 1 February 1941:

By the time I've reached Shakespeare the bombs will be falling. So I've arranged a very nice last scene: reading Shakespeare, having forgotten my gas mask, I shall fade far away, and quite forget . . . They brought down a raider the other side of Lewes yesterday. I was

8

cycling in to get our butter, but only heard a drone in the clouds. Thank God, as you would say, one's fathers left one a taste for reading! Instead of thinking, by May we shall be – whatever it may be: I think, only 3 months to read Ben Jonson, Milton, Donne and all the rest!

She called this last book 'Turning the Page' or 'Reading at Random', and according to her biographer Hermione Lee it was planned as 'a collection of essays which would make up a version of English literary history'. She only completed fragments of the first two chapters.

What survives the air raid? The imagination, and then the scrunching and scrambling as the mind seeks to re-create itself. Hermione Lee records an anecdote told by Somerset Maugham that reveals much of Woolf's appreciation of bombing. 'After a dinner party in Westminster,' he recalled, 'she insisted on walking home alone during an air-raid. Anxious for her safety, he followed her, and saw her, lit up by the flashes of gun-fire, standing in the road and raising her arms to the sky.' She is beckoning to them, come closer.

In my childhood, I had only one grandfather. One was there, although already dead by the time I knew what that might mean. Grandparents are myths: their lives are the stories they suggest and we are told, and the one I had was myth enough to make up for the lopsided genealogy. He was Australian, a writer who left suburban Melbourne in the hot slow years before the Second World War to become a war correspondent in Europe, and he built a big house on the side of a hill in Tuscany, planted eucalyptus trees, entertained with a servant in a white jacket. There is a photograph of him having lunch with Hemingway. He was my mother's father, and my young cousins and I spent every school holiday in that house, playing badminton and lighting fires and never learning to speak Italian. This was my grandfather; I grew up in this myth.

But everyone has two grandfathers. I had another. My father's father simply wasn't there, and my father never spoke of him. He was not there and when I started writing this book, I did not know his first name.

My father and I are in his car, driving to an airport, and I have at last asked about the day his father died: about 12 June 1943. I don't remember what it was, but I do remember a catastrophe, my father says, and it must have been bad because that night he was allowed to sleep in his mother's bed. My father was three years old. At six, he was sent to boarding school. This felt like punishment. Later, he wanted someone to tell him what had happened, but he did not ask. You do not talk about this. Maybe everyone has this, says my father, this unease about where I was from. Maybe it is a standard emotion.

Later, my father sends me something he has written. It might be useful, he says, and I open it:

Aged five or six, just after the war and I think for several years after, I had a favourite bedtime story. I made my mother read it every night for months. In the story, a Russian family, mother and two children, are driving home at night in a pony-drawn sleigh through the forest in the snow, under the bright stars. As they near home they hear a pack of wolves behind. They hurry, but the wolves are faster. The family is crossing a clearing in the forest when the wolves catch up with them, leaping and snarling at the sleigh. At the moment all is lost, a dark figure steps silently from the surrounding forest, raises his gun and shoots the wolves. It is the children's father.

A few years later, he was at school, and learning the Lord's Prayer. 'Our father, which art in heaven,' it begins, and he imagined this was his father. He survived school, and then university, and in the autumn of 1962 he moved to France. 'Having always vaguely imagined as a child that my father might have survived the war – shot down and memory lost – this idea firmly rooted itself in my mind when I moved to France,' he writes: 'I had fantasies about the day I would meet him and recognise him. Sometimes he recognised me, and stopped me in the street. Quite soon further layers added themselves: he was not only alive, but very rich.' In time, my father marries, and has children, and one day as a small boy I am doing a project on ghosts for my homework. I don't remember when, but I asked my grandmother about ghosts and she said, of course. We were in her house, a thatched cottage in Sussex, and she pointed to the tree in the curve of the drive. A long time ago, she had seen my grandfather sitting there, and she was delighted, because she was not expecting him to have returned yet from the base. It was the day he died.

After the air raid, in the place of ceremonies, there are only stories. On 12 June 1943, the Wing Commander of 83 Squadron at RAF Wyton wrote to my grandmother. Such letters have a genre, a work they now must do, and he begins: 'I am writing to express my sympathy and that of my Squadron over the news that your husband is missing from an operational flight. He was Captain of an aircraft detailed to attack Münster on the night of 11/12 June, and after leaving base nothing more was heard.' Nothing more, that is, until now, for Wing Commander Searby is not only consoling. He is starting to raise a fiction. He continues: 'It is to be hoped that we shall have further news of them as it is possible that they may have been able to bale out or force land in enemy territory', and I have read of this before: a forced landing at night; an injury perhaps; far from home. And then a journey, trials, alliances, the occasional kindness of strangers. A night in a haybarn. A borrowed tweed coat. The letter struggles between finality – the past tense, nothing more was heard – and the fantasy of continuation. 'This is indeed a great loss to the Squadron,' Searby writes, for 'He had altogether carried out 38 sorties and his experience was a valuable asset to the Squadron at this stage of the war.' When I later read his logbook, I count thirty-nine. Münster was his thirty-ninth raid, and his thirty-ninth raid is not yet complete. He is not yet back from bombing Münster.

I would like to tell you, here, about a death, but as I sit reading these documents sixty-five years later, I find I can't do anything quite that simple. On 5 January 1944, there was another letter: this time to my great-grandparents, and from the Air Ministry Casualty Branch, on Oxford Street in London. 'I am directed to inform you with regret,' it begins, and then sets out another fiction: 'in view of the lapse of time and the absence of any further news regarding your son, Acting Squadron Leader J. E. Swift, D.F.C., since he was reported missing, action has been taken to presume, for official purposes, that he lost his life on 12th June 1943.' In the absence of a corpse, he leaves a corpse-shaped space and some trouble for others to finish. The Wing Commander imagined him alive, and the Casualty Branch presumed him dead, and only later, eight months after he was lost, came another letter. 'Recovered from the shore at Callantsoog, Holland, on the 17th June, 1943,' it says at last, 'the body.'

After the air raid, Virginia Woolf walks the city. She kneels to collect a dusty fur coat, and elsewhere in the ruins someone is pushing the shards of blue green glass, clean against his finger. After the air raid, Wing Commander Searby writes a letter, and my grandmother smiles at a ghost. There are fictions which cluster in the moment of trauma, but after the air raid one particular kind of literary imagining is richest of all. Virginia Woolf was not a poet, but after the air raid, she wrote, scraps of poetry return to us, and when she thought of being bombed she thought too of reading the great poets, of Shakespeare, Donne and Milton.

Here is our first missing: an absence of poetry. They said, and they say still to this day, that there was no poetry for this war. On New Year's Eve of 1939, four months into a war that would last five years, the *Times Literary Supplement* called on the poets of England to join the battle. The *TLS* was and still is the most influential literary journal in England, and addressed its editorial 'To the Poets of 1940'. 'What can the poets do with the year 1940, when the world seems to be threatened with a new dark age?' begins the editorial, and ends by insisting: 'The monstrous threat to belief and freedom which we are fighting should urge new psalmists to fresh songs of deliverance.'

They were soon disappointed. By November 1940, the same editors declared that 'the creative imagination to-day is, not non-existent, but put on the shelf for the duration', and in the Christmas round-up of 1940 books they return to the theme, explaining: 'It is probably true that war has inspired little poetry of lasting value except in retrospect, that the imagination can only grasp its deeper meaning when the torrent of sensational violence has swept by.' This torrent of sensational violence was the Blitz, as London had been bombed each night during the autumn and winter of 1940, and in their first issues of 1941 they note the burning of Stationer's Hall and Paternoster Row, 'the old bookselling quarter' of London. No fragile papery thing such as poetry could survive the flames, and the literal fires of London – three million books burned in one warehouse in one night – were reflected by the poets themselves. In late 1941, Stevie Smith wrote a poem which elegantly refuses its own subject. Called 'The Poets are Silent', it is only four lines long:

> There's no new spirit abroad,
> As I looked, I saw:
> And I say that it is to the poet's merit
> To be silent about the war.

Cecil Day Lewis agreed. 'It is the logic of our times, / No subject for immortal verse,' he wrote, in a short poem called 'Where are the War Poets?', and when in late 1942 T. S. Eliot was invited to contribute to an American book on the destruction of London, he was hardly more enthusiastic. 'It seems just possible that a poem might happen / To a very young man,' he started, and then snapped shut even this most tentative suggestion. 'But a poem is not poetry – / That is a life,' he concludes, and 'war is not a life: it is a situation'.

The poets in London did not simply turn away: they felt the need to explain, and to give a theory to the absence. They began to tell a story about the war, about how it was ignoble and somehow did not deserve their poetry. In October 1941, Robert Graves – famous for his bestselling memoir of service in the First World War, *Good-Bye to All That* – gave a radio talk on the question of 'Why has this war produced no war poets?', and explained that the answer lay with the difference between the two wars. During the first, 'Poems about the horrors of the trenches were originally written to stir the ignorant and complacent people at home', but now, he insisted, nobody has any doubts 'about the justice of the British cause or about the necessity of the war's continuance'. If there is no injustice, there is no need for poets 'to draw attention to the evils of war'. This war is a duty, and the soldier a policeman on the beat. It lacks drama, and in its practice is a messy thing, part of a disappointing age. 'It should be added that no war poetry can be expected from the Royal Air Force,' he continues, as 'The internal combustion engine does not seem to consort with poetry.'

We see here the thickening of a theme, as patterns of thinking harden into assumptions and as poetry is pushed from the war. 'Where are the poets of this war?' begins the *TLS* editorial of 8 August 1942: 'This question is often asked by those who remember that the last war threw up a fair amount of notable poetry.' A couple of pages on in this same issue is a review of a new book that might apparently settle the editorial question: called *Poems of This War by Younger Poets*, the volume collects exactly what the title promises, some slim sentimental verses by soldiers, young men fighting. But again, we are told to look elsewhere. 'The tone and temper of the poetry so far published during this war are inevitably distinct from that of a quarter of a century ago,' insists the anonymous reviewer, and goes on to refuse even to name the poets collected in this anthology. 'In a short review it is impossible to pick out any of the thirty-six contributors for special notice,' the review waspishly ends: 'Nor does the anthology tempt us to do so.'

No war poets: the chant goes up. No Wilfred Owen, no Siegfried Sassoon, no Rupert Brooke: again and again, the trinity of Great War poets is invoked to condemn the failings of this moment in verse. By 1945 the claim had stuck, safe enough now to be dropped in passing. 'The last war has had neither its *Iliad* nor its *War and Peace*,' wrote George Steiner in *The Death of Tragedy* (1961). 'None who have dealt with it have matched the control of remembrance achieved by Robert Graves or Sassoon in their accounts of 1914–18,' he concludes, and in the bibliography to his influential textbook *English History 1914–1945* (1970) the historian A. J. P. Taylor notes: 'Works of literature are fewer and less enlightening about the second world war than about the first.' Close to the end of his 1975 study *The Great War and Modern Memory* the literary historian Paul Fussell describes the 'conventionality' of Second World War poetry, part of a larger process of young writers 'eschewing the Second War as a source of myth and instead jumping back to its predecessor'. In turn, writing in the *New Statesman* in 1978, Peter Conrad argued that 'This was a war to which literature conscientiously objected', and when in 1989 Paul Fussell came to write a study of the psychology of the Second World War he dismissed in a single sentence the possibility of poetry. 'It was a savage, insensate affair, barely conceivable to the well-conducted imagination,' he insisted, and then added, in parentheses: '(the main reason there's so little good writing about it)'. 'It is true,' declares Martin Francis in *The Flyer: British Culture and the Royal Air Force, 1939–1945* (2008), 'that the RAF failed to produce an outstanding verse writer during the war', and as claims these have the reassurance of each other.

On the shelf behind my desk as I write there is a small stack of books: they are anthologies of Second World War poetry. Here in faded maroon, its spine attached by tape, is *Poems of This War by Younger Poets* (1942), and beside it in more martial grey *The New Treasury of War Poetry* (1943). *The Terrible Rain* (1966), edited by Brian Gardner, shows streets and rubble on the cover while *Poetry of the Second World War* (1995), edited by Desmond Graham, is illustrated with green- and orange-tinted shots of refugees. Most recently and demurely, *Poets of World War II* (2003), part of the Library of America series, is small and pale green, and carries by the contents page a photograph of its editor, Harvey Shapiro, smiling in a flying suit.

The fact of anthologies does not still this debate, for these are judgements of value, not of quantity. What is being asked, and what is being denied, is the possibility of testimony: whether poetry can add to the record of this war. The same query troubled the poets themselves. In his anthology *The Poetry of War 1939–1945* (1965), Ian Hamilton includes a section of what he calls 'War Poet' poems, and here the claims by the *TLS* and famous poets find answer in the worries of writers in verse as they seek to define their own place in the chaos. Some are defensive, such as Donald Bain of the Royal Artillery and Gordon Highlanders – in his 'War Poet' he writes: 'We do not wish to moralize, only to ease our dusty throats' – and some are ashamed. Robert Conquest, who served with the Oxfordshire and Buckinghamshire Light Infantry and as an intelligence officer in Bulgaria, begins his 'Poem' of 1944 with an apology. 'No, I cannot write the poem of war,' he admits: 'Neither the colossal dying nor the local scene'.

They are asking for a role in this; they are considering how to witness. 'I must believe / That somewhere the poet is working who can handle / The flung world and his own heart,' continues Conquest, for the poet now must do both, and must pay particular regard to the jumbled landscape of this war. 'I offer him the debris / Of five years undirected storm in self and Europe,' Conquest concludes, and as he imagines the possible poetry another will write he is also giving instructions on how this may be done. It will be a poetry of debris and storm, of the flung world; a poetry of pieces. 'How to draw altogether to a purity / To a rarity?' asks Richard Eberhart in 'War and Poetry'. He spent the war with the US Naval Reserve, teaching air gunners to shoot .50 calibre Browning machine guns from planes, and answers with advice: 'The poem should be the things we lost'.

The war poets debate is a footnote to the history of the Second World War, but it is mirrored in a second tradition of silence: the forgetting of the bombers. For in the place of a full record of bombing, there is also a curious absence. In the autumn of 1997, the memoirist and novelist W. G. Sebald gave a series of lectures on the subject of air raids and German literature; they were published in England as *On the Natural History of Destruction* (2003). The RAF, he explained, attacked 131 German towns and cities, and destroyed three and a half million homes during their bombing campaigns; they dropped close to a million tons of bombs and yet 'The images of this horrifying chapter of our history have never really crossed the threshold of our national consciousness.' Sebald went on to suggest that 'There was a tacit agreement, equally binding on everyone, that the true state of material and moral ruin in which the country found itself was not to be described', and points particularly to the refusal of writers to break 'the well-kept secret of the corpses built into the foundations of our state'.

In Britain, too, many turned away. At the House of Commons in London on 12 March 1946, during the first debate on the future of the RAF after the end of the war, Wing Commander Millington, the MP for Chelmsford, rose to speak. He had completed a tour of operations with Bomber Command during the war, and he began: 'We want – that is, the people who served in Bomber Command of the Royal Air Force and their next-of-kin – a categorical assurance that the work we did was militarily and strategically justified.' He then gave a catalogue of the loss. 'When I first reported for operational duty, the average expectation of life for nine crews out of 10, in the group to which I was posted, was less than six months,' he said, and listed 50,000 men in Bomber Command killed and 15,000 serious casualties, of a total of 110,000 trained.

Millington's speech that day was motivated by what he feared was the beginning of an institutional disregard, 'an undercurrent of thought that the strategic work of Bomber Command was wasteful of our manpower and over-destructive in its effect upon the enemy'. The great firestorms of Hamburg and particularly of Dresden on Valentine's Day of 1945 – when the roads and windows melted in the blaze and tens of thousands of civilians were either burned or suffocated as the flames sucked the oxygen out of the city centre – had attracted criticism in the English press. That spring, there began to be reports of the damage in Germany: approximately seven million left homeless, and 42.8 cubic metres of rubble in Dresden for every surviving resident. All the reckonings vary greatly, and always will, but somewhere between 300,000 and 600,000 Germans, mostly civilians, had been killed by RAF and USAAF bombs. But what is perhaps most frightening about this scale of destruction is how it has been met with silence. 'In the safety of peace,' writes Max Hastings in his 1979 history of Bomber Command, 'the bombers' part in the war was one that many politicians and civilians would prefer to forget.'

Perhaps this chill is even worse than simple condemnation. On 13 May 1945, Churchill addressed the nation and announced victory in Europe. He thanked the Royal Navy and the Merchant Marine; he thanked the army, and the fighter pilots, but did not mention Bomber Command. 'When it came to awarding medals,' writes Patrick Bishop in his study *Bomber Boys* (2007), 'care was taken not to identify the strategic bombing offensive as a distinct campaign.' There is no memorial to Bomber Command in central London. 'You would think the fury of aerial bombardment / Would rouse God to relent,' wrote Richard Eberhart, but:

> the infinite spaces
> Are still silent. He looks on shock-pried faces.
> History, even, does not know what is meant.

All around the bombers falls a kind of quiet.

At the start of the new year, my father and I get back into his car and drive to Gloucestershire to meet the Squadron Leader. Tony Iveson is eighty-nine years old, and before he was a bomber pilot he had flown fighters in the Battle of Britain. He wears a grey jumper, with a logo that says 'Aérospatiale'; it was given to him by a friend who was a test pilot for Concorde. Later in the year, he is planning to give a lecture on courage. I ask him what he is going to talk about. 'You can only talk about your personal experience,' he says.

The Squadron Leader is now running a campaign for a memorial to the things that he, and others like him, did: to the 55,000 lost – when the bombers talk of the dead, they call them lost – and the ground crews that put the bombers in the air. 'There's a memorial in Park Lane to animals,' he says: 'Come on.' The Bomber Command Association have a polished website for the memorial campaign, and are supported by the *Telegraph* newspaper, and the publicity materials return often to the same set of claims. 'Bomber Command flew missions on almost every day and night of the war,' they say, and 'It was the only arm of the British forces to continually attack the German homeland throughout the war.'

This afternoon in Gloucestershire, the Squadron Leader speaks in practised phrases of what the air war meant. 'The bombing offensive prevented attack in our country,' he says. 'For more than four years' – between the retreat from Dunkirk and the Normandy landings – 'you could not leave the country for more than twenty miles in any direction.' For more than four years, that is, the war was a conflict fought in the east between Germany and Russia, and to the south in North Africa. Apart from the bombing campaign, there was no western front. 'If we had lost in 1940,' he says, 'and the Germans had got here, there would be nothing the Americans could have done.'

What the bombers fear is silence, and what they want is witness. Why is bombing controversial, I ask him. 'Because we killed civilians,' he says. Early in the war it was a waste of time, he tells me: they did a lot of dead reckoning, over a blacked-out Germany, and the truth is that they often did not know what they were bombing. I asked if he was scared. 'It was a long time ago,' he says, and the waiting was the worst part: 'once you got on the job, you were very busy', busy up in the air, and no time to think of what was below. Most of the time, they just wanted to get home. 'You get used to things,' he says.

The problem was that the bombers got better as the war went on. 'The night of Dresden everything worked perfectly,' he says: 'the weather was right, the marking was right, and 5 Group wrecked the place.' One million tons of bombs was no mistake, and this is the trouble the bombers face when they speak of memorials. 'Bomber Command was a terrible weapon,' he says. The fire hisses, and outside, the watered-down English winter light. From the other room I hear my father say, this grief distorted my childhood.

Later in the afternoon, the Squadron Leader does a German accent, and tells funny stories he has told before. My father drives me to the local station, and I take the train back to London, and it occurs to me that I have asked this man questions I would scarcely ask of an old friend – I have asked him if he was scared, and if he thought of the civilians he had killed – but I did not ask him what he did after the war. I had not thought he had a life, after the air raids. On the train, I look out of the window, but it is getting dark, and all I can see is my own reflection. The next day, I go to the library.

Because I did not trust this story of decline, I went back to the *TLS* and read everything else. I avoided the headmistressy editorials and looked instead at the advertising banners, the 'News and Notes' section on the front page, the regular features. Here, in the announcements of minor publishing news from sixty years ago, I found another story of the war and literature, and another way to memorialize the bombers.

On Saturday, 2 December 1939, 'News and Notes' announced the following: Magna Carta had been moved from Lincoln Cathedral to the Library of Congress in Washington, DC, for the duration of the war; *Cornhill* magazine was suspending publication; and *Gone with the Wind* was the most popular novel in Germany. Coverage of the war sneaks into these pages in echoes and allusions, as on page 2, during a brief review of Leonard Woolf's new book, *Barbarians at the Gate*. 'Things have changed much in 2,500 years,' observes the reviewer, but there is no doubt 'that the civilization we are defending today, with all that it implies in liberty, justice, tolerance, humanity and truth, is at bottom the civilization of Athens'.

If this were all you knew – if the only historical memory available of the Second World War were a complete set of the wartime *TLS* – you would see a struggle between forces of light and dark, waged in cultural terms: the civilization of Athens and Magna Carta on one side, faceless barbarians reading *Gone with the Wind* on the other. But you would see also a war dominated by one particular unknown and terrifying form of fighting. The front cover of the Christmas Supplement of 16 December 1939 ran a complete poem by Dorothy Wellesley, called 'The Enemy', which is at the same time a bloodthirsty ode to aerial bombing and a baroque nightmare of this terrible technology. 'There is some delight in bombing an Enemy / Whom all mankind must hate,' it begins, and rouses itself through fifty leaden lines to a final exclamation:

> Kill off the living, Enemy!
> For you have raised the dead.
> They come with clanging sound, and phosphorescent eyes,
> With the worm that never dies,
> They rise, they rise, who care no more for pain!
> Pale Enemy, hail!
> The nations are bombing the cemeteries of the slain.

The ghosts of old soldiers, killed in earlier wars, have been woken by the bombs, and they are coming back. This is a horrible poem, with its dodgy rhymes and awkward meter, yet it has a mesmerizing force to it, and establishes a theme to which the *TLS* will return, apparently unconsciously, again and again: that bombing is a particular threat to civilization, and yet may provoke poetry.

I read on, into 1940, and while the pressures of war occasionally intrude upon the grey pages – in a mention of a book of wartime recipes, or an essay on the policies of the Prime Minister, Neville Chamberlain – literary London appears largely unruffled. In January of 1940, as war is spreading across Europe, a note insists that 'no-one who respects the high tradition of literature would willingly let the hundredth birthday of Austin Dobson pass without a tribute of gratitude and reverence.' A couple of weeks later, in a short notice about the closure of libraries in London, the editors report: 'Nothing could be more disastrous to us as a people, or lead more certainly to our downfall, than the impoverishment of our cultural and artistic life.' They hold to this ideal of cultural continuity in the face of war, and the essays continue, on Chaucer, on Irish drama, on the achievement of the seventeenth-century playwright Philip Massinger. Dickens's birthday is duly noted, and there are illustrations of English scenes: of meadows in Somerset, the Ashmolean Museum at Oxford. Every now and then, the war does throw its shadows, and where those fall, they tend to form a pattern. The Spring Books Supplement for 1940 runs on its cover a poem by Edith Sitwell, called 'Lullaby', which begins:

> Though the world has slipped and gone,
> Sounds my loud discordant cry
> Like the steel birds' song on high.

The illustration shows three bombers over a burning ruined house, in flames. There is a wolf howling into the night, and a baboon holding a baby; beneath, a drowned woman with a skull.

To read these pages now is an exercise in tragic irony, for we know what the *TLS* does not: that the Blitz is coming and that London will burn. On 22 June 1940, there is a positive review of a history of the Great Fire of London of 1666, in which the reviewer notes 'a strange and universal fascination' with the Great Fire. There was good weather that summer, and the Stratford Shakespeare Festival went ahead as planned, although with smaller audiences than anticipated, and on Saturday, 7 September 1940, a special issue is dedicated 'to the purpose of spreading the spirit of our literature abroad'. There are essays on the relationship between European and English literature, and on reading habits in the Commonwealth, but presumably nobody read them, for at four o'clock that afternoon the Blitz began.

There is no mention of the raids in the next issue, of 14 September 1940, and the issue of the following Saturday, when half of London was on fire, led with a praising review of a new dictionary of clichés. 'It is possible to welcome so powerful an ally in the defence of good English in an hour when official English is using unparalleled opportunities of destroying it,' the reviewer notes, and there is the usual recommendation for Novel of the Week: the historical romance *Basilissa*, by John Masefield. On 12 October, 'News and Notes' mentions a slight delay in the publication schedule for the four-volume *Cambridge Bibliography of English Literature*, and adds that the Reading Room of the British Museum has reopened, after a brief closure 'for protective work'. However: 'the Manuscript Reading Room will be closed until the danger of air attack is passed.'

As I read them now, these issues of the wartime *TLS* are snugly bound in blue mock-leather, in the upstairs reading room of the British Library known as 'Humanities 2'. These survived, but once, in their unbound form, they were nervous loose pages and surely, in the burning city, they participated in a larger worry that fire would take all. I can only read the survivors, but once they must have worried that they could be lost, and I warm to their little acts of defiance.

I read on, through 1941 and the following year – 'Notwithstanding the war the "Twickenham" edition of the Poems of Alexander Pope, which is to be completed in six volumes, continues its scholarly course' – and in time I come to 12 June 1943, the day my grandfather was lost, and I find, of course, that the world goes on. Novel of the Week is *The Serpent*, by Neil M. Gunn. The cover celebrates a new volume of traveller's memoirs, and there is a crossword, opaque to me (6 across: 'A nail-biting giant', 4 letters), and then, on page 284, a short review of two airmen poets.

They have been forgotten now. Thomas Rahilley Hodgson was twenty-six when he was shot down, in May 1941, but before then he had written a wintry poem called 'Nocturne':

> The grey sky overcast, and dying, the sun
> red tangled, huge among
> the bare branches of trees. Last call
> of birds, and night coming,
> cries of children slim and clear
> along dusk.
> Fear of mortality.

He shares this fear with the second poet in the review, Alan Rook, who wrote:

> The living are dying
> daily. And death shall come
> not in the moment of expected danger
> but only
> when the reaper is ripe for the corn.

On this day of unexpected death, in a small town in Sussex fifty miles from London, my grandmother waited for news, and, further away, my grandfather fell from the sky. Nobody noticed, but two sentimental poets in the pages of the *TLS*.

Again and again, in reading my way after the poets of this war, I have a sense of another conversation, just submerged. I hear the speeches, by the editors and the famous literary men, loud and certain; and yet, as from another room, a hum; of people speaking softly, of something more or less unspoken. In May 1946, a year after the war ended, Edmund Blunden wrote an essay for the *TLS*. 'The second war with all its novelty of aspect and its shifting of emphasis has not weakened the commanding position of Wilfred Owen in the poetry of the age,' he insisted, and went on to elaborate the familiar music:

'nor have its own poets varied the themes so powerfully as to throw upon his pages any shadow of supercedings.' Blunden was himself a poet of the First World War, and had edited the 1931 edition of the poems of Wilfred Owen. He wrote: 'Owen's imagination, artistry, and compassion remain, now that the fumes and the volleys have left the daylight to itself and us, as a practically perfect achievement', and approvingly quotes Sir Osbert Sitwell on Owen: 'If he can be properly called a War Poet – since, greater than that, he was a Poet – he may be the only writer who answers truly to that description.'

The emblematic story of British war poetry in the twentieth century is that of Wilfred Owen, perfect and dead. He wrote the poems that war poetry is supposed to sound like, and that children can recite:

> Bent double, like old beggars under sacks,
> Knock-kneed, coughing like hags, we cursed through sludge,
> Till on the haunting flares we turned our backs
> And towards our distant rest began to trudge.

Like every generation, I learned these at school. They make ideal reading comprehension exercises, for they ask not that you know much, but that you feel deeply; their rhymes are inviting and sad, and they have a wistful urgency that is very hard to refuse. 'Above all I am not concerned with Poetry,' Owen wrote in the famous preface to the first collection of his poems: 'My subject is War, and the pity of War. The Poetry is in the pity.' The work these poems do, then, is to elicit from us our sympathy, and they do so as they rhyme emotion with location. Owen made a landscape famous – mud, sludge, trudge, the trenches along the western front of the First World War – and rendered it as poetry.

Owen's distinctive poetic achievement lay in the meeting of his place and his verse, and his own life was a sad paraphrase of the war as a whole. He was killed on 4 November 1918, one week before the end of the war, and, as the myth records, the bells were ringing the

Armistice when the telegram reached his parents in Shrewsbury. He wrote this, too: in 'Anthem for Doomed Youth', when he traces 'The shrill, demented choirs of wailing shells; / And bugles calling for them from sad shires'. And since he wrote his own death, we are in the presence not of an individual but of a principle, and perhaps we need not look any further. Owen lived an idea about poetry, for his admirers and his editors, which was made perfect by his death. 'All that was strongest in Wilfred Owen survives in his poems,' wrote his friend and mentor Siegfried Sassoon, in a brief introduction to the first collection of Owen's poems. The man has become the poems, and Sassoon goes on to insist: 'any superficial impressions of his personality, any record of his conversation, behaviour, or appearance, would be irrelevant and unseemly.'

But this is too strict, for people do not really live as ideas. We live by accident and once, Wilfred Owen imagined that he might be someone else. In his letters, we meet a variable young man, and in August 1916, during military training, he thought he wanted to be an airman instead of a soldier. As he wrote to his mother, he was applying for transfer to the Royal Flying Corps:

> Flying is the only active profession I could ever continue with enthusiasm after the war.
>
> Once a certified pilot, the pay is £350. The Training lasts three months.
>
> By Hermes, I will fly. Though I have sat alone, twittering, like even as it were a sparrow upon the housetop, I will yet swoop over Wrekin with the strength of a thousand Eagles, and all you shall see me light upon the Racecourse, and marvelling behold the pinion of Hermes, who is called Mercury, upon my cap.
>
> Then I will publish my ode on the Swift.
>
> If I fall, I shall fall mightily. I shall be with Perseus and Icarus, whom I loved; and not with Fritz, whom I did not hate. To battle with the Super-Zeppelin, when he comes, this would be chivalry more than Arthur dreamed of.

Perhaps the weather was fine, that August in Essex, and perhaps ground training was dull, but he was looking at the sky and considering what might be, and his motives are a strange blend of the practical and the mythic: the £350 pay, the echoes of Hermes. We can follow his jittery associations: from a worry about work to flight, and to sparrows and eagles over the town where he grew up, and then to his own poetry.

He had written 'The Swift: An Ode' more than three years earlier, in imitation of Keats's 'Ode to a Nightingale', and it is clumsy – 'to be of all the birds the Swift!' it longs – but suggests some of the possible glamour Owen saw in learning to fly. 'Waywardly sliding and slinging, / Speed never slacking,' it wonders:

> Easily, restlessly flinging,
> Twinkling and tacking;
> – Oh, how we envy thee thy lovely swerves!

Owen is collecting the materials for a poetry of air war. When he thinks of Zeppelins, he thinks also of the swifts, of Greek myths and Arthurian heroes and the inevitable fall; and of what he will write; and of how others shall marvel at this airman poet above.

The Royal Flying Corps rejected Owen's application for a transfer, and on New Year's Eve of 1916 he was sent to the mud of northern France, to the trenches he then made famous in what Cecil Day Lewis later called 'probably the greatest poems about war in our literature'. The earlier, doubtful Owen – envious of the swift, of the airmen – was soon forgotten. 'During the weeks of his first tour of duty in the trenches, he came of age emotionally and spiritually,' continued Day Lewis, in the preface to his 1963 edition of Owen's poems, collapsing the man into the landscape: 'The subject made the poet.'

The poet needed the trenches, and Day Lewis continues: 'though this ubiquitous landscape surpassed all the imagined horrors of

Dante's *Inferno*, it provided the soldier poets with a settled familiar background, while trench warfare gave them long periods of humdrum passivity.' Without the trenches, then, there could be no poetry, and he elaborates:

> Such conditions – a stable background, a routine-governed outer life – have so often proved fruitful for the inner lives of poets that we may well attribute the excellence of the First-War poetry, compared with what was produced in the Second War – a war of movement – partly to the kind of existence these poets were leading: another reason could be, of course, that they were better poets.

This is a strange and poignant claim to make in what is, after all, the introduction to a collection of First World War poetry, but Day Lewis is here not really writing about Owen at all. He is writing about himself, and explaining his own failure to become a similar poet of the Second World War.

Cecil Day Lewis was supposed to be a war poet. In his 1935 collection *A Time to Dance*, he writes poetry about his own obsession with war as a form of poetry:

> In me two worlds at war
> Trample the patient flesh,
> This lighted ring of sense where clinch
> Heir and ancestor.

He is the heir of the First World War poets; Wilfred Owen is his ancestor. He continues, in imagery that is again borrowed from the poetry of the previous war:

> The armies of the dead
> Are trenched within my bones,
> My blood's their semaphore, their wings
> Are watchers overhead.

The gesture towards the air is more fully developed in his next collection, *Overtures to Death and Other Poems*, published in October
1938. In the poem 'Bombers', he imagines a flight of planes overhead:

> Black as vermin, crawling in echelon,
> Beneath the cloud-floor, the bombers come:
> The heavy angels, carrying harm in
> Their wombs that ache to be rid of death.

The image here of a womb is continued in the next stanza, where
the 'iron embryo' of the bomber longs to give birth to 'fear delivered and screeching fire'.

Here is the promise of a poetry specific to the Second World War.
It builds upon the tight fury and intensely physical metaphors of the
First World War poets, and yet the form of its menace is particularly
modern. 'Children look up,' he writes, for this type of war is no
longer bound to a single landscape; it is in the air, and as the 'Earth
shakes beneath us: we imagine loss'. He begins to sketch a new
poetry, of terror bombing, and to imagine the broken fields of London, Hamburg, Coventry, Dresden; and yet once the war broke out,
he rapidly abandoned this line of imagery. At Easter 1938, he bought
a cottage in Dorset, and by the end of the summer had withdrawn
his membership of the Communist Party in London and moved his
wife and two sons to the countryside. He started an affair with the
wife of a local farmer, and spent the autumn of 1939 finishing the
latest in a series of pseudonymous thrillers he wrote to make money.
'*Malice in Wonderland*, the tale of a deranged murderer running riot
in a holiday camp,' notes his biographer, was 'published in the summer of 1940'.

The poetry he wrote in these years embodies this turn away from
the war. In October 1940, as the Blitz was beginning in London, he
published a translation of *Georgics*, Virgil's cycle of instructional
poems about farming, with a prefatory poem that opens: 'Poets are

not much in demand these days'. He goes on: 'Where are the war poets? the fools inquire', and concludes that 'We have turned inward for our iron ration'. The cycle as a whole glorifies the pastoral scene, apart from the preoccupations of war.

> Oh, too lucky for words, if only he knew his luck,
> Is the countryman who far from the clash of armaments
> Lives, and rewarding earth is lavish of all he needs!

exclaims one stanza, and surely here Day Lewis found an echo of his own retreat. Always in these poems he is distracted from the war. In May 1940, he enrolled in the local platoon of the Home Guard, and wrote of his military experience in a collection published as *Poems in Wartime*. 'The farmer and I talk for a while of invaders,' one poem begins: 'But soon we turn to crops'.

We have been at this moment before, when a poet comes suddenly aware of a new poetry of this war; and yet, in the moment of suggestion, turns away, made self-conscious by the task. We have seen the theme of a poetry of air war raised, and dropped, and yet it is at this pause, when I hear the poets saying, no war poetry, that I start to listen for the rumble in the distance, as the earth shakes beneath us and we imagine loss. The bombers are never far behind. In the spring of 1941, Cecil Day Lewis took a job at the Ministry of Information, in a building near the shattered squares of Bloomsbury that haunted Virginia Woolf. Some nights the raids on London were so bad that Ministry officials slept on bunk beds in the basement, and Day Lewis went on writing, a series of pamphlets for popular distribution by the Ministry as well as his own poems that would then be published in his collection *Word Over All* of 1943. In the brief window between Woolf's suicide at the end of March 1941, and my grandfather's first bombing raid six weeks later, Day Lewis returned to the suspended theme of bomber poetry, and became a secret war poet.

'I watch when searchlights set the low cloud smoking / Like acid on metal,' Day Lewis wrote in 'Word Over All':

> I start
> At sirens, sweat to feel a whole town wince
> And thump, a terrified heart,
> Under the bomb-strokes.

But it is not enough, yet, to report of what he saw, for he knows that where he may have had a terrified night, the truer sufferings were elsewhere. 'These, to look back on, are / A few hours' unrepose,' he continues: 'But the roofless old, the child beneath the debris – / How can I speak for these?' The poetry of air bombing requires a particular imaginative sympathy absent from other war poetry, and it must play between telling and deferring the tale: between the poet who survived and the others who died that night. And it is only in this fine balance, pitched between condemnation and celebration, between terror and relief, that the poem may also invoke the bombers themselves. They are above, of course, out of the burning city, but they are initiating the bomb-strokes, and so they too must be invited to speak. A little later in the collection, in 'Airmen Broadcast', Day Lewis challenges the bombers to compose a poetry of their own, and since it encapsulates so much of this moment it is worth quoting this poem in its brief entirety:

> Speak for the air, your element, you hunters
> Who range across the ribbed and shifting sky:
> Speak for whatever gives you mastery –
> Wings that bear out your purpose, quick-responsive
> Finger, a fighting heart, a kestrel's eye.
>
> Speak of the rough and tumble in the blue,
> The mast-high run, the flak, the battering gales:
> You that, until the life you love prevails,
> Must follow death's impersonal vocation –
> Speak for the air, and tell your hunter's tales.

If we read these two poems side by side, we see Day Lewis imagining himself as both bomber and bombed. And yet, by isolating himself from each – he is not with the roofless old, nor hunting through the ribbed and shifting sky – he is forming a space for the poet in this war, one who is partly a victim, shivering in his basement bunk, and yet conscious also of the greater loss; and one who partly longs to be an airman. 'How can I speak for these?' he asks, and commands: 'Speak for the air'. Cecil Day Lewis is summoning the double-subject into being. It was not automatic. The *TLS* and the guardians of English literature said, no verse, but here perhaps before them, in the quiet between the bombing, another poetry was beginning.

Perhaps this is what a poetry of air bombing might mean: perhaps it is always of the near distance, its sufferings always at a remove. Perhaps the poets are the voices from the other room, almost overheard, and the poems never quite take the form we anticipate. While Day Lewis was working for the Ministry of Information in Bloomsbury, he was not writing only the poems that appear safely now in his *Collected Poems*. He was working also on a series of cheap pamphlets that sought to celebrate the war effort, and in one of these, called simply *Bomber Command*, he returns to the air war. Like all government documents, it appeared anonymously; it never invited anyone to read it as a poem.

The pamphlet presents itself as a strict narrative history of the first phase of the bomber war. The title page promises 'The Air Ministry Account of Bomber Command's Offensive Against the Axis, September, 1939 – July, 1941', and it begins quite routinely at the beginning, with a flight by a Blenheim to take reconnaissance photographs of the German fleet on the first day of the war. Accompanied by maps, and statistics, and glossy photographs of grinning bomber crews, solid in full gear, it tells of the early raids on the German fleet, of the first winter and spring of the war, and then the first attacks on a land target, the seaplane base at Sylt, off the Danish coast, in March 1940. There are leaflet drops, and crash landings, and as Holland falls to the Germans the British raids follow them. By May 1940, Bomber Command is raiding mainland Germany, particularly targets 'in the district of the Ruhr, which is the most important industrial area in Germany'. Through the summer of the following year, the raids intensify, and by the end we are assured that 'the aircraft of Bomber Command were over Germany twenty-six out of twenty-eight nights.'

It makes compelling reading, this modern epic of industrial war, and yet apologizes for the repetitions of its subject. Bombing operations are 'not dramatic in the accepted sense of the word', the pamphlet insists, and explains:

> To describe every bombing attack carried out against Germany would be to transform this narrative into a catalogue of raids. Such makes dull reading. This should be so. The most successful raids are those in which no incident occurs; the best crew, that which takes its aircraft, unseen and deadly, to the target, bombs it and flies home again through the silence of the night. In essentials all bombing operations are the same.

Told as a story rather than a catalogue, the bomber war demands characters and a setting, so we meet the members of an abstract crew: the pilot, who 'must be imaginative, yet not be dismayed by his own imagination', and the navigator, 'the key man in a bomber aircraft', who directs the plane and aims the bombs. He has the hardest job of all, for 'Darkness, clouds, air currents, all singly or together, are his foes.' Life on base is not half bad, we are told, and the atmosphere 'may be likened to that found in an inn frequented by mountaineers'. We see pictures of these men in their planes, often looking away from the camera as if to feign duty, and of the operations rooms, and because a story needs not only a cast but also a crisis, we are told about a night that almost went wrong.

'Münster, an important railway junction, was bombed five nights running from the 6th to 10th July,' the stirring anecdote begins, and goes on:

> The crew of a Wellington have good cause to remember one of the recent attacks on Münster. When on the way home it encountered and shot down an enemy fighter, which, however, set the bomber's starboard wing on fire. It was over the sea and the crew stood small chance of being picked up if they baled out. One of them, a sergeant, volunteered to climb out on to the wing and extinguish the flames. He climbed out of the 'Astro' hatch, kicked hand- and foot-holds in the fabric and beat out the fire with an engine cover. He had a rope round his waist when out on the wing; but had he lost his hold it would either have snapped or, helpless in the slipstream, he would have been battered against the tail fin. The Wellington reached its base safely.

I stop here, stunned not by the surreal bravery of this scene but its familiarity. I know what happened this night, because my grandfather was bombing Münster in July of 1941, on the night of the 3rd, and then again on the 5th, and on the 7th and again on the 8th, and on the 7th his Wellington was attacked by an enemy fighter. 'Sgt Swift claims enemy aircraft shot down by rear gunner,' runs the clipped official history told in the Operations Record Book for 57 Squadron, and goes on: 'Attacked by Me. 110, causing damage to rear turret and stbd [starboard] aileron and elevator. Front gunner + rear gunner fired long bursts, believed secured hits.' Nothing here indicates surprise, but this moment was exceptional enough to form the basis of my grandfather's citation for the Distinguished Flying Cross four months later, and the citation tells another slightly different version of the same night, placing its emphasis now on the combat and not the damage. 'Whilst participating in an attack on Münster, Pilot Officer Swift's aircraft was engaged in a 15 minute encounter with a Messerschmitt 110,' the official citation runs: 'After six attacks the enemy broke away in a vertical dive. It was most certainly damaged, if not destroyed.'

What moves me most now, reading of these wild heroics more than sixty years later – more than a lifetime later – is that after this night, he went out again, to Münster on the 8th and then to Cologne on the 10th. Perhaps my grandfather's raid was not even the same as the one in the pamphlet: perhaps another Wellington raiding Münster was attacked by another Messerschmitt, and another starboard wing was burned; and another crew trailed home, relief whistling through their teeth. Perhaps this was simply a busy season for such frisky heroics. 'In essentials all bombing operations are the same,' wrote Day Lewis, and perhaps in the poetry of bombing there are no certain heroes, but only repetitions.

At the end of Day Lewis's pamphlet on Bomber Command is a short section, called 'One Thing is Certain', which celebrates precisely this quality of repetition. 'The attack on the enemy continues without pause,' he writes at the close, and moves into a flurry of quotation. 'They plod steadily on, taking their aircraft through fair weather or foul, night after night,' he promises, following the witches in Shakespeare's *Macbeth* as they chant: 'Fair is foul, and foul is fair, / Hover through the fog and filthy air'. 'These twentieth-century "gentlemen of the shade, minions of the moon" have accomplished much in twenty-two months of war,' he continues, and now the bombers are paraphrasing Falstaff's crew in Shakespeare's *Henry IV*, misbehaving with charm. 'By day they will go out in these new aircraft with their comrades of Fighter Command ever farther into the confines of the foe. By night they will take them "aloft incumbent on the dusky air" to the farthest town and city of Germany,' he vows, and now they are with Milton's Satan in *Paradise Lost* as 'with expanded wings he steers his flight / Aloft, incumbent on the dusky air, / That felt unusual weight'. Day Lewis's bombers fly at the end of a history of echoes, and their war has the glamorous logic of a poetic image, flying and fighting by the moon. After the air raid, wrote Virginia Woolf, a scrap of poetry returns to us: because the poets were waiting for this kind of war.

The question of war poetry is a question of landscape. 'The First World War took place in a fixed imaginative landscape,' wrote Vernon

Scannell, himself a poet who fought in North Africa during the Second World War, in 1975: but 'The Second World War had no fixed habitation.' We find this claim elsewhere, a rattling echo between the poets. Writing in the *Listener* on 16 October 1941, on 'War Poetry in This War', Stephen Spender opens with the common complaint. 'The war of 1914–1918 provided a great stimulus to the arts, especially to painting and poetry,' his piece begins: 'The present war has had comparatively little effect on either.' He goes on to explain why: 'In the last war, tens of thousands of men lived for weeks and months at a time on the Western Front', and 'It was the Western Front which produced the best poetry of this war.' However, the second war has no single geography: now, 'This war has no stage setting easily visualised by the imagination of the whole world.'

Within a year he had changed his mind. During 1942 and 1943 Oxford University Press published a series of thin volumes: called *War Pictures by British Artists* they collected recent paintings by theme and presented them with an introduction by a poet or writer. The volume *Air Raids* was published in early 1943 with an introduction by Stephen Spender. Here, there are paintings of the damage to London, incendiaries in the suburbs, the House of Commons in rubble. 'For years before the war, European cities were unreal, with the unreality of a landscape sunlit and unspeakably silent before a storm,' Spender writes, and now that the cities have been bombed they have become centrally the subject of war art. 'The background to this war, corresponding to the Western Front of the last war,' he concludes, 'is the bombed city.'

The bombed city was a place of poetry. 'O see the wasted city by morning / When the bombers have gone,' commanded Emanuel Litvinoff, early in the war, and in a more satirical mode John Betjeman summoned: 'Come, friendly bombs, and fall on Slough'. Again and again, in the poetry of this war, we find the new landscape of a bombed city, and as the poets reflected upon their verse they returned often to a shallow pool of images, of bombs howling down, of fired streets, of formal ruin. 'When I reach for the wind / Cast me not down,' wrote Sidney Keyes in 1943, in 'War Poet': 'Though my face is a burned book / And a wasted town'. The poets of the Second World War saw in bombing a promise of verse, and a force as fierce as gravity pulls them back, time upon time, to its scenes. In his 'Rhyme of a Flying Bomb', set in an air raid in 1941, Mervyn Peake tells of the 'boisterous tune' of bombs falling:

> a singular song it was
> As it rattled its ribs and danced,
> Had a chorus of doors that slammed their jaws
> And a chorus of chairs that pranced.
> And the thud of the double-bass was shot
> With the wail of the floating strings,
> And the murderous notes of the ice-bright glass
> Set sail with a clink of wings.

There is a music to this damage: a balance to the loss of bombing, and here in poetry the raids were answered. Bombing is at first a story of loss, of damage, but it is not itself an ending; what follows is the starting of meter and rhyme. 'Ruin is formal,' wrote Emily Dickinson, and poetry deals in the arrangement of fragments; each poem has a kind of fractured architecture. The proper term for a unit of poetry is a 'stanza', which in Italian means a 'room', for poems like houses are built from pieces. This warfare, so involved in breaking and in rubble, asked for an art form that too had at its heart an embrace of the incomplete.

The bombed city was quick with literary imagining, and most of all with poetry. In October 1944, the quasi-governmental group known as Mass-Observation – an affiliation of surrealists, ethnographers, social historians – conducted one of their esoteric surveys. Their agents called six major bookshops in central London, and the editors of leading poetry journals, to ask what impact the war had upon poetry. Without exception, each described a marked rise in the buying and reading of poetry during the period in which London was bombed. At Collett's Bookshop, the manager reported: 'Our sales of poetry have gone up considerably.' An assistant at Foyle's replied: 'Well, I sell the poetry, and I can tell you there's an enormous demand for it', and at Zwemmer's the manager said: 'Oh yes, poetry's in demand.' In 1940, Stephen Spender's and J. B. Leishman's translation of Rilke's *Duino Elegies* and T. S. Eliot's *Book of Practical Cats* were doing good business. John Donne was selling well in 1944, and Rupert Brooke was constantly in demand. 'The outstanding thing,' said the sales manager at Faber, 'is that there has been an unusual demand for poetry.'

This is one half of the story, for the scene beneath depends upon the bombers above. 'There has been a wonderful revival,' said the editor of *Poetry Review* in October 1944, when Mass-Observation called him, and explained that people from all over the world were sending him their poems to publish. 'We haven't got such fine verse from the men in the field this time,' he added, but there is one exception to the trend of disappointing poetry from the forces. 'The best of it is from the RAF,' he said: 'Oh yes, it's certainly the RAF that has flowered into poetry this time – perhaps their greater freedom accounts for it.'

Bombing was to the Second World War what the trenches were to the First: a shocking and new form of warfare, wretched and unexpected, and carried out at a terrible scale of loss. Just as the trenches produced the most remarkable poetry of the First World War, so too did the bombing campaigns foster a haunting set of poems during the Second. But this is no simple process, for they are not equivalent geographies. Bombing, if we take the whole of it, is always double. It was a kind of war conducted in the cities and the planes, shared between the bombers and the bombed, and so it asks a split reckoning, a thinking in two places. 'Children look up,' wrote Cecil Day Lewis: and think upon the bombers above.

All of my grandfather's remains that are not in a sandy grave in Holland sit now in a dark blue shoebox on a shelf in my father's house in Wales. Here are his shoulder flashes, his braid insignia, and a copper plate for his visiting card. Here is his civilian logbook, the record of a hobby in the year before the war, and a small red notebook of his operations and training flights. Here is his Distinguished Flying Cross, with a purple and white ribbon, and fifteen letters to my grandmother, dated between 22 May 1941 and 9 June 1943. Here are two letters to his son, my father, with a drawing of a Lancaster bomber, and the accounts for the final distribution of his estate.

His disappearance and death are an obvious theme of these last traces. There are clippings from the *Times* of 21 August 1943, reporting the crew as missing, and of 21 April 1944, listing them as 'Now Presumed Killed in Action'. Their story of his slow death is amplified in the letters from the Casualty Branch, also here, with the heavy folds of use, and the photograph of his grave.

Some things are unknown: a photograph of a small sincere boy, and another of a young woman in a bathing suit by a lake. Perhaps it is Lake Geneva; perhaps the small boy is my grandfather, or my great-grandfather. Here is a ticket for admission to Buckingham Palace for the investiture ceremony of my grandfather's DFC, on 14 April 1942, and here, amongst the rest, is a shabby blue hardback book: *Air Force Poetry*, edited by John Pudney and Henry Treece.

The book was not my grandfather's. It was published in 1944, after his death, and the inscription reads 'Betty Bruce', which was my grandmother's name after her second marriage, in the autumn of 1945. But the binding is worn and the spine is broken, which tells that once, somebody turned to it and looked it over again.

Air Force Poetry is a prison: its poems and its poets are fiercely bound. They know they will die, and around their bases:

> Through flat, damp fields call sheep, mourning their dead
> In cracked and timeless voices, unutterably sad,
> Suffering for all the world, in Lincolnshire.

I have never read a more mortal book than this one. Every line knows death, and every poem does the work of elegy, and even those which momentarily hint at the freedom of airmen – 'O! The great joy of it!' – know where it will end:

> Along the pillared streets of cloud
> the wide unceilinged skies across
> we sweep on slim swift wings, and pass
> among the stars no stain of blood;
> for borrowed is our flight, and earth
> reclaims from all the skies her dead.

The airmen here are imagined on the steps of heaven, or in 'a pilots' paradise' 'at your log-books' end', and even as they briefly live they are the agents of other deaths, for:

> The moon in the star-laden sky
> becomes a thin smile, as the hand moves
> the bomb-release, and others, compacted
> of bone and blood the same even, die below.

Above, they are mortal, and below, 'the dark drizzle of the smoky city', 'the ruins of this screaming town'. Of the thirty-three airmen poets collected in this book, six had been killed in action by the time of publication.

This is what airmen do: they are reported missing – as in the title of one poem here – and they disappear.

> Fetch out no shroud
> For Johnny-in-the-cloud;
> And keep your tears
> For him in after years

instructs the middle stanza of John Pudney's 'For Johnny', and I fear in reading these that my grandmother was called again and again back to one particular.

If they die they'll die,
As you should know,
More swiftly, cleanly, star-defined, than you will ever feel

writes H. E. Bates on the first page of this collection, and starts an echo. For these airmen 'Unwarmed by the short swift rushings / Of human happiness' on page 19 are on page 23 victim of 'the doubts to which swift death gives birth', although on page 27 'their swift fame need fear no tarnishing'. Even while they 'sweep on slim swift wings', there is upon them a threat as 'suddenly life leaps up to a swift crescendo', and these poems buckle here around the pattern of one man.

'On my grave no name remains behind,' wrote John Bayliss in one of his poems in *Air Force Poetry*, for what airmen do is disappear, and in their absence they leave a challenge to those who would tell their story. In 1928 the Russian literary critic Vladimir Propp published a study, called *The Morphology of the Folk Tale*, in which he identified thirty-one basic elements of the plot structure of folk tales. He called them 'functions', and they are the primal pattern of all stories. This does not mean a story may not be phrased in any other way, but this is what the telling wants from us, when we kneel before a child, and with a dip we begin, once upon a time.

We open with the first function, as 'One of the members of a family absents himself from home.' On 18 October 1939, six weeks after the start of the war, my grandfather enlisted in the RAF Volunteer Reserve in Uxbridge. In the third function, 'a new personage, who can be termed the *villain*, enters the tale', and through the following four functions challenges the hero, by committing murder, declaring war, or tormenting by night. Through 1940 the Luftwaffe bombed the airbases and cities of England, and my grandfather trained. In the eighth function, the hero 'either lacks something or desires to have something', and in May 1941 my grandmother sent a parcel – 'One fine cake, one mess dates, one box assort. cigs, one letter, one coupon' – to my grandfather at RAF Feltwell. By the ninth function, 'the hero is approached with a request or a command; he is allowed to go or he is dispatched', and on 11 May 1941 my grandfather goes on his first bombing raid, on Hamburg in a fabric-covered Wellington bomber.

The order is imperfect, but the story continues. In function fourteen, 'the hero acquires the use of a magical agent', and on 4 May 1943 my grandfather changes his plane, moving from a Wellington to the faster and more powerful Lancaster bomber. 'You would like daddy's new aeroplane it is bigger than the old one,' he wrote to my father. In the sixteenth function, 'the hero and the villain join in direct combat', and on the night of 7 July 1941, and then again a week later, my grandfather engages with and shoots down a German night-fighter. As a consequence of the combat, in the following function, 'the hero is branded', as he receives a mark upon his body or a ring. On 14 April 1942, my grandfather was decorated with a DFC at Buckingham Palace.

In the twentieth function, 'the hero returns'. The functions continue, as a folk tale may go on – the hero may be tricked once more, and yet ultimately triumph, and be rewarded with the kingdom – but my story stops here on the night of 11 June 1943 as one crew did not return, were presumed missing, found, marked as dead, named, lost. From my grandfather, I inherit a fractured fairy tale. The bombers who fly and do not return threaten our need for stories because they thwart the possibility of an ending. The bombers who kill civilians in foreign cities threaten our demand for goodness in our heroes, and it is for both of these reasons that the poetry is theirs.

Chapter 2. It was Not Dying

23 December 1940

There is snow on the ground in Cambridgeshire. Out on the ice by the hangar the boys of 25 Course gather for a photograph. They are done with lessons now, and in the front row some wear mittens for the cold. This is not really uniform, and the boys are playing a little. He sits at the far right and he has bare hands. He did six years in the City – the slow time of a commuting job, and no boast there, for Father is on the board of directors – but now there is a war on, and the war wants pilots, and he wants to fly. On the day of the photograph, he has his flying badge and the rank of Sergeant, and he is joining 11 Operational Training Unit at RAF Bassingbourn. 'Character: Very Good', they write on his service record. Out on the ice, the boys start to settle for the shot. Some of their grins turn a little. He crosses his legs, his left boot crunching the snow, and raises his eyes, and folds his hands, and they take the photograph.

My grandfather learned to fly in the year before the war. He spent Saturdays with the Cinque Ports Flying Club at Lympne aerodrome in Kent, but five days a week he parked his car at Haywards Heath and took the train into London. Kaufman Heyworth & Co. was a rubber brokerage firm with grand offices in London House on Fenchurch Street, and my great-grandfather Jim was a senior partner. The company did not take his name, but every day of the week Mr Kaufman, Mr Heyworth and Mr Swift had lunch together. Jim Swift told his family that they considered him the best accountant in the City, and the rubber business made him a rich man. He drove a blue Daimler, badly, and when in 1926 he built his own house in north London, there were a cook and a parlour maid and a tennis court and a billiards room with a full-size slate table. He had three children, and for twenty-first birthdays they pulled back the billiards table and had dances on the parquet floor.

Later, Mr Kaufman, who was a German Jew, will change his name to Merchant, but England has not yet so finally and violently turned itself away from Germany, and in these years there is good business in trading rubber with the Continent, so in 1929 my grandfather Eric was sent to the École Supérieure de Commerce in Neuchâtel to study business and to learn German and French. In 1932, he spent the evening at a party in Neuchâtel, talking to a dark-haired girl called Mary Rymer. Many years later, his sister will tell me that the day after the party, my grandfather sent flowers to this girl; and her sister will tell me that he took her sailing. In time, they hire architects and builders to make them a house, and two years after that, from a white hotel by the sea in Devon, she writes: 'My husband!'

These are my grandparents: both went by their middle names. Where he was Eric, she was Betty. They were the children of another age. He was from a family of rubber brokers, in the time before synthetics when rubber was an important commodity. She was born in Wellington, India, at the end of the British Empire, and when they came to name their house, they called it Honeysuckle Cottage.

They are characters of an old world, but a new world is forming around them. In July 1936, the Air Defence of Britain was divided into four separate commands – Bomber, Fighter, Coastal and Training – and the next year, the Civil Air Guard was formed, to train military pilots on civilian airfields. My grandfather swore an oath – 'I undertake to present myself for entry in the Royal Air Force Volunteer Reserve as an airman pilot if and when called upon to do so' – and wore a badge, and now his flying lessons were paid for by the Air Ministry. At the start of 1939, he took a week off work and flew every day, and on 28 January, after he had flown a little over ten hours, he passed his civilian A licence. Through March, and April, and into the summer, he flew only at weekends, and the last entry in his civilian logbook is on 27 July 1939 and reads simply: 'climbed to 5000 ft.'

'Britain has drawn on the winged gauntlet,' wrote A. G. J. White-house in his bestselling pamphlet *Hell in Helmets: The Riddle of Modern Air Power* (1940). The youth of Britain, he declares, are obsessed by the Royal Air Force, and for every young man in England, 'All his eyes see are Hawkers, Bristols, Spitfires, Handley Page bombers, and Short naval flying boats.' This generation dreams of flight. 'I have seen them walking the streets of London and the towns of the Midlands,' Whitehouse goes on: 'They are ever looking upwards, and only turn away when they pass a newsvendor's stall. There they gorge their eyes on the latest weekly air paper, or the cover of their favourite air monthly.' Now, with the war, these are not only stories. 'It will be the Royal Air Force that carries the weapons to the enemy, not the Army or the Navy,' Whitehouse vows, and somewhere in this overblown martial rhetoric is a slightly bored young man who does not want to work in his father's rubber brokerage any longer.

The first myth about my grandfather is that he hated his work in the City, and longed to escape. This was a story my grandmother told my father, before she died, and that my great-aunt repeated to me, and it is of course a story of great convenience, if you wish to explain the absence of a loved one, for it gives him motive. I have no evidence beyond a further detail. In the summer of 1939, my grandfather bought a beautiful car: an MG TB Midget, soft-top, low to the ground, in British racing green with green leather seats. This is not a sensible car for a man with a wife and a baby – my father was born in May – and its price was almost a third of what it had cost him to have a house built three years earlier. But it was his, and even on a cold day he drove with the top down, and it might show a man in love with machines, who wished their flair and glamour to echo his own.

There are many ways to date the start of the Second World War. On 1 September 1939, the Luftwaffe bombed Warsaw at dawn, and two days later, when Chamberlain declared war, there were air raid sirens over London. Churchill did not become Prime Minister until 10 May 1940, but the next day he ordered the bombing of Germany, and the United States did not enter the war until its fleet had been bombed by the Japanese at Pearl Harbor on 7 December 1941. These are all versions of the war, but my grandfather's story might begin on 18 October 1939, when he enrols in the RAF Volunteer Reserve at No. 1 Recruiting Centre at Uxbridge, just outside London. He waits, during the autumn and winter, and the following May he reports to Padgate, in Lancashire, and is sent to No. 5 Initial Training Wing in Hastings, on the south coast. In July, he moves on to RAF Kidlington for flying training, and he passes through these lessons a little faster than some, for he already has his civilian pilot's licence. On 23 December 1940, he arrives at RAF Bassingbourn, where he will complete operational training – flying out in bombers, trial runs – and at the end of April he is posted to 57 Squadron at RAF Feltwell.

At the start of July, a month after our trip to Holland, my father and I go to the 57 Squadron annual reunion. It has been a wet summer, and there are floods by the motorway as we drive north-east from London. In March 1935, following RAF Expansion Scheme C, the Air Ministry began to build airfields in locations that allowed the bombers to reach Berlin in a latitudinally straight line. RAF Feltwell was established that year, but it is now an operational United States Air Force base, so the reunion takes place a little further north. We drove for a while through flat Lincolnshire, fields of blue flax and yellow rape, and it was on this journey that we pulled over by a village shop to ask directions and I first heard the old nickname for these eastern reaches of England, closest to Holland and then to Germany, where every country lane ends in an old airfield. Bomber County is where the bombers left from and where they came home to, and, every summer, the 57/630 Squadron Association holds its reunion, with dinner at a mock-Tudor hotel followed by a day at East Kirkby airfield. Because I wanted to know what became of the bombers, I came here too.

The halls of the hotel are thickly carpeted, and on the walls there are prints of Lancasters and famous raids, the Dambusters, Peenemünde, and the heroes, Gibson, Cheshire. The old bombers wear blue blazers, with rows of medals at their left breast pocket; they have askew teeth, and always wonderful posture, and every year they come back here with their grandchildren to see again their crews. In the hotel bar before dinner, with brass fittings and low chairs, my father and I both dressed in suits walk between them, lighting upon the oldest ones. Each time, we ask, were you at Feltwell in 1941, and each time there is a pause before they answer, no. These are survivors, and they joined later, in '43 and '44, and so their stories are of the last raids of the war, when Berlin was lit with fire.

We go through to dinner, and I sit next to a navigator. After the war, he made a fortune in electrical wiring, and he does not mind when I take out my notebook. 'The girls everywhere were all over you,' he tells me: 'You were like a film star', and these are for the most part happy memories. On the base, there was always food and always a bed, better than most four-star hotels in England. They were young men. He knew one thirty-year-old pilot, he said, and they called him grandpa for his age. When my grandfather died, he was thirty.

In the fog and rain of Lincolnshire and Norfolk, with their low cloud base, there were times – seven, ten, twelve days – when operations were called off. 'The birds couldn't fly,' he tells me, and sometimes they would not know until the last minute, until they were ready, and twice his plane was called back with a red flare when they were already at the end of the runway. 'Pissed off you were,' he says. You had been ready all day. At nine o'clock, on an ordinary morning, they say that you are flying tonight. You go to the rec room to get your kit, and you go to the plane, and fly out over the North Sea. The gunners pop their guns, and the pilot notes engine temperature; the navigator checks his equipment. You fly for twenty minutes, but it takes another twenty to get wheels up, and another twenty for wheels down.

You get back to base at 1130, and then to the mess for bacon and eggs. At 1230, you report to the briefing room, and are told your target. The navigator knows first, but soon the rest of the air and ground crews calculate tonight's mission, because everyone knows the distances, and how much fuel that asks: five hours to the Ruhr, eight to Berlin, ten to Munich. In the afternoon, the phones on base are disconnected.

In the dusk, you go out to the plane, and sit on the grass, and smoke. You know that you will have no real food for ten hours. You have a Thermos of tea, and a piece of chocolate, but it will be so cold in the plane that you have to hold the chocolate in your mouth to warm it up. It will feel like minus fifty degrees and your teeth will ache, and so you get dressed up. Uniform, then a woolly, a thick jumper, then a fur-lined flying suit, with zips, so that if you are wounded they can unzip it from your body; on your feet, silk socks, then air force socks, then wool socks, then flying boots. The planes take off close. As one lifts, another is beginning to roll along the runway, and the next is joining the queue.

He can tell me all this, and how the flak hits you all at once, like a sledgehammer; and about a night in March 1944, a raid on Munich when ninety-seven planes failed to return; but the navigator knows that there is only so far telling can take you, and so after dinner, when there is an auction to raise funds for the association, and one of the prizes is a joyride tomorrow in a Lancaster, he bids and bids, and after he has won he turns to my father and says, that's for your boy.

In the morning, we sit for the Lord's Prayer under the wings of the Lancaster in the hangar, with rain tapping on the roof and housemartins nesting in the far corners. 'Just Jane' is the Lancaster that lives at East Kirkby, a restored Mk VII model built in the spring of 1945, too late to see service in the war. This plane can no longer fly, but for a fee takes anyone willing to relive a little of the past on a short taxi up the runway, turning before take-off and rolling back to the hangar. Standing by the plane now, looking up at the wings, it is a strain to imagine that this could fly at all: it is a children's toy, blocky like Lego, a clumsy fit. In the shadow, as we wait for the rain to pass, I speak to a gunner. He had once sat in the little Perspex bubble on top, and I ask him how it was up there. Bloody awful, he said: cold, and hard to stay awake. It was like driving a motorbike, he told me, with handlebars to twist to left or right, but it was hard work.

The service ends, and the rain clears, and they bring out the Lancaster, and a foot-ladder, and ducking my head I step up and into the barrel of the plane. All is clean, and oiled, and green. On his service record, my grandfather's height is five feet seven inches, and he must have been grateful that he was not a tall man, for there is only a narrow, low crawl-space up past the radio and the navigator's equipment to the left, and into the cockpit.

There are thirty-eight dials in the cockpit of a Lancaster. They have the faces of old watches, and they give simple readings, whether you are level or not, which direction you are heading, how much fuel you have left. There are four channels on the radio, and a dial to choose the colour of the day – red, amber, or green – for the lights on the undercarriage. These were to show the gunners on the ground that you were a friend, not an enemy plane; something for the Royal Navy to aim at, the pilot joked, for there are many stories of Lancasters shot down by their own defences.

The cockpit of a Lancaster is an idea of power and restraint. Everything is metal, and everything is rattling with noise as the Merlin engines turn and thrash, but the pilot's seat is strict, straight-backed. There is no cushion here, and the pilot must sit upright and look down, out of the windows, at the crowds who are standing below and waving. It was cold and cramped inside a Lancaster on operations, and many died in just this space, but with people watching all around it is the centre of the world. The gunner told me it was bloody awful in his turret, but still he comes back to the reunion and looks at the Lancaster every year, and during dinner the navigator said it was 'a fantastic aeroplane'. 'Anything else was pathetic,' he said, and today along with me on my ride are another old navigator, who has not been inside a Lancaster in the sixty-two years since the end of the war, and an ancient, shaking pilot with his grandson.

Imagine a school you have read about in old-fashioned books, but now the toys – the footballs and the cricket bats – are great weapons, and this is close to the bomber base. Inside the control tower at East Kirkby is a small museum, with solitary tattered items on show. The Christmas menu from the officers' mess in the last year of the war was turtle soup, turkey and pork with roast potatoes, Brussels sprouts, Christmas pudding and mince pies, and this is the dated food of British institutions: solid, fixed, in place. All is familiar, even the prospect of terror.

A little later in the afternoon, I sit and talk with an old WAAF, from the Women's Auxiliary Air Force, in the canteen known as the NAAFI. The NAAFI has plates with pictures of bombers on them, crew photographs on the walls, ketchup in plastic bottles, and tea and cakes. It is always 1943 in here. Alma Leedham is eighty-five years old with a grey bob and glasses, and her eyes light up when she talks about 4,000 lb bombs and incendiaries. She was a bomb loader on Lancasters, at East Kirkby for the second half of the war, and the airmen used to chat her up while she was trying to work. For her, this was not the physics of total war but a job, and a fun one. She drove a little tractor to pull the carts of bombs out to the planes, at their dispersal points, and once in a while when they needed a hand she would clamber up into the Lanc to help out with the stacking.

The bombers keep their own history. Their affection for the weapons, for the bombs and the planes, comes from familiarity, and this is why they pause when they answer my questions, waiting for me to finish my notes, for me to get it right. They might never say this, but they do not quite trust the official narrative of the strategic air offensive against Germany, in four thick black volumes, and the books they sell at the reunion, and often press upon me, are not published by famous publishing houses in London but usually photocopies, bound at home. These stories have titles like 'A Night to Remember' and 'Simply the Best', and they talk about fate, and luck, and sometimes there are ghosts.

In the hangar at East Kirkby, a man has set up a stall. He has a moustache and a blue blazer, and red folders of losses and crashes, and a map with blue and red string. These are his notes on all the planes from Bomber County during the Second World War, each of their operations, each of their losses, and, he tells me with a slight laugh, 'quite a few mid-air collisions'.

This is an almost futile project, for the information is more reliably recorded elsewhere, and there is little he could tell me that I could not find by reaching for the books upon my shelf. But like everyone at East Kirkby, he is holding on to a history he considers his own, and possession involves the responsibility to tell. I found him macabre, but my father pauses at his stall and asks for the folder of losses for the night of 11 June 1943, the night my grandfather died. Under the serial number of my grandfather's Lancaster he has noted, 'Swift and crew POW.'

On Sunday afternoon, the reunion closed with a looping fly-past by a Spitfire and a few jokes about next year's advance bookings, 'for the optimists among us'. I went back to London, and on to America, where I started a new teaching job in a small town a few hours' drive north of New York City. In the long light of an upstate autumn, and as the snow came in November, I read about the bombing campaigns, and I wrote to Alma Leedham. We agreed that when I was next in England I might call upon her, and so on a perfectly clear winter's day at the end of the year I took a train to the south coast, past stubbly fields and lines of trees.

Alma Leedham lives in a pink bungalow called Green Pastures, with a cat called Casper and eleven fish in the pond. There are Christmas cards on the mantelpiece, and we sit on stools in the kitchen, drinking weak instant coffee. She shows me how she recycles teabags. She calls her husband Terry, although his nickname is 'Lofty' – he was a tall man, and the forces love nicknames – and although he is long dead, she mentions him constantly.

She met Terry at RAF Scampton in 1943; sunny Scampton, they called it, where it always rained. He was with 57 Squadron in France at the start of the war, and when France fell in the summer of 1940 he stayed behind with a couple of others to blow up the bomb dump. He rowed back across the Channel, she tells me, and rejoined the squadron at Lossiemouth, and from there to their new base at Feltwell in November 1940, where the Squadron was re-equipping on Wellingtons.

My grandfather came to Feltwell in April 1941 as a Wellington pilot. By September, he had flown thirty-one raids, and was sent on as an instructor. Terry was there a little longer. He wanted to be a navigator, Alma said, but he suffered from vertigo, so he became a flight sergeant with the ground crew, maintaining and arming the turret guns. The vertigo probably saved his life, she says, and he stayed with 57 Squadron after their move to Scampton in September 1942, and for another twenty years. He was posted to Iraq, and Singapore, and later he and Alma worked for IBM. He died long after the war, with children and grandchildren.

Alma believes she has a guardian angel. On April Fool's Day, when she was nine, she was run over. She was crossing the road and a cart hit her, crushing her right leg; her foot was caught in the spokes of the wheel, and she bit down so hard on her tongue that it nearly came off. She wanted to be a driver anyway. She left school at fourteen, and worked for a dressmaker in Kingston-on-Thames, but she got sacked for sliding down the banisters just after her seventeenth birthday. She got a job in the office of a spark plug factory, and she joined the WAAFs on 2 December 1941, but was too scared to tell her mother until three days before she left. They sent her to Bridgnorth. 'You wonder what you have done,' she says, and most of the girls cried themselves to sleep. From there to Morecambe, to learn to march, and then Blackpool, to learn to drive lorries. In the spring of 1942, she was sent to Pwllheli, in north Wales, where she saw dolphins for the first time and learned to drive cars. The town is on a hill, over a bay, and one of the girls crashed into a baker's van during practice. In late May, she got 95 per cent in her exams, and joined 57 Squadron at Scampton in June 1942.

The story of bombing does not have to be a tragedy. Alma is often laughing as she tells me of pub crawls in Lincoln, starting at the post office and working all down the high street to the Assembly Rooms, a dancehall by the cathedral with a live band, and if they missed the half-past-ten bus back to base, then six girls would pile on to a bicycle. She talks about Jean, who asked a Scottish captain what was under his kilt, and her friend Vivian from the bomb dump, and then one night in early June 1943, when she went to the post office to meet the girls, only Terry was there. In the first ten days of June 1943, my grandfather was waiting to fly his last raid, on Münster, and he is almost dead, but this is not Alma's calendar. She and Terry used to eat tomatoes on toast for dinner, and when they were engaged they danced the tango at the Assembly Rooms.

This is Alma's favourite war story. She is driving her tractor out to the dispersal point, to bomb up the Lancaster for operations, but the tractor bumps over a stone, and a box falls out. She calls to some boys – there are always a few boys in Alma's stories, waiting by the planes to chat her up – to help her straighten the boxes, and they ask, what are these, and she says, 'Incendiary', and before she says, 'bombs', they are running, over the runways.

Alma knew the bombs, as well as anyone could, and she told me too that she sometimes wanted to hide away on a Lancaster. Once, a pilot took six WAAFs up, and it was very bare inside the plane, she told me, and she was sick, and because there were no pilots in her stories I asked her then, were you friends with any airmen, and she says, no. No: 'Most of us steered clear of the aircrew because they weren't coming back.'

I think that Alma did not want to talk about the pilots, but because I had taken the train to see her that day, and because in some way it mattered that I was writing a book, she tried to go on, and if before she was telling slapstick, then when she started to talk about the airmen her anecdotes assumed some of the apartness of fairy tales. They sometimes took a flowerpot with them on the raid, she said, because when you drop them they make a whistling noise to startle those below, and so soon there were no flowerpots in the gardens near the base; and when the Americans came, there was fresh ice cream sent every day. But by then it is clear to both of us that I am looking for something else, and I think she did not want to disappoint me, so in the middle of these stories she paused and said, quite quietly, it was terrible. I asked, what, and she said that once a Lancaster had come home 'with so little of the rear gunner they had to hose it out'.

Alma drove me very fast back to the train station. She calls seatbelts 'stupidity belts', and told me how she likes to watch Formula One. She knows which drivers are good, and which use too much caution. It's knowing when to take the risks, she said, and told me to marry someone with a good heart. Later, I sometimes joked that I was having a flirtation with an 85-year-old woman, and this is not wholly wrong, for Alma's war was a love story.

There was something more I wanted to ask Alma, but a mix of manners and superstition prevented me. So I waited, and then in the new year I wrote to her, and in time she wrote back. January had been a busy month, she said, with three pantomimes, a Big Band Concert, her son's birthday, and the death of two old friends. 'But at our ages that is only to be expected,' she wrote, and went on:

> Your question regarding the hosing out of a rear gunners turret on the return of a Lancaster's raid on Germany was an expression used by my husband, Terry. Being the Flight Sergeant in charge of the guns and turrets he and his men had the awful job of checking everything on the aircraft when they returned from a raid. The rear gunners were often targeted by the German fighters as being the easiest to reach and when the crews came home many were dead before they got back to base. I only heard Terry use the expression (hosing) on one occasion when he came into the hangar in tears. On that particular morning when we went in to work, we heard that our planes had had a really rough trip/sortie.

She signed off, Cheerio for now.

'When I died they washed me out of the turret with a hose,' wrote Randall Jarrell in one of his most famous poems. The speaker is a gunner on an American bomber, either a B-17 or a B-24, and he sits in a Plexiglas sphere hung below the body of the plane, known as the ball turret. This moment, of a man's wet remains washed coldly away, is acutely and specifically nasty, but that does not mean it happened only once. Alma was remembering RAF Scampton, in 1943 or 1944, and a Lancaster; and Randall Jarrell was writing of an American bomber, from far away in Texas or Illinois; and both are awful; and both are unreal. Alma's telling is perched somewhere halfway between a fable and a real thing. It was an expression, she said, a habitual pattern of language, and also a specific episode, the morning Terry came into the hangar in tears. And Jarrell's poem as a whole has some of the smoothness of myth, a fate for all men instead of a story of one. Everything, even the worst thing you can imagine, can be a cliché.

'The Death of the Ball Turret Gunner' is a short poem –

> From my mother's sleep I fell into the State,
> And I hunched in its belly till my wet fur froze.
> Six miles from earth, loosed from its dream of life,
> I woke to black flak and the nightmare fighters.
> When I died they washed me out of the turret with a hose

– and what is perhaps most striking is its haste. There is so little time here, only fifty-two words. We begin with what is apparently a birth. 'From my mother's sleep I fell,' the poem opens, and while this might make sense – where else to place a birth than at the start? – the birth is suspended here by what follows. He is born into the State, and still waits, 'hunched in its belly'. The birth is delayed, even in this brief poem, but in the third and fourth lines the unborn child becomes an airman in combat, six miles above the earth. Here the flak will wake him; and yet this is a cruel reversal, for anti-aircraft fire does not wake airmen but kills them, and in the nowhere moment between the end of the fourth line and the start of the fifth, he is dead.

The birth of the ball turret gunner is no more than a preparation for his death; there is nothing in between. When my grandfather enlisted, in the third week of October 1939, he was measured like an infant: five feet seven inches, black hair, grey eyes, and a chest thirty inches around. He has, his service record explains, moles on his right arm and to the left of his navel, a birth mark on the nape of his neck; the dip of a vaccination on his right arm, and scars on his right elbow and his left knee. These details build an identity, but the description is imagining his violent death: in such precision it prefigures the body blasted, and the need to know this single man among other likely corpses. The list brings a man to life only in the case of his death.

For the moment, this is fiction, and for the moment we must wait. In England, the war began on a Sunday morning, and a couple of days earlier my grandfather's parents, Jim and Agnes, and his two sisters left London for Sussex, where they stayed with my grand-parents in Honeysuckle Cottage. My father was only four months old, and the house not big, but they shared bedrooms and, in the evenings, listened to the radio. My grandfather enlisted in October, but was not called to training at once, so he returned to his job in London. Each morning, he drove his sister Brenda into Haywards Heath, where she had begun a secretarial course at Miss Hosta's Academy, and where he took the usual train. He carried a little bag with him, ready for service, but they did not call him yet, and so he waited. Each evening, Brenda would finish at Miss Hosta's, and sit in the car until his train came in.

By the end of the year, no bombs had fallen, and no German troops had stormed the south coast. The house was feeling smaller, and my great-grandparents and great-aunts returned to London. Through the winter, my grandfather waited like a toy soldier; invisible to us, for a while, but we can guess him commuting, and watching his son grow, and carrying his satchel. Some Saturdays, he flew from a nearby airfield, to keep in practice, but still only on a little plane. Historians call this period 'the phoney war', for while Britain and Germany were technically at war, there was no fighting, long through the winter. January 1940 was exceptionally cold, and then on 9 April Germany invaded Denmark and Norway. Two days later, according to Sir Charles Webster and Noble Frankland, the official historians of the strategic air offensive against Germany, 'six Wellingtons and two Blenheims of Bomber Command, operating under the control of Coastal Command, attacked the aerodrome at Stavanger in Norway. This was the first Royal Air Force bombing attack against a mainland target in the Second World War.' On 10 May, Germany invaded the Netherlands, and Winston Churchill became Prime Minister of Britain. By 14 May, the French front at Sedan had collapsed, and on 15 May ninety-nine RAF bombers attacked east of the Rhine for the first time, targeting the oil works of the Ruhr. In the words of the official history:

> Thus began the Bomber Command strategic air offensive against Germany. For many years it was the sole means at Britain's disposal for attacking the heart of the enemy, and, more than any other form of armed attack upon the enemy, it never ceased until almost exactly five years later Germany, with many of her cities in ruin, her communications cut, her oil supplies drained dry and her industry reduced to chaos, capitulated to the invading armies of the Grand Alliance. It was probably the most continuous and gruelling operation of war ever carried out.

But we are getting ahead of ourselves. In the third week of May, my grandfather finally received his orders. He resigned from Kaufman Heyworth, and took the train to 3 Reception Centre, at Padgate in Lancashire.

I think he starts to leave us now. From now, all his story will be a tumble of leavings, and we will know him more by what he puts away than by what he keeps. The categories of a traditional storytelling – of possession, of ambition, of desire – will mean nothing. It will no longer be possible to tell his choices from what he is told to do, or his decisions from his orders. From now on, he is always rushing, and in the fabric of everything I can recover is the tug of borrowed time. But this necessity will permit a strange and wonderful luxury, for now his entire existence is in the interest of the great recording machine of the British military bureaucracy, and everything is recorded. If we can find him then it is precisely because he gave so much away and became the property of someone else.

The first stage at the Reception Centre is the clearance of civilian clothing, and he is issued with identity discs, a respirator, and eating irons, a knife, spoon and fork, which he carries with him, as well as a mug and sheets. On the first day, there are vaccinations for typhoid and tetanus, lectures on personal hygiene and venereal disease, and a mathematics exam: fractions, decimals, square roots. He went to a private school in north London, and then an expensive business school in Switzerland; he passes this exam without pause. He sleeps in a wide Nissen hut with twenty other men. The stove is in the centre, and it is cold in the morning, and the washrooms are a hundred yards away across the yard, but there is a day of drilling to warm him up, and in the evening he can buy a pack of cigarettes and Blue Label beer in the noisy NAAFI, where others play billiards and darts, and write letters home.

I know this scene in its detail because in the archives of the Imperial War Museum in London there are two fat bound volumes, on crinkly paper, of the never-published memoirs of an airman: 'Here Today, Bomb Tomorrow: The Saga of a Bomber Pilot', by Denis Hornsey, DFC. As he recounts with occasionally excruciating precision, Hornsey took the train from Euston to RC Padgate on 21 May 1940, three days before my grandfather; the two men left on the same day a week later. Because of Hornsey, I know that my grandfather spent much of his time drilling, once naked in what they called the 'FFI Parade' – 'This is, for the uninformed, a "Free From

Infection" inspection' – and that the tea tasted funny. There were rumours that this was because 'bromide was added to keep the men from thinking too actively of chasing after women', and I know the exact list of kit issued to the new arrivals. They were given 'three heavy woollen vests and pants, and a heavy woollen Guernsey; three service shirts, three service collars; clothes brushes, hair brushes, boot brushes and button brushes' – but we must break here, for sixty-seven years and a couple of weeks later I am sitting in a high-ceilinged hotel room in Haarlem, Noord-Holland, with my father. We have spent the day in my grandfather's cemetery, and now my father is brushing his hair slowly, before he goes to bed, and I laugh and say, you brush your hair like a little girl. He looks at me and says, I brush my hair like my father.

For a moment, he is visible; we are with him. But Hornsey can only take us so far. He pauses from his complaints about the food and constipation to confess:

> I find it hard to remember the names of most of those who were with me at Padgate, from May 21st to May 28th during 1940. Their faces, too, are hard to recall. If I concentrate I can picture some of them in my mind, cheery and smiling, as they crowd round in my memory. But they are dim faces now, and most of them are dead faces.

On 29 May, Hornsey was posted to 31 Initial Training Wing, and my grandfather was posted to 5 ITW, at Hastings on the south coast. He walks a mile to Padgate train station, carrying full kit. Or perhaps he drove his deep green MG, fast, with the top down. It was the day after his son's first birthday, and I only guessed he took the train because Hornsey did.

The Initial Training Wing was based in a row of old hotels between Hastings Pier and Warrior Square, and on the day he arrived, it was still setting up. Hastings is a seaside town, all flaky white Georgian buildings and shabby genteel hopefulness, and further round the coast, at Margate and in the Thames Estuary, the

British army were evacuating from Dunkirk. He could hear the guns from France, that week, but the air was salty, and there was a bucket-and-spade atmosphere to even the training orders. 'When the barrack rooms are close to the beach cadets and airmen are to undress in their quarters and proceed direct to the shore with great-coats over their bathing costumes,' instructs one ITW memorandum dated 7 June 1940, and continues: 'Respirators are to be taken on the beach on these occasions and laid carefully on the greatcoats and not on the sand.'

Lessons start at half past eight the next morning. There is more advanced mathematics, now: algebra, the substitution and trans-position of formulae, maxima and minima; the language of geometry, the parallelogram of velocities, vector and scalar. There is rifle drill, and he learns to shoot a Browning gun and spends an hour each week on the Morse buzzer. There are lectures on air navigation: the form of the earth, longitude and latitude, bearings, Mercator's pro-jection, magnetic north. The whole of the world is waiting to be described, in lectures eight hours a week, and four hours of organ-ized games, and he is learning to make foreign things familiar. He watches films about meteorology and the internal combustion engine. He memorizes the silhouettes of friendly and enemy air-craft, and they tell him too about the physical effects of service fly-ing: lack of oxygen, exposure, glare, noise, discomfort. There is a lecture on first aid – the treatment of haemorrhage and shock, the treatment of burns – and another on how to pull an injured body from the wreckage of a plane. These things may be useful later.

The war is coming close; but in the afternoon he pulls his great-coat over his bathing costume, itching his legs, and walks down the stony beach – careful to fold the greatcoat, and sit the gasmask on top – and treads in the soft brown English water. Later, there is a boxing match in the Adelphi Hotel. They have put up a temporary gym in the basement, and the airmen gather in and smoke, and in the air the broken smell of rubber and sweat, and on a night like this it might be hard to recall the war, here in this holiday town. But

on a night like this, the war still steps a little closer. According to
the Operations Record Book for 5 ITW, on the night of 19 June, at
2330, 'a Whitley Bomber of No. 77 Squadron, which had been on a
bombing flight over Germany, returned with one engine unservice-
able & crash landed in the sea off Hastings Pier. The crew of 5 were
landed, but slightly wounded.' It was safe, this time, but it was also
near: the low bomber, an engine whining out; then the splash, and
shouts as men run down the beach to boats to pull the crew from
the sea.

No-one was ever so far from the war as Randall Jarrell, deep in
Texas. He registered for the selective service draft in October 1940 in
Austin, but was not called. So he went on teaching at the university,
and writing reviews, and seeing his poems into print. His letters
from 1941, full of worry about the *New Republic* and *Partisan Review*,
say nothing of the war elsewhere. In the autumn of 1942, after the
publication of his first collection of poems, *Blood for a Stranger*, he
was ordered to join the Air Corps, and in October wrote to a friend:
'You should see me sitting in a Trainer with the hood down anx-
iously trying to get airspeed, altitude, and direction all right at the
same time. It's a pathetic sight.' A couple of weeks later, he wrote
to Edmund Wilson: 'Flying is pretty dull and I'm bad at it.' At the
end of the year, he was rejected as a pilot, and in January wrote to a
friend: 'Did you ever figure out how we (we means Congress and
such, here) got into the war on the side we're on?' In February, he
was sent to Sheppard Field near Wichita Falls, a training base for the
United States Army Air Force, where he worked in the mail room
and was later transferred to the Interviewing and Classification
Department. It was hardly a heroic war. In March, he wrote to his
wife to ask her to send him his tennis shirts and shoes, and in the
summer, when he earned a medal for qualifying as pistol marks-
man, he told her he would give it to their cat, 'to wear it around his
neck on a ribbon on special occasions'. He writes at length about
the food on base, and on Friday, 11 June 1943, the last day of my

grandfather's life, he declared: 'I went to bed about 8.15 last night, and feel swell today. The war's certainly going well.'

This was a careful pose. Jarrell was a poet, and his particular resistance to the war came from the war's apparent resistance to poetry. 'I don't think I'll be able to do any writing much,' he told his wife not long after arriving at Sheppard Field. The problem was not that he lacked time, but that he lacked a subject. 'The trouble with writing a story about the army is this: people expect something to happen in a story,' he explained to a friend, 'but the whole point of the army is that nothing ever does happen.' This is one of his favourite themes. 'Trust the army to make anything meaningless,' he wrote to his wife; and 'I'm just a needle in 75,000 haystacks'; and he reports a joke he made for the boys. 'I asked them if they knew the profession the Army really does prepare one for,' he wrote: 'The answer is being a convict.'

Jarrell had to learn that bombing was a subject for poetry, and his poems about the base are full of images of schooling and of schoolchildren. 'What we do mostly is stand in line,' he told his wife: this is not incidental but essential to the experience of military training, and so he wrote a poem about it, a scene of soldiers waiting

> To form a line to form a line to form a line;
> After the things have learned that they are things,
> Used up as things are, pieces of the plain
> Flat object-language of a child or states;
> After the lines, through trucks, through transports, to the lines
> Where things die as though they were not things.

Later, in a letter to Robert Lowell, he called this 'the armiest army poem I've written'. This is the first lesson of Randall Jarrell: in lining up we learn our own repetition. 'You are something there are millions of,' he writes in his poem 'The Sick Nought', and training teaches this precisely with one eye on the possibility of death. At the front, in combat, 'things die as though they were not things', and while we may pause here – surely these are people, soldiers? – the logic is coldly simple. In training, we move towards death, after which we are only ever a thing.

'I don't think I'll be able to do any writing here,' Jarrell had written, in February 1943, and again: 'The conditions aren't very good for writing.' Yet by August 1944, when he was invited to contribute to an anthology of war poetry, he replied to the editor: 'if anybody can write a good poem about anything, he ought to do it about a war he's in.' In 1945 he published his second volume of poetry, *Little Friend, Little Friend*. The collection is dominated by poems about life on the base and the details of air war, and its title alludes to the bombers' nickname for their fighter escort, the little planes that would accompany and protect them. By 1944, Jarrell had been convinced that this war, and particularly the mechanics of bombing, presented a fine subject for poetry.

In April 1943, Jarrell transferred to Chanute Field in Illinois, to qualify as an operator on link trainers, indoor model aeroplanes which simulated flying conditions for students. In October, he met a pilot called Northrop, 'the 19th Bombardment man', who was heavily decorated: 'the Distinguished Service Cross, the Silver Star, the Air Medal, the Purple Heart, several citations, and something else I forget'. As he wrote to his wife:

> He was telling me about battles; he said he had swell motion pictures he'd taken of the battles of the Java Sea and the Coral Sea, but they confiscated them before he got home. He said he dropped a 4,000 pound bomb on a transport at low altitude, and the transport broke in two and completely disappeared before the plane was out of sight of her. He saw a rugby stadium (a concrete one holding 35,000 people) in which a 4,000 pound bomb had been dropped; it was completely leveled.

Here, bombing runs are marvels, tall fantastical tales, and this is the second lesson of Randall Jarrell: the planes and their bombs are a spectacle of engineering and design, in their force so close to nature and yet so new and strange. In working as an instructor, Jarrell belonged to the US Second Air Force, and in a poem called simply 'Second Air Force' he describes an outsider to a base, a mother visiting her son stationed there:

> She sees a world: sand roads, tar-paper barracks,
> The bubbling asphalt of the runways, sage,
> The dunes rising to the interminable ranges,
> The dim flights moving over clouds like clouds.
> The armorers in their patched faded green,
> Sweat-stiffened, banded with brass cartridges,
> Walk to the line; their Fortresses, all tail,
> Stand wrong and flimsy on their skinny legs,
> And the crews climb to them clumsily as bears.
> The head withdraws into its hatch (a boy's),
> The engines rise to their blind laboring roar,
> And the green, made beasts run home to air.

The base is a new world, where war and landscape are bound together – the planes move 'over clouds like clouds' – and where the awkwardness of men, clumsy like bears, can be made clean in their machines. The planes themselves, the Flying Fortresses, can be awkward too, on their skinny legs, but when they rise off and up, then they are home. And this scene, when 'green, made beasts run home to air', is wonderful to tell.

Men can lose their selves; and terrible, powerful machines can carry them and bombs great enough to level a concrete rugby stadium; there is danger here, and a trace of horror. In 1961, at an arts festival at Pfeiffer College, Jarrell spoke about his bombing poems, and his talk was recorded. 'To tell you the truth, I didn't like the war much,' he began, in a wry but childish voice, and continued with familiar reluctance: 'If I had my way, they just wouldn't have wars.' Then he begins to address the poems themselves. He talks about standing in line, and about the daydreams of soldiers, and in discussing 'The Death of the Ball Turret Gunner' he folds himself down and over, and reaches between his legs, to demonstrate to his uneasily giggling audience the exact posture. As he talks and as the audience both laugh and are afraid, he is enjoying his theme for its wild blend of horror and humour, its absurd and violent promise. In this lecture, he returns to a conversation he remembered with a decorated bomber pilot, who 'told me in great detail how he was responsible for a raid that completely wiped out a small Swiss town. It was an easy error to make, just a navigational error, they turned right when they should have turned left', and as he rambles on, the audience, expecting a joke, laugh.

He may be remembering the bomber Northrop from Chanute Field, transformed in time and reflection to a slapstick villain, or this may be a different meeting on a different base, but its essential idea is the same. 'Inside the infallible invulnerable / Machines,' writes Jarrell in 'Siegfried':

> the skin of steel, glass, cartridges,
> Duties, responsibilities, and – surely – deaths,
> There was only you.

For the bombers are still men, and under all of Jarrell's war poetry hums an uneasy pun: when we say 'bombers', we often mean the planes themselves, the Fortresses on skinny legs, the tight Lancasters. But we may also mean the men who flew them, and in this new and possibly perfect kind of technological war – 'the transport broke in two and completely disappeared before the plane was out of sight', 'a raid that completely wiped out a small Swiss town' – men still die. Human fallibility and loss were not in the plan; and this is the third lesson of Randall Jarrell.

'It was not dying: everybody died' is the opening line of Jarrell's poem 'Losses', and here is the struggle. Even in training, which he elsewhere calls 'these rehearsals of the raids', there are deaths. The poem tells of crews learning, on a base somewhere in unnamed America, and:

> It was not dying: we had died before
> In the routine crashes – and our fields
> Called up the papers, wrote home to our folks,
> And the rates rose, all because of us.
> We died on the wrong page of the almanac,
> Scattered on mountains fifty miles away;
> Diving on haystacks, fighting with a friend,
> We blazed up on the lines we never saw.

These are not-quite-airmen, and this is not-quite-war, and deep in the poem is the knowledge not simply that this new type of war may mean new types of deaths, but more than this: we die by analogy; we rehearse our deaths; and if there never before has been a bomber war, then how can we know how to die in this one? Our lessons have limits. We can only learn so much. 'We died like aunts or pets or foreigners,' he writes, for these are the only ways of dying a young man might have seen, until now.

All is new. In October 1945, Jarrell wrote that 'most of them were kids just out of high school', but bombing was young too, and the poem goes on, and the students begin operations. Then, he writes:

> In bombers named for girls, we burned
> The cities we had learned about in school –
> Till our lives wore out.

Perhaps the greatest tragedy of bombing was that so much had to be learned, and in the lessons the war approaches. One day, my grandfather met the war face to face, and it did not leave him. On 11 July 1940, he reported to RAF Kidlington, to begin first Elementary and then Service Flying Training. He stayed until almost the end of the year, at lectures on airmanship and forced-landing procedures, and here he begins navigation exercises and is introduced to the bombs. There was a demonstration by a staff pilot of high- and low-level dive-bombing. Near the end of his time here, he took the Pilot Navigator Test – 'A cross country flight over a triangular course with each leg approximately 50 miles' – and it was here, at about half past eight on an evening at the end of September, that a training exercise miscarried. A Harvard trainer on a practice flight from RAF Kidlington crashed in a field near Begbroke, and the pupil who was flying the plane burned to death.

After passing his flying training course, on 12 December 1940, my grandfather drove home for ten days' leave, and two days before Christmas reported to RAF Bassingbourn, near Cambridge, to join 11 Operational Training Unit. Twenty-one other pilots arrived on the same day, and at twenty minutes past ten that night a Wellington stalled over the runway and crashed into a field next to the village. The crew of six were killed. On 16 January, just after midnight, a German bomber dropped a landmine on the married airmen's quarters. On 15 February, an instructor and pupil on a local flying circuit crashed and were both killed, and ten days later, at half past two in the afternoon, a Wellington landed badly, killing the crew. Just after lunch on 1 March, another Wellington crashed, with all crew killed. Twelve bombs fell on Steeple Morden, the satellite station to Bassingbourn, a couple of hours before dawn on 31 March, and there were attacks by German bombers on four different nights in April.

The war is so close now, but perhaps he is still naive, untouched somehow. I do not know when it began for him, but if not already, then it is soon. On 29 April 1941, he will join 57 Squadron at RAF Feltwell, and a fortnight later, as pilot of a Wellington, he will bomb Hamburg. We burned the cities we learned about in school, wrote Randall Jarrell, and my grandfather had been to Hamburg once, when he was a student in Switzerland before the war, and he had met my grandmother there. I know this because a couple of weeks after his first bombing, he wrote her a sweet note. 'I am just as impatient and bouncy to see you as in the Hamburg days,' he said. But that was earlier, before he was a bomber.

Alma mentioned Lofty's old billet-mate, John Holmes; they shared a hut at Feltwell in 1940 and '41. He no longer came to the reunions, but she said he had stories, so one day my father and I drove from Wales, in the mist, south to the English Riviera. Paignton is a town of raffish hotels and faded concrete, palm trees and the traces of holidays. It looks like it is trying to be somewhere else. Mr Holmes lives in a little white cottage, number 45, but here all the houses have names, and his is called Easterly.

They used to call him 'bosun' because before the war he worked in the shipyards, and in the upstairs room is a gas fire and two small chairs with a telescope between them, looking out to sea. He joined the air force in 1936, and went to France with 57 Squadron; he wanted to fly, but was roughed up in the retreat from Dunkirk, and when he rejoined 57 Squadron at Feltwell he worked as a rigger, on all the plane except the bombs and engines. He said he knew each plane by the sound of its motors, and in his kitchen sixty years later he pushes his lips and does an impression of one.

There is a sadness in his constant joking. He walks with a cane, and has a chairlift to take him up the flight of stairs; he says: 'The only way for old people to keep in the picture is to be awkward.' Twice in two hours he says, 'Trust me: I'm a used-car salesman', and later he describes himself as 'halfway through my ninety-third year and a keen freemason', but I had already seen the ring with the antiquated mathematical device.

They believed in signs and symbols, on the base. The pilots were tense, he said, 'keyed up like a violin', and sometimes they cracked. 'At night, you just imagine,' he said. They liked to fly the same planes, but in the planes you were 'twenty thousand feet nearer your maker than ever you have been in your life', so the planes were part of the problem, and so they held on to what they could. He remembered the drinking – 'four of us used to drink half a bottle of brandy for breakfast' – and the crazed parties. Once, the officers took all the furniture from the mess and set fire to it on the lawn. But mostly he remembered waiting. He went into the flight office at four, before it was light, to have tea and to wait for the incoming bombers. Holmes was the first to check them in, and if they did not return, then he wiped the pilot's name and aircraft number off the chalkboard. Perhaps because this was his job, at the crossroads of loss and life, or perhaps because he had a connection to the sea, and that is lucky, the airmen used to give him things, before they went: a fountain pen, a folded photograph of a girl, keys, and they promised to come back for them. In time, he said, this became so popular that he had to buy a tin cash box to keep them in. I asked what he did with the unclaimed pieces. I was never left with anything, he said. I was lucky.

I had read about the superstitions before. On operations, some saved their ration of chocolate, to eat when they came back, and some took talismans with them: a scarf, a pipe, a cross. The base was a place of heavy ritual, bound in a timeframe of coming and going; luck was simply repetition, and loss a break in the rhythm. In Randall Jarrell's poem 'Eighth Air Force', published in his third collection, *Losses* (1948), a bombing crew are in their hut:

> The other murderers troop in yawning;
> Three of them play Pitch, one sleeps, and one
> Lies counting missions, lies there sweating
> Till even his heart beats: One; One; One.

They are counting and waiting, counting and waiting. 'This is a war . . .' he goes on, and a long pause in the line – three dots of an ellipsis, tick tick tick – tells much of Jarrell's sense of the bomber war; as readers, we wait too. The scene spools out, and 'these play, before they die, / Like puppies with their puppy', and here is the challenge of bomber poetry and of Randall Jarrell. The shock of the accusation – these are 'murderers' – is only lightly muted as he sees them also as puppies, playing with their puppy. The real trick of sympathy here comes in the detail, given only in passing, that they will die for this, in this universe of awkward counting, this childish war, this unlearned lesson.

John Holmes did not know my grandfather. I asked this first of all, a formality to get out of the way, and he paused as if he might say, yes, but he said, no. My father and I had brought a photograph, just in case, of my grandfather scowling in his MG. The top is down, and his cap sits a little large for him, and for a moment Holmes looked at the car. MGs consume a lot of fuel, he said; and fuel was rationed. But he had fuel. He was pumping 60,000 gallons a night, into the planes out on operations, and the odd gallon wouldn't be missed, so sometimes the officers came to him with their sports cars to borrow a little, so they could roar off in the black-out to see their wives and girlfriends. The Wellingtons took high-octane fuel, a richer mix than civilian petrol, so the engine runs hot and the plugs would blacken with carbon; you need to get it cleaned, every now and then, but this is not a problem, for on the base you are working every day with engineers.

For a moment, a scene sparkles before me: of my grandfather and this man, of John Holmes siphoning off a little plane fuel into the shining green car, and my grandfather makes a joke, and waves as he shifts up gears and rolls away. He is a pilot, and when he leaves the base he is still flying along in the dark, on that same fuel. I can't touch him, but I can see him in this exchange; but then I know that this is only a fiction and, like all of Holmes's memories, it is a story about being left behind.

It was only ever fiction for Randall Jarrell, for he was always left behind. His journals from the bases are now in the New York Public Library, and they are the standard composition books used by schoolchildren. He writes his name on the cover, and here are first drafts of some of his poems. In the pencil draft of one, 'Soldier', he writes:

> Find an answer for yourself
> Who taught you why we should die; or why we are dying?

When he came to publish this poem in *Little Friend, Little Friend*, the phrase appears as:

> Here what they teach is other people's deaths;
> Who needs to learn why another man should die?
> Who has taught you, soldier, why you yourself are dying?

Jarrell's slippery pronouns, with their awkward slide between 'he' and 'we', between 'I' and 'you', betray his own position. We never know exactly who is speaking. He can be a mother, watching her son clamber into a Flying Fortress; or in the hut with the troubled airmen; or inside the infallible invulnerable machine. In 'The Truth', he is a child, remembering a bombed city – 'I used to live in London till they burnt it' – and as the ball turret gunner, he is already dead.

Jarrell imagined all. We burned the cities, he wrote; but of course he never had. It was not dying, he wrote; but for so many, it was. 'We are dying' in the first version of 'Soldier' becomes 'other people's deaths' in the second, a little further from him. On a Tuesday morning in February 1943, Jarrell wrote to his wife. 'I miss you ever so much,' he told her, 'and don't worry, I'll stay safe and on the ground to come back to you. You have to ask for flight duty to get it, and I've lost any inclination that way.' Randall Jarrell, who imagined every aspect of the bombing, can only take us this far. By the end of April 1941 my grandfather is crewed up, an operational pilot on Wellington bombers with 57 Squadron, and if we are to follow him we must go up with the planes, and into the cities.

Chapter 3. B is for BOMBERS

29 April 1941

RAF Feltwell is a base like many others. It has the same rough shape – a lopsided diamond, tipped by the cluster of low concrete buildings, and a great cross of runways at the centre, the longest angled into the prevailing wind – and off them curl stands for the planes. They called these dispersal points, but from the air they look like branches, or fingers reaching out. Its structure is common, but its history is particular, and for the history of RAF Feltwell we have the tower log, and the Operations Record Book, and the letters and notes of airmen. They sent me to Feltwell, ran the joke: but I felt awful.

By April 1941, this was a base accustomed to war. After their rough evacuation from France, 57 Squadron re-formed here in the middle of November 1940, where the weather was squally all winter, and the night-flying programme for the new Wellingtons often interrupted by passing enemy aircraft. It started to snow on New Year's Day, 1941, and some days the temperature rose above freezing only in the afternoon. 57 Squadron Wellingtons bombed Ostende on 13 January, and Emden two days later, but on the 19th and again on the 21st, the airfield was attacked by low German raiders. On 4 February, after an unsuccessful operation on Le Havre, two Wellingtons returned to find an enemy raid under way on their home base. The sergeants' mess was bombed, and they had to land at Huntingdon instead. The pattern continues. On 27 February, the Operations Record notes, 'Aerodrome defence exercise abandoned halfway due presence of E.A. [enemy aircraft] in vicinity', and on 19 March, just after half past one in the morning, 'aircraft diverted to Wyton owing to enemy activity over station.' The nights are quieter in April, but on 26 April the Wellingtons are called back after they have already taken off, and on 29 April my grandfather reports for duty.

He starts to fly the next day. On 5 May, he flies for the first time in T2962, a Mk I Wellington, but he is only second pilot. On 8 May, he is up for two hours and forty minutes, to test petrol consumption, and the next day for two hours to test the oil. Just after midnight on Sunday, 11 May, an enemy plane drops incendiary bombs on Feltwell, and in London that was the final night of the Blitz. It was a full moon, clear for bombing, and at five on Sunday afternoon the crews were briefed.

T2962 lifted off at 2250. There were five Wellingtons flying that night from Feltwell, of a force of ninety-two planes from 1 and 3 Groups of Bomber Command; each Wellington carried just under 3,000 lb, a mix of 4 lb incendiary bundles and 500 lb general purpose bombs, fused to explode a quarter of a second after impact. They looped north and east, and as they crossed the North Sea the few clouds that had collected over Norfolk evaporated. They kept the Waddenzee and the northern archipelago of Holland to their right, and in the moonlight with a slight ground haze they passed between Heligoland and Sylt and reached the German coast at Meldorf.

There were Messerschmitts active round Meldorf: another Wellington from 3 Group reported an attack by two Me. 110s at quarter past one, and over the next hour there were further combats with a Junkers and a Messerschmitt. My grandfather's plane was early in the stream, and at just after half past one, flying from the north-east at 15,000 feet, they bombed Hamburg. The target was the Blohm and Voss shipyards, and as they scrambled west and then north for their return they could see the fires behind them.

The Air Ministry's Interceptions and Tactics Report, now declassified and in the National Archives at Kew, tells all this in lists and figures, but even their stark accounting – Group, Time, Average Bombing Height, Average Bomb Load – preserves a sense of strangeness. 3 Group reports nine separate attacks by enemy night-fighters, and at the target there was heavy flak, and three Wellingtons were never heard from again, and yet the violence of the night does not quite dissolve a counter-tone that sounds at times like wonder. Section 7 records the observations of aircrew. Ten miles north-east of Hamburg a Wellington described 'Bursts of tracer observed and something seen on fire in the air'; twenty miles to the west, another recalled 'ball of fire as from burning aircraft falling into sea', and to the south an hour later, 'Falling object bursting into flames.'

This was my grandfather's first night in what the poet John Ciardi called 'the jungle skies', a strange new world of moonlight and a light haze and objects falling in great bursts of flame. In the next three weeks, he flies almost every day and many nights, and twice he bombs Cologne, and then on the 27th he flies his first daytime raid, a mine-laying operation aimed at German battle-cruisers lying off the French coast. By the end of May he has spent more than twenty-four hours – more than a day of his life – inside Wellington T2962, and it is now that we can read his words.

The first of my grandfather's surviving letters was written on the morning of Thursday, 22 May 1941, from the sergeants' mess at RAF Feltwell, and is to my grandmother. 'Dearest Tigger,' he begins, and thanks her for a parcel she has sent but that he has not yet collected, and continues:

> As we settle down they seem to be giving us more time off which is very nice but owing to lack of petrol and any alternative means of transport we are more or less confined to the camp & village. The latter contains about four pubs selling indifferent beer, a small cafe & fish & chip shop that also does quite a decent egg & chips. There is a small library in the mess containing mostly cowboy books & I find I am getting a little old for that sort of thing.

His last bombing run was four days before, on Cologne, but the previous night he had been out on a flying practice. 'I seem to be getting plenty of sleep these days & nights & am feeling quite bouncy,' he writes. The next night, he was again on a practice run for half an hour and then bombed Cologne between two and three in the morning, but in the clouds no-one could see where the bombs had fallen. In the letter, he gives her advice on what to do with some troublesome hens, and pauses to collect the parcel. 'One fine cake, one mess dates, one box assort. cigs, one letter, one coupon,' he notes, and 'Thank you very much my darling.' He signs off: 'Bless you look after yourself.'

The letters go on like this: they are affectionate nothings. On Monday, 26 May, he thanks her for her recent letter, and 'the dates were very good.' Before signing off, he adds: 'Must leave you my darling, it is getting quite dark', and there was night training that evening followed by his first daylight raid at dawn the next day. On 3 June, he apologizes for writing in pencil – 'I appear to have lost my pen' – and complains that he is tired. 'I have done quite a lot of flying to-day,' he explains, and in a postscript, an in-joke: 'Have you got a new bowler hat yet?' In the logbook, he flew on 1 June, and the 3rd, and there were night-flying runs on the 4th and the 8th in preparation for a big raid on German warships at Brest that finally took place on 10 June, but on 9 June he writes to his sister: 'There is no news at all.' On 16 June, he writes to my grandmother, thanking her for her letters and apologizing he cannot call that evening. 'In two hours time I shall be otherwise occupied I fear,' he writes, and according to his logbook he flew for four hours that day and then at twenty minutes past two the next morning dropped three 500 lb bombs, one 250 lb bomb, and six canisters of little incendiaries on Düsseldorf. On 19 July, after a week in which he bombed Münster three nights out of four, dropping close to 9,000 lb of bombs and starting fires that could be seen a hundred miles away, he writes to his mother. 'I expect I shall be seeing you all again rather soon,' he says, and he writes again on the 29th thanking her for some money. He always signs off, 'Love', and he never forgets to ask after some family news, their recent holidays, what someone wants for their birthday. There is a joke in every single one of his letters.

For a long time, these letters saddened me. It was not because they traced a long-dead set of emotions – I was glad to see my grandparents had nicknames, and shared a vocabulary of flirtation that was completely their own – but because they struck me as dishonest. They are remarkable most for their resistance. 'I think of you nearly all the time,' he wrote in that first letter to my grandmother, and even here in the gesture of love, there is something held back. I thought the letters could tell me nothing of the life of my grandfather. I thought that he was refusing to write, and that whatever it was that he was not saying was what I was searching for: the inner life of a bomber pilot, the imaginative trail of an inconceivable job, the last remains of a man so hurtfully lost. I thought that the point was the terror and the mess that had been left out. I was wrong. On Monday, 16 June, he wrote to my grandmother, and again he apologized for his handwriting. 'Can you read all this – my writing my dear is getting worse and worse,' he wrote: 'Doing too much flying I expect.' That is what he meant to write, but on the page he first put 'writing' and then crossed it out:

> Can you read all this – my writing my dear is getting worse and worse. Doing too much ~~writing~~ flying I expect.

The letters are sparse, and I might have liked more, but they tell a pure story of an occupied man.

He wrote to my grandmother on 22 May, about the village and the cowboy books, and again four days later, to wish her happy birthday; he wrote to his sister on 9 June, to thank her for issues of *Punch*, and on 16 June to my grandmother to apologize for not calling. Then there is a pause in the letters, until he writes to his mother twice in late July, but in all this time his life's constant was the war. After the unsuccessful daytime search for German warships on 27 May, operations are cancelled the next day and again at teatime on Sunday, 1 June. He is flying with his usual crew – Martin as first pilot, and Andrews as the observer, Buckley on the wireless and Lane on the guns – and they prepare to bomb on 4 June, but in the afternoon they stand down. Four days later, they make the practice run, and bomb up the plane, but at half past nine, as they are waiting to go, they are called back. On 10 June, they go out into thick clouds, but cannot find their target – German warships moored at Brest, an impossible aim as all around was water – and very early in the morning of 13 June they drop six 500 lb bombs on the railway yards at Hamm, and report 'A large fire seen several miles to the south of the estimated position of the target.'

The bombing war goes on, a round of night testing and operations, bomb loads and practice; they see fires as they fly home from Düsseldorf three hours before dawn on 17 June, and the next night they return for the warships at Brest but the target is obscured with smoke-screens. When there are operations, they are flying much of the night, from take-off at ten or eleven until half past four or five the next morning, not long before the summer dawn, but even on the down days there are short test runs, for the oil and the radio, often in several different planes in a single day. He lands home at half past five on the morning of 19 June with his usual crew in their accustomed plane, and later that day takes a different Wellington – W5704 – up for ten minutes. This is his wedding anniversary, and he had been promised leave, but it was cancelled, and the next day he is again in W5704, for almost three hours, with a different crew. He is trying them out; these six men are seeing if they can work together. In the evening of 21 June they take two different planes up for forty-five minutes each, and at eleven that night my grandfather is first pilot on an operational sortie. The plane is T2959, and the crew are Butt, Dick, Whitton, Maskell, Cox. At just before two on the morning of the 22nd, they drop seven 500 lb bombs on Cologne. The Operations Record notes the crew's collective opinion of the raid, and while they admit 'Bursts not seen', another 57 Squadron Wellington that night reports 'a good fire which seemed to be in the centre of town', so perhaps the new crew might fairly have considered this a success.

At the reunions and after, I often heard the bombers speak with tenderness about their crews and about a particular plane; their stories of the war have a cast of characters and a standard setting. My grandfather's war is not yet so fixed – there are minor substitutions to his crew, over the next week, and he moves between planes – but now it begins to take a form. The day after his first raid as pilot he is back again in W5704 for an hour-long air test. He will fly this plane almost every day for the next fortnight, bombing Düsseldorf on the 24th and Bremen on the 27th. On the afternoon of 28 June, the Station Commander holds his summer sherry party, and operations that night are cancelled. On 3 July, my grandfather bombs the Friedrich Krupps steelworks at Essen, and two days later, at quarter past one in the morning, the railway station at Münster. Forty-eight hours later he is again over Münster, and then twenty-four hours after that he drops a further seven 500 lb bombs on the same place.

Münster was not the city he bombed most often, but it was where he bombed most intensely, and it was where he bombed last; on that third night, he lists a target for the first time in his little red notebook. 'Mun,' he wrote, and that night another 57 Squadron Wellington reported the railway station ablaze. In Münster this week, my grandfather's war took on a new rigour and fury, as if all the war were Münster. On a single day, 8 June 1941, he arrived back at Feltwell from Münster at half past four in the morning and then just after eleven that night lifted off again to go back.

This heavy repetition was no coincidence. Like my grandfather changing planes the war is restless, and as the official historians of the strategic air offensive explain: 'The German spring campaign in the Balkans and, above all, the invasion of Russia on 22nd June 1941, presented Britain with new allies, new dangers and, perhaps, also with new opportunities.' The Russian front forced the Luftwaffe east, and so Bomber Command followed, improvising not only a new target list but a new kind of warfare. The plan to focus upon German transportation centres was not a new one – it had been discussed since at least the autumn of 1940 – but at the end of June 1941 this ambition moved to the centre of Bomber Command's operations and, with it, my grandfather's war assumed a new logic. On 9 July 1941, the Deputy Chief of the Air Staff sent a directive to Sir Richard Peirse, Commander-in-Chief of Bomber Command. 'Sir,' it begins, with the mix of familiarity and formality that marks so much military talk, and preserving a strange fiction that this is a letter rather than an order: 'I am directed to inform you that a comprehensive review of the enemy's present political, economic and military situation discloses that the weakest points in his armour lie in the morale of the civil population and in his inland transportation system.' The twin objectives of transport and morale are knotted together as railway yards tend to stand in cities and railway workers are often not soldiers but civilians. 'The main effort of the bomber force,' the Deputy Chief of the Air Staff continues, should consequently be directed 'towards dislocating the German transportation system and to destroying the morale of the civil population as a whole and of the industrial workers in particular'.

Long after the war, and still today, debates will run over how we may measure such an aim. Morale is counted out in rates of factory production, but its index may also be the nightmares of children and their parents, and there is no statistic for the quality of fear. On the morning of 9 July 1941, my grandfather's crew reported on last night's raid: '0128 hours. 7 x 500 lb. Bombed on course 350 degrees. Bursts seen and one small red fire started.' They were 14,000 feet up, almost three miles, so they could hardly know. One small red fire could be ten, or none. But they were not only aiming at railway yards and the structures of a city; they were targeting too the kinds of loss that cannot be archived, and if what they sought was civilian morale, then this too is part of the story. My father said his mother would be surprised that we would want to go to Germany, after everything that had happened, but at the end of July, almost exactly sixty-seven years later, he and I got back into his car and drove to Münster.

In the morning, my translator and I walk across Münster, past the old town down cobbled lanes to the diocese archives: inside, it is church-cool, and benches like pews. We are reading the chronicle of a church, during the war, and she says in passing that her great-grandfather was a communist, and sent to Dachau. Later in the day, I ask more. He was her father's grandfather, and did not talk about it. Her grandfather, his son, worked as a driver for the state train company during the war. She does not know what was in the trains. Later still, sitting outside a student bar with a dark beer, on a sloping street by the university, I ask how she was taught German history at school. Guilt, she says, always guilt: in history lessons, in religious studies, in politics, always guilt. It is not easy to be a German born in the second half of the twentieth century.

Münster was a city of music and churches, and it was close to the country. July 1941 began with a harvest festival in the Domplatz, the cathedral square, and that week the Hitler Youth arranged a trip for high school students to go out and collect herbs from the fields around the city. A folksy melodrama called *The Village Poet* was showing at the Schanburg cinema, and on Saturday the cathedral choir gave a concert in the gardens of the castle. In the first week of July there were air raid sirens at night but no raids, and the headlines of the *Münsterische Zeitung* told of Soviet losses on the eastern front and 109 British planes shot down in the last seven days. There had been a raid on Münster in May 1940, six bombs falling at half past one in the morning, but since then so little that the flak batteries were moved elsewhere, to the cities to the south-west that were bombed nightly.

Like vegetables, bombing is seasonal, and although the summer nights are short, there are fewer clouds in western Europe than in the winter. Like the tides, it follows the moon, and this week the weather was warm and clear and the moon was filling out. On the night of Saturday, 5 July 1941, the sirens started at just before one, and in twenty minutes the bombs were falling. Bomber Command sent sixty-three Wellingtons this night, with a total bomb load of twenty-six 1,000 lb bombs, 396 500 lb bombs, fifty 250 lb bombs, and almost 6,000 4 lb incendiaries. My grandfather reported dropping seven 500 lb bombs at 0115 hours, but they are keeping English time inside the plane, and down below in Germany the bombs fell from just after one until almost three. The numbers do not quite match. The municipal police record lists only 240 heavy-explosive bombs and 3,000 incendiaries, but this was enough to kill twenty-one people and start fires across the city. On Monday, the newspapers announced the death that night of Käthe Pohlmann (37), Ernst Pohlmann (11) and Ingeborg Pohlmann (3), of Dorotheenstrasse 26, not far from the cathedral, and there were accounts of a strange howling noise as the bombs fell. Perhaps it was flowerpots.

On Sunday, thousands of citizens took a stroll to look at the burned houses. For Münster, bombing on this scale was new, and the municipal police report issued in 1946 stressed the novelty of the night. 'Because this was the first time the citizens came into contact with the new image of waging war, and because of the fire and thunder of explosions, many people have this in mind when they think of war,' the report states, and emphasizes: 'Every new attack made them experience the horrible progress in the area of air bombing.' My grandfather did not bomb on Sunday night, but there was a small raid at half past two, and just as the people of Münster were experiencing a new image of war, so too were the German defences learning. Each night the bombers came in from the north-east, and on Monday my grandfather was flying again. He took off at just after eleven, passing Southwold on the English coast and then crossing over into Holland south of IJmuiden. This route runs an almost perfectly straight line from Feltwell to Münster, but this night the Luftwaffe night-fighters were waiting, and south of Apeldoorn a Messerschmitt attacked at 14,000 feet, as the crew recounted in the briefing the next day, 'causing damage to rear turret and stbd. [starboard] aileron and elevator. Front gunner + rear gunner fired long bursts. Believed secured hits.' The plane sank to 7,000 feet, and this night they dropped their bomb load short, at Burgsteinfurt thirty kilometres north-west of Münster, and turned for home.

The flak batteries came to Münster on Tuesday, 8 July, but this night was the worst of all. The sirens howled up at a quarter to one in the morning, and half an hour later the bombs started to fall and did not stop for an hour and a half. My grandfather was in a new plane, after last night's damage, and at half past one dropped seven

500 lb bombs. The reading room of the state archive and all the costumes in the theatre's warehouse burned; bombs fell on the post office, in the Domplatz, and on the eastern wall of the cathedral. Paul Roosen, the priest of the little Church of St Aegidius on Aegidiistrasse, noted the damage in his chronicle. He speculated that the raiders knew there was no flak at Münster, and this was why they returned night after night, and he guessed that 10,000 incendiaries had fallen. He was grateful that his parish had been little damaged, other than shop windows, and where a few of the old stained glass panes on the north wall of his church were blown in he commented: 'This is not bad luck as they needed to be renewed anyway, and the plans are already finished.' Noting that twenty-five incendiaries had fallen on the Church of the Holy Cross on the other side of the city, he added: 'One cannot but wonder whether the pilots have actually aimed at the churches', and the next day he held a crowded mass in the chapel to give thanks for the survival of the church and parish. During the service, some of his congregation cried, and he promised that God would reward them for their sacrifices.

Faced with chaos, Roosen chose to imagine cause; he tried to give a logic to the damage, as the fiction of malicious pilots aiming at churches was somehow easier to bear than the acceptance that the bombs fell where they willed, without a sense or order. In Münster, in July 1941, it was not impossible to see beyond the rubble to the structures of the city beneath, and if you crunch on glass underfoot, maybe it was time for new windows anyway. For a while, the rubble can be swept away.

In the spring of 1940, the city archive hired Dr Franz Weimers, an old soldier and the former editor of a military newspaper, to chronicle the war. He had a press pass, allowing him to walk the streets during the air raid sirens, and he carried a camera. His little black-and-white snapshots, each the size of a matchbox, are held in the new city archive. Here, a man and woman arm in arm stroll down a street towards the camera, and over their shoulders we can see into the rooms of half a house. There are women in hats, on bicycles, and men in suits, and children running with a ring, and often they are looking at the strange neat ruins. The gutters are clean, and their outfits proper, and the pieces in marked piles. On 8 July 1941, a woman in a floral print dress, holding a bicycle, looks down the Prinzipalmarkt past a broken shop front and towards the Lambertikirche, and in another a little girl in a pinafore stands under a horse chestnut at the centre of a square. Behind her, a whole world away, a house has collapsed, and its skeleton roof shivers in the sky.

On the morning of 9 July, Dr Weimers left his house at Aegidiistrasse 60 at eight. The air was brown with acrid smoke, burning the eyes, and the famous old Gasthof Levi on the corner had been burned to the ground. At ten, he saw women carrying their laundry out of their homes. On Klosterstrasse the paper shop had burned, and there was still fire on Telgferstrasse, so a fire engine blocked the street. 'Thousands of firebombs must have been dropped,' he wrote:

> The poor people who stood at corners and in the squares with their few retrieved belongings but did not know where to go were a pitiful sight to behold. The authorities responsible for providing accommodation, such as the Red Cross, the security service, and deployed battalions, were all working at it at full speed, and consequently all homeless people could be accommodated in the evening, even if some of the solutions were only provisional.

At noon, children were collecting at the train station to be evacuated to the country, and Weimers saw people with blankets walking out of the city. But in the photographs, they are still smiling wanly, and there are teams of men to push the rubble from the streets.

After the archives, I went out to the suburbs to talk with people who had been there. In the prim apartment above what had been her husband's medical practice, a lady who reminded both my interpreter and me of our grandmothers – we realized this afterwards, as if she were the ideal vision of grandmothers everywhere – remembered the first bomb, in May 1940, because it was two days before her four-teenth birthday. It fell on an agricultural warehouse near the har-bour, and there was so much dust; nobody knew what it looked like to be bombed, so they all went to see. In 1941, it was safe in the day. Before going to bed she would pack a little bag and leave it by the door, but her dancing lessons went on until Stalingrad at the start of 1943 and even in the shelters she could see friends, and gossip. In October 1943, the bombers started coming in the day, and by 1944 there were often corpses in the streets and it was hard to walk any-where because of the rubble, but she started studying law at the university in the summer of 1944, as well as working shifts on the telephone exchange in one of the two big shelters under the city. The last air raid was on Palm Sunday 1945, six weeks before the sur-render, and then she and her mother left.

Their stories take a formal pattern. At first, the bombing was a spectacle. One woman told me that they called the red and green marker flares dropped by the bombers 'Christmas trees', and through 1941 the old city life went on with light adjustments. The children learned to put out fires, with a bucket of sand for the phos-phorus and a broom wrapped in rags for the flames, and they some-times pulled the furniture out into the street. In 1941 and the next year, the raids were at night, as if they could not touch their days of school and singing, dancing lessons and church, and although each person I spoke to told me their story of a bomb that fell too close – one had seen a woman with half a face, another heard the howling on the house next door – this was still presented as a separate anec-dote, their war not the war. It was not until October 1943, when the daylight raids began and the planes were higher, that their ways of growing accustomed came under threat; and then it seemed that this was for ever, and the city was overwhelmed, insensible.

What the people in Münster are telling is the story of childhood, and its sequence of diminishment might be specific, but its larger moral is not; they were young and foolish, and then they learned. Perhaps this was why I so admired the Reverend with whom I spent a morning, for although he too had composed his history into a careful artefact, he wished to tell me that the bombing had saved him. An elderly woman let us into his house, and then we sat in a darkened room to wait. There were framed pictures of saints, a menorah, and he came in, very tall, with soft white hair and a soft beard and a soft look in his eyes. He shook hands, and sat, and stared ahead only; he held his head a little lightly, as if it were only just attached to his shoulders, as if something were about to fall. The only sign that he was blind was that the room was dark.

On 15 February 1943, when he was fifteen, he became a flak assistant along with his whole class from grammar school. He joined battery no. 3, a couple of kilometres to the north of the city. There were three parts to a battery, with fifty people: the administration, who worked in the kitchen, or keeping the guns and clothes in order; the gunners; and the observers, who calculated the range and target on Kommando Machine 40. This was his duty. I asked if he was good. He was very good, he said, and he won two medals, the flak battle medal and the flak action medal, but he never fired the guns.

When the air raid siren started, they moved to the trenches around the batteries. This was a good system, he says: they were well-organized, and they always moved fast, and he has been telling me carefully about the mechanics of target and range, but I ask him, were you afraid. For a long time he waited, with his head held, and then without stopping he said, for the first time in English:

When I was younger, and not yet in the flak, there were bomb raids and we used to sit in the cellars. I was there when the light was going out and the walls were coming nearer and then I was afraid. But in the flak battery we were so busy that we were seldom afraid.

He speaks so precisely that I write this down.

The Reverend's history is composed because it is for him a sensible one; he understood this world, on the flak, and he did not resent it. In 1937 he started grammar school in Münster. He liked the new schoolbooks they gave out at the beginning of each year, and he read everything he could, the German books, history, geography, and then the English books, and later Latin. 'I hungered for reading,' he told me, but twice a week they had to spend an afternoon with the Hitler Youth, and twice a week there were piano lessons, and then confirmation lessons, and all of this was a distraction. He often received a 1 in mathematics, he told me, and sometimes in music, and he was good too at languages, and social sciences, and drawing. Some lessons were so easy that he did not think at all, he says, but he was bad at sports and did not like to march, and in 1941 and 1942 the Nazi party were not much impressed with idle, intelligent boys like this one.

The Reverend tells me he could not have stayed in school, but after the great defeat at Stalingrad over the winter of 1942 the Wehrmacht needed men, and all ages were called up, and so in February 1943 his grammar school class rotated on to duty on the flak battery, and he stayed with the unit until August 1944. The daylight raids began on 10 October 1943, and he served through an autumn of almost continual bombing, but he remembers it now as an ordered time. The students stayed together in the barracks, and in the mornings their teachers would travel out from the city to give lessons. At noon, the teachers returned to their homes, and the flak helpers were on duty, but there was not much to do apart from watch over the plotting mechanism of the machine, making sure the location of the enemy plane corresponded to the aiming point, and after five on days when there were no raids he was free, and he would read. The Reverend completed his high school diploma here, in the mornings and evenings around the bombing war.

This is a smooth and pragmatic way to tell a history, as a tale of work and reward, but I asked the Reverend what he was reading, those evenings on the flak. He was looking at the night sky, as flak assistant B4, and balancing target and aim, and he told me that he liked to read books of astrology, and Dante's *Divine Comedy*, and most of all he loved Karl Immermann's version of the Münchhausen tales. Immermann's *Münchhausen* was published in 1841, and was a four-volume reworking of the popular stories of the misbehaving Baron von Münchhausen. The Baron tells of his journeys to Africa and across Europe and the east, and here are often bears to fight, and ludicrous escapes, and a great bridge that spans the world; the stories slip the confines of physics or truth, and revel in their excess.

If in Immermann the Reverend found escape, then the opposite may be true of the other great work he read on those afternoons. Dante's *Divine Comedy* describes a world divided into the three parts of the Christian cosmology, heaven, Purgatory and hell, but its most famous scenes are of urban fires and a state of almost war. Walking through the City of Dis, Dante sees 'the flaming walls' of 'the city of pain', and pauses in what he calls 'a countryside of sorrow and new torment' where heretics are bound in burning tombs. Later, Dante travels on to the burning desert, where:

> Enormous herds of naked souls I saw,
>   lamenting till their eyes were burned of tears;
>   they seemed condemned by an unequal law,
>
> for some were stretched supine upon the ground,
>   some squatted with their arms about themselves,
>   and others without pause roamed round and round.
>
> Most numerous were those that roamed the plain.
>   Far fewer were the souls that stretched on the sand,
>   but moved to louder cries by greater pain.
>
> And over all that sand on which they lay
>   or crouched or roamed, great flakes of flame fell slowly
>   as snow falls in the Alps on a windless day.

One night on the battery, the Reverend told me, they saw the bombs falling, and they lay down in their trenches as the second gun was hit.

The *Inferno*, Dante's book of hell, imagines punishment in all its forms – those who were violent on earth shall now be trapped in violence, and those who were gluttonous shall now feed only upon filth – and imagination too may be a kind of suffering. One afternoon in Münster, my interpreter took me to visit two sisters who had been teenagers in the war, and in their proper life they tried not to think too much of the bombing, but its terrors had not quite left them. I meet them in a bungalow covered in creepers outside the city. One lives here, and the other is visiting, and there are two cats, and in the garden, flowers and stone animals; not like an English garden, the older of the two apologizes. She has been to England, and she likes the Cotswolds. In the sitting room, she serves coffee and homemade biscuits called Raspberry Coins. Better not to serve tea to an Englishman, she says; better to serve coffee than the wrong kind of tea.

The older sister has put some books out. There is a map of Münster as it was in 1925, and a magnifying glass, and another called *Bomben auf Münster*, which is filled with photographs and lists and which she later gives to me, because she says we are new friends. She asks how old my grandfather was when he died. He was thirty, I say, and they grimace; that is too young. A little later, they tell me about their cousin, who was a pilot in one of the night-fighter squadrons, and who was killed. After, nobody mentioned him. Last year, the older one tells me, they talked about the war for the first time, and a couple of weeks ago, when they knew I was going to come and ask about the bombing, the younger one had the nightmares again, which she had not had for years.

They laugh, these two women, at their stories, and there are photographs of one, the older, in a nurse's uniform, and she is laughing then too. Their father had been wounded in the First World War, and he was a funny man who made a fortune in scrap metal but then lost it all in the hyperinflation of 1924. Later, there was a handsome priest at the cathedral, so they attended services there, and in the evenings their father read to them. When the younger one cried at the end of *Uncle Tom's Cabin*, her father gave her liquorice.

Their stories had no sequence. They told me of moving eleven times during the war, and of taking chocolates to class for the first day of school, and they said that Münster was much cleaner now than it had been before the bombs. They never spent the whole night in an air raid shelter, and the worst was the howling of the sirens. When the younger one heard that there was going to be war, she was afraid, and she stayed that way until the end. She had the imagination, she said, and she was scared of being trapped in the cellar at night, of being sent to Siberia by the Russians, and then later of the Americans who came to Münster. The older one was not afraid because she could not imagine what might happen, and the younger one told me she likes cloudy days, because the bombers cannot come.

Most of all theirs were sweet comic stories, of the time when their father found a corset in the rubble and asked if it was a Panzer tank, and of when the bedroom windows were gone and they replaced them with boards because you need no light in there anyway. They could save only a few things from the raids, and they laugh because they saved a big glass punch bowl, and their best china. They tell me that the city archive where I read the church chronicles is where the public shelter used to be, and they ask about the Blitz in London, and whether the English had food shortages too. They are surprised to hear about rationing, and she gives me a glass of brandy, and a tin of homemade biscuits to take away with me. Mostly we have been laughing here, so I leave with an ache in my cheeks.

The imagination was trouble. In Münster, it was better to be the older sister, who could not think of what might come, than the younger, who was always scared, and I had read this before. 'More life may trickle out of men through thought than through a gaping wound,' wrote Thomas Hardy in *The Dynasts*, his epic drama about the Napoleonic Wars, and in the trenches of the First World War Wilfred Owen agreed. 'Happy are those who lose imagination,' he wrote in his poem 'Insensibility': 'They have enough to carry with ammunition. / Their spirit drags no pack'. Imagination is alternative thinking – the ability to see that in a darkened room, a clothes-covered chair is a crocodile, a bear – and perhaps it is a peacetime luxury. In 1945, Lord Moran published *The Anatomy of Courage*, a study of 'how courage is born and how it is sustained among an army of free people'. Moran had fought in the First World War, and then been Churchill's private doctor, and during research had interviewed bomber pilots about their fears. 'Men wear out in warlike clothes,' he concludes, and argues that courage is a finite substance; to sustain it, 'we have to put away any thought of an alternative to the dangerous situation in which we are.' Again, he insists that 'the idea of another way of life' is a 'chronic danger' in wartime, and approvingly quotes the great bomber pilot Guy Gibson. 'The worst thing is seeing the flak,' said Gibson: 'You must leave your imagination behind you or it will do you harm.'

Literary critics call this a trope, when an idea falls into a pattern of language, across times and places, and the sisters in Münster in 2008, and Owen in 1917, and Hardy in 1908 were only agreeing with John Ciardi, who was a rear gunner on B-29s bombing Japan and who one night in 1945 on the island of Saipan in the Pacific wrote in his diary: 'The trouble with wakening the imagination is that it makes you afraid in advance.' What scared him was precisely one possible future. 'Thinking too much of death by curves of chance,' he wrote in his poem 'Expendability':

> Imagination's curse (the nearest ghost)
> Sees all too readily the falling dance,
> The motion down and lost.

He does not know how he will die, but he does know how he might die, and the trouble with the imagination is that it is always ready to fill the gap between those two: to show him as a horror movie his own plane moving down and lost. The imagination brings nearer the ghost.

> I beg of chance the green and living day.
> I wheedle numbers, plot new averages,
> Alchemize probabilities

writes Ciardi a little later in this poem, counting out a consolation for the falling dance in his mind.

Ciardi was born in the Italian North End of Boston, the son of immigrants from Naples. He had fights in his childhood, and his uncles took him poaching pheasants. His family were always worried about money, but he learned to be a poet as an undergraduate at Tufts, and then at graduate school at Michigan, and part of his pleasure at winning the Hopwood award for poetry there in June 1939 was the large cheque that came with the prize. In January 1940, he moved to Kansas City to teach English at the university. His letters boast about girls and about his communist sympathies and here at some point in 1940 the FBI opened a file on him as a subversive. In the autumn of 1941, he started taking civilian flying lessons, and wrote to a friend in October that he hoped to earn his pilot's licence by Christmas as an escape from teaching freshman prose composition to undergraduates. 'In a year or so I can pile up 200–250 hours of solo,' he wrote, 'and pull down a job as a flight Instructor at $375 per month. Egad.'

Although we are in Kansas, this is not a wholly foreign story: a young man, restless at work, and an amateur pilot, and war breaks out. In December 1941, the Japanese bombed Pearl Harbor. Ciardi applied to enlist in the United States Army Air Corps, and spent the spring and summer of 1942 working on a manuscript of poems and waiting. In late October he was called to the AAF Classification Center in Nashville, Tennessee, for pre-flight training, but by the summer of 1943 his commitment to the army had begun to unravel. His biographer, Edward Cifelli, struggles to explain what happened.

'Considering that Ciardi had done well in the army through 20 March 1943, the sudden turnabout that led to his dismissal five months later is curious at best,' he notes, and while Ciardi later blamed the FBI and their investigation into his communist sympathies, Cifelli suggests that it may equally have been due to his engrossing affair with a married woman during the same time. At the start of September, he was dismissed from officer training.

This was not the end of Ciardi's war, for within a month he had re-enrolled at Lowry Field in Denver to train as central fire control gunner on B-29s, in charge of the twin guns at the upper rear turret. 'Indications are that he liked his new location and his new work,' observes Cifelli, and in April 1944 he transferred to Walker Base in Kansas. Like my grandfather, he was twenty-eight years old when he completed training, and the oldest man on his crew. In October, his biographer notes, 'just before shipping out for combat duty, he tempted fate by taking out a three-year renewal to his *Poetry* subscription.' In November, as he left the US with the 882nd Bomb Squadron for Saipan, he began keeping a diary.

Saipan is one of the Marianas, a strand of fifteen volcanic islands in the Pacific south of Japan. It is twelve miles long, and five and a half miles at the widest point, and when he arrived there in the middle of November 1944, it was an island blasted by war. Thirty thousand Japanese soldiers were garrisoned here by the summer of 1944, and on 13 June the American bombardment had begun; by 9 July, when the island fell, more than 3,000 American troops had died in taking an island of forty-six square miles. Yet the early days of Ciardi's diaries are marked by an air of role-play, as if this were not for real.

He began the diary, he said, as 'a sort of human study', an ethnography of men in war, and the subject occurred to him precisely because it appeared so unlikely. 'The Army is the last place in the world to observe human nature,' he wrote. 'The reason is, I think, that no-one acts like himself', and, at first, his characters are fitting themselves to roles occasionally forced upon them and occasionally enjoyed. They were 'playing cowboys and Indians with our new toys', and when at the end of November a Japanese fighter machine-guns the base, he is surprised: 'No-one had ever shot at me before, and I couldn't quite understand anyone beginning to.' He compares a hangar to a stage-set, with B-29s parked in the moonlight, and jokes about being a member of the 'Saipan Hunt Club – hunting parties twice weekly (weather and mechanics permitting)'. He worries about where to get cold beer, and on his first operation, bombing Tokyo, he looks out to sea. 'Someone always seems to have just finished a terrific pillow fight,' he writes. On 7 December, he heard that *Poetry* magazine had awarded him a prize, and in the envelope was a $100 cheque. The next morning, he goes out and drops 10,000 lb of bombs on Iwo Jima, and in the evening he has a haircut and then goes to the base theatre 'to see a program of native dances', but he finds the girls ugly. A few days later, after a bomb run, he notes: 'It's hard to judge from 25,000 feet', and in these early days he is always 25,000 feet from the war.

'It began with one of those chemical anxieties,' he wrote, on the day the war turned. It was 16 December 1944, and 'time swallowed and disappeared.' That day, his crew were set to bomb the Mitsubishi engine plant at Nagoya, but he could not sleep the night before, and on their way out the plane had engine trouble. They bombed an alternative target, and jettisoned everything they could, and tried to make it home, 'and the Pacific stayed endlessly below.' That night, when he sat to his diary, there was a new mix of horror and fear in his tone: fear at what might have happened, and horror at what has. 'Nagoya is the third largest city of Japan with a population about that of San Francisco,' he wrote: 'Unlike Tokio, it is comparatively unmodernized and consequently highly inflammable.' Suddenly, the war has rushed too close. He compares the target to a city at home – he imagines, that is, bombing San Francisco – and more than this, he recognizes the awful efficiency of what he is doing, setting fire to a flammable city.

Maybe Ciardi was only tired that day, and maybe it was only

chemical, but after 16 December his diary scrambles into a fit of anxiety and disgust. 'Whenever my imagination runs cold and deep I go out and look at a B-29 for five minutes and I'm cured,' he wrote: 'It's a good thing to look at, a beautiful thing to look at, and it's pointed the right way.' But as the raids continue the planes falter – the bomb doors freeze one night, and the guns on another – and can no longer offer their cure. Soon, he is writing: 'In every engine there is fire and death in more places than any eye can find, and it waits forever.' He counts – thirty-five missions make a tour, and two planes lost per mission equals 75 to 1 odds on returning, and 2 to 1 that a crew will complete a tour – and catches himself doing it, 'as if reducing it to a number made a wall against machine guns'. At the start of the new year, he writes a single line: 'Stay Alive in '45.' On 23 January, he again addresses himself: 'Ciardi seems to be having combat nerves.' At the end of February, 'I sat down and wrote a letter home to be mailed in case I didn't come back.' The diary stops at ten o'clock in the morning on 10 March 1945. Its last word is 'waiting'.

Ciardi survived the war, and forty years later in an interview with the oral historian Studs Terkel he did nothing to narrow the fairy-tale relief of his escape. In the second week of March 1945 he was approached by 'the colonel in charge of awards and decorations', who said: 'We need somebody with combat experience who can write. You've taught college English, you've published a book. You're now working for me.' Three missions later, his original crew were all killed when their plane exploded over Tokyo Bay, and Ciardi wrote the official letters of condolence that were subsequently sent to their families. He spent the next six months in an office at the base on Saipan, writing condolences and citations, and in September 1945 he was shipped home. On the way back he stopped off in Oahu, where he won $4,000 in a craps game.

In a time of war, there is torment in the notion that there might be other places. In the office on Saipan, Ciardi had gone on writing poetry, and when he came to publish his second volume in October

1947, he called it *Other Skies*. As his biographer counts, Ciardi published twenty-five poems in American magazines – *Poetry*, and the *Atlantic Monthly*, and the *Yale Review* – between joining the air corps in late 1942 and 1 January 1945. The war was good for his writing, and by the end of his diary, after one of his last bombing runs, he notes an awkward little rhyming couplet of relief: 'Fighters and flak may break my back, but searchlights'll never hurt me.' In *Other Skies*, Ciardi assembled his war poems, and ordered them into the whole story of bombing.

The poems collected in *Other Skies* tell the arc of Ciardi's war. The first section is of school and civilian life, carnival times on a teenage beach: 'In sunburn, tights, limp sandwiches, warm beer, / Prowling boys, orange peel, family groups, and lotions'. Here are poems of college and graduation, and in the second part we move to training. Here he disposes of civilian clothes – 'Look back, inanimate, serene, / Tie, shirt, scarf, gloves, and gabardine' – and starts upon the stations of a soldier's life. He goes to 'camptown' and begins his training in lessons:

> Where even murder must be learned at school,
> And sky, a shadow to be memorized,
> Charts the shadows we had not surmised.

Soon, he is flying. 'At first the fences are racing under,' he writes, on take-off, and the world changes: 'Horses and men / Are different yet – we see men look up'. Soon after this, in a poem called 'Death of a Bomber', he sees his first training accident. The poem opens:

> We saw the smoke. The blue skull of the sky
> Scarred on the black trail of the running fire.
> The world came out of doors and every eye
> Turned on the afternoon, while higher and higher
> The sirens mounted and the watchers' breath
> Drew in and waited to be first with death.

The cadets are looking up to a plane on fire, but they are thinking of themselves. 'We stood and watched and each man watched his own / Possible future flaming to arrive,' he writes, for this could be each of them. In the next poem, he is waiting to embark for Saipan, and again is thinking of what might come: 'We see ourselves on a burning other sky.'

It is a common story, from far to close, and familiar from the Saipan journal and the careers of other poets, other bombers; perhaps it is the inevitable story of this war. He travels by boat to Saipan, what he calls 'this coral rock behind the world', and here he goes on the first bombing runs to the Japanese cities:

> Where cloud rained fire, and we were in the cloud –
> Its climate, dark, and deluge. And we spread
> Simple as rain, like thunder loud,
> To be the following weather of the dead.

But thinking of bombing as somehow natural, 'simple as rain', can only last so long. In 'Poem for My Twenty-ninth Birthday', the raids are occupying his daydreams as, he writes, 'We waken, and the cities of our day / Move down a cross-haired bomb sight in the mind'. His mind turns again upon what he is doing, repeats the raids in dreams, and he writes:

> I cannot lose my darkness. Posed and dressed,
> I touch the metal womb our day will ride.
> We take our places while a switch is pressed,
> And sun and engines rise from the hillside –
> A single motion and a single fire
> To burn, return, and live upon desire.

The bombing men are becoming part of the bombing planes, and he is folding his own separate self into the war. The crews and their weapons present 'a single motion and a single fire', for there are no individuals here, no line between men and machines.

The chronology is common, and yet Ciardi's war was specific to him in one dramatic moment. He survived, and the closing poems bring him back from the Pacific and into civilian life. In 'V-J Day', he writes of the strange peace of flying home on the day Japan surrendered, when 'No fire-shot cloud pursued us going home. / No cities cringed and wallowed in the flame', and in these last poems there is often an air of slight surprise at the absence of bombs. He writes of his hometown, and a local drugstore, and we are safely back in domestic America.

Yet it is perhaps too neat to say that Ciardi's war was made complete in poetry. *Other Skies* tells a perfect story, from training to fighting, from distance to fixation, and then the return to the old life, but the bombing stayed with Ciardi. He was discharged from the army in October 1945, and within a year was married. He took a teaching job at Harvard, published poems in the *New Yorker*, and edited an influential anthology, *Mid-Century American Poets*. His was a powerful voice in American poetry of the moment, and in 1959 he published *How Does a Poem Mean?*, a how-to-read poetry textbook with well-known verses and exam questions. 'Every poem makes some demand upon the reader's sympathies,' he argues, and goes on: 'In addressing his subject, the poet takes an attitude toward it and adopts a tone he believes to be appropriate. His sense of what is appropriate, either in tone or attitude, is of course a question of values.' In Ciardi's own poetry of bombing, his attitude and tone are always mixed; his 'sense of what is appropriate' remains unclear. It is remorse, perhaps, when he writes, 'cities cringed and wallowed in the flame', and yet he only rarely thinks of those below. In *Other Skies*, his subject is the bombers not the bombed. 'Nothing we do except to stand and wish / Will serve,' he writes: 'Nor ever stop the fear', and if there is a sympathetic attitude played out here it is of pity to these men. Yet it is never an easy pity. 'Our wheels touch and our waiting lives return,' he writes in one poem, of landing again from a raid, but 'Far off the dead are lying in the rain, / And on their dark the ruined cities burn'.

For Ciardi, the bombing remained unsettled. Its points of sympathy stayed unclear, and in the same interview with Studs Terkel long after the war he spoke of precisely this division. 'We were in the terrible business of burning out Japanese towns,' he said: 'That meant women and old people, children. One part of me – a surviving, savage voice – says, I'm sorry we left any of them living. I wish we'd finished them all.' This is one voice, but almost without pause he continues. 'I have some of my strike photos at home,' he says, and explains:

> Tokyo looked like one leveled bed of ash . . . Some of the people jumped into the rivers to get away from these fire storms. They were packed in so tight to get away from the fire, they suffocated. They were so close together, they couldn't fall over. It must have been horrible.

He could not have seen this, but he can by imagining know it, and this is the double voice of the poems and the journal, violent and horrified, reported and daydreamed.

In 1967, as high-altitude American planes were again involved in a firebombing war in the east, Ciardi published an odd, large, limited-edition book of what might be seen as children's verse. *An Alphabestiary* is an unclassifiable work, and close to the start of its list of letters Ciardi writes:

> B is for BOMBERS, our national pride.
> And also for BOYS who like Bombers to ride.
> And also for BLESS in 'God Bless Our Side.'
> B is for BAD (the Enemy) whom
> we Bless our Boys' Bombers Bravely to Bomb.
> And for BELLS we ring out when we welcome them home.

He may be thinking immediately of B-52s and napalm, the technology of a later war, but here is a return to an earlier theme, and the mocking, saddened double voice. The bombers are children, in a children's poem, and yet they are violent; we must welcome them home and also see that patriotism is absurd.

The poetry and the war of John Ciardi are a double story, about surviving and never quite getting away; about the imagination, and what you saw. In early 1947, as he readied his collection of war poetry for publication, he started on another project, one that would take twenty-three years to complete. That spring, he began to translate Dante's *Inferno*, and it is Ciardi's version that I quoted earlier in this chapter. At a conference in 1965, Ciardi spoke of his own attachment to Dante, and opened with a rhetorical question. 'Why should a 20th-Century American poet spend many years working on an American-English version of the 14th-Century Christian Florentine allegory?' he asked, and answered simply: 'Whether or not we know how to say it to ourselves, there is something in the darkness of our age's own mood that responds at great depth to the darkness of Hell.' Dante, he continued, 'entered the activity of his life-imagination at a heat of passion beyond most men, yet saw through diamond eyes; he could burn and still see'. The *Inferno* is a war poem, but it is also a poem about reflection and consequence, and about imagining another time to see our own.

> I, one man alone,
> prepared myself to face the double war
> of the journey and the pity

wrote Dante at the start of the second canto, like Ciardi out on a bombing run and after, both watching the burning city and yet not of it, here and there, almost on fire.

To be a bomber is daily to war against an alternative version of your own story. At half past ten on the night of 24 July 1941 my grandfather took off from Methwold, the little satellite base down the road from Feltwell. He was flying the Wellington N2841, in which he had spent much of the previous two weeks, and the target was the Deutsche Werke shipyard at Kiel. At 0145 the following morning, from a higher altitude than he had ever raided before, he dropped five bombs, and as they swung for home could see the fires a hundred miles away. He landed just before six at Feltwell, and the news was bad. Another 57 Squadron Wellington on the same run, under the pilot Sergeant Green, was lost. Within an hour, a rescue team has assembled, and at half past eight the same Wellington N2841 takes off again with a different pilot. They find nothing, and the next day the weather turns to rain and cloud. Operations are called off on 28 July, and again the next day, and again the next. On 5 August, news reaches Feltwell that Sergeant Green and his crew washed up in Holland. All were drowned.

My grandfather is out on operations on the night of 6 August, and again two days later, and on the 12th he sits to catch up with his letters. He has fallen behind with replies, and is even more apologetic than usual; he writes to both his sisters and to his mother, thanking them for issues of *Punch* magazine and for their recent visit to see my grandmother at Honeysuckle Cottage. 'You should see me next week,' he writes to his mother, and to his sister, 'There is no news.' She has plans to go riding, and he advises: 'Don't fall off the 'orse too much.'

'A flying officer should live in the mess, he should not live with his family,' wrote Lord Moran in *The Anatomy of Courage*. He continues: 'We must practise a prudent economy in emotion in time of war if we are to remain sane. Where there is a lavish display of feeling the mind is not at peace; it is divided against itself.' The strain in my grandfather's letters is that of a man remaining sane. 'My dear Mother', 'Thank you for your letter which came this afternoon', 'Love to Father', 'Love Eric', 'Don't fall off the 'orse too much'. All letters from the base are love letters because that is all they can be. They can report no news so they are every time the same, and each one acts as what John Ciardi called an 'Elegy Just in Case'. His poem of that name takes the form of the last letter that airmen leave behind to be sent on by others, and in this genre there is only one message:

> Darling, darling, just in case
> Rivets fail or engines burn,
> I forget the time and place
> But your flesh was sweet to learn.

To tell of his days on the base – for my grandfather to explain the story of the drowned Sergeant Green, how close it came – would have been to acknowledge that he himself had been claimed by war.

After writing the letters on 12 August, my grandfather went out that night on a bombing run to the railway yards at Hanover. He bombs the same target two nights later, and three nights after that they are over the station at Duisburg, but the weather is terrible and visibility poor. This is his twenty-fifth raid, and a tour in Bomber Command is a minimum of thirty. On 18 August, Bomber Command received a report from the War Cabinet. A member of the secretariat, Mr Butt, had spent much of the first half of August examining 650 photographs taken by night-bombers between 2 June and 25 July, and concluded that Bomber Command were hardly bombing at all. His first finding is the most stark: 'Of those aircraft recorded as attacking their target, only one in three got within five miles.' For French ports, the proportion was two in three, but this sharply falls for German targets. Only one in ten planes that claimed to have bombed targets in the Ruhr had in fact done so, and these figures are only for those aircraft which recorded an attack upon the target. When he calculated from all sorties, he found that 'only one in five get within five miles of the target, i.e. with[in] the 75 square miles surrounding the target.'

My grandfather flew fifteen raids in the period covered by the Butt Report. Following their calculations, only three of these nights did he come within five miles of the target. Some nights, he was bombing far away; some nights, he was not bombing at all. The bombers knew what they were doing, and in the briefing reports by other crews from 57 Squadron in June and July of 1941 there is often uncertainty. 'Bursts only seen,' the returning crews reported, and 'Bombs were aimed at estimated position.' On 10 July, one crew 'Bombed town believed Bonn', and another described 'Big flash from bombs, but position uncertain.'

This is the secret history of bombing: much of it was imagined. While the British bombed by night, the Americans bombed by day from higher altitudes: they claimed this made them precise, but it was not so. In the middle of January 1945, John Ciardi wrote in his diary: 'Our precision bombing has everything but precision', and a postwar report on the efficiency of American bombing in Europe during the first half of 1943 concluded that 'the Eighth Air Force put only 14 per cent of their bombs within 1,000 feet of the target.' The Butt Report simply made this visible.

The official historians of the bombing war conclude that 1941 'brought Bomber Command to the nadir of its fortunes', but for one airman the closing weeks of that summer were not so bleak. On 21 August, my grandfather is commissioned Pilot Officer, and a week later is his twenty-ninth birthday. The night of 5 September is a full moon, and he bombs the chemical works at Huls in a new plane, then Kassel, then Kiel, then Brest in the next week. On 15 September 1941 he bombs the main railway station at Hamburg. This is his thirty-first operation, and the next night is a farewell dinner at Feltwell. He has ten days' leave, to go home, and on 26 September reports to RAF Bassingbourn. He had finished his training there and now returns as a flying instructor, a veteran pilot with a completed first tour, now relieved from operational duties.

Chapter 4. England and Nowhere

30 May 1942

There were summer storms in the morning, but they cleared, and that night a full moon. My grandfather, as pilot of Wellington R1252, took off at eight minutes before eleven. He was twenty-fourth to leave, of twenty-five bombers from Bassingbourn and its satellite base Steeple Morden, and the target was Cologne, but he was the first to return. On lifting off, the crew ran tests on the guns and radio, and then, only minutes into the air, there was the accident. As they reported later: 'Task abandoned, returned to Base due to explosion of IFF detonator in W/OP's face.' The wireless operator was Flight Sergeant Sills, and he was blinded when the radio warning device known as Identification Friend or Foe blew up before him in the thin corridor behind the cockpit. The Wellington landed at twelve minutes past eleven, twenty minutes after taking off. In his notebook against this raid, my grandfather notes simply: 'NoG'. No good; no go.

He was not meant to be on operations. He came to Bassingbourn on a fine autumn day in late September 1941 and was flying by the end of the week, but now as Pilot Instructor with D flight. 11 Operational Training Unit, housed at Bassingbourn and Steeple Morden, was comprised of four flights and thirteen student crews. On 30 September 1941 they reported a strength of twenty-six serviceable Wellingtons, five Ansons and two little Lysanders, and my grandfather flies in a whole alphabet of planes during the autumn and winter, up every two or three days for ten minutes or three hours, teaching, training. He has done this so many times, by now, and his private logbook for this season is a calm string of numbers, air test and cross country, circuits and bumps, flying out across England and home.

I have none of his letters from this time, but in the RAF archive at Hendon are the papers of another airman, Sergeant Francis Robert Edwin McCarthy, who was stationed here in the autumn of 1941. In McCarthy's descriptions Bassingbourn is a holiday camp, with lessons in the day and evenings spent listening to records in the mess, or walking to the village of Royston for a drink and darts in the pub. On 15 October 1941 there was rabbit for dinner, and for special occasions in the officers' mess they sat down to cream of asparagus and trifle, roast goose and roast pork, oxtail soup. There was so much food they kept pigs on the leftovers, and sometimes after dinner the officers handed round the printed menus for each other to sign. There were football matches, and the station library was open until half past seven each evening. On 9 May 1942, after my grandfather had flown for four hours with two trainee pilots, there was a concert on the base in the evening, and in the spring of 1943 the Air Ministry compiled a report on conditions here. 'More personnel are using the gymnasium in the evenings for badminton and apparatus work,' they conclude, and 'The Station Cinema continued to show excellent films which were changed every two days.' In the photograph album kept by a WAAF who spent part of the war here, now also in the archive at Hendon, is a crisp black-and-white scene with the caption 'Bassingbourn 1942'. In the foreground are men in shirtsleeves sitting on the grass, looking on as wary couples dance to a band set up on a flatbed truck.

He was at Bassingbourn for the third birthday of his son, in May 1942, and for the first birthday of his daughter in February, but now he is closer to home, for my grandmother had rented a farmhouse in a village to the south-east of the base. The house at Barley was bare, but it was less than ten miles from the officers' mess, so he could spend the night there, and one weekend, when his sister came for lunch with my grandmother, he flew past and tipped his wings. They waved back up to him, low above them.

I went to Bassingbourn in the summer of 2008. I took the train to Royston and the Major met me at the station, a soldier in a family car. Bassingbourn is now an army base, where the recruits go for Phase One training; where they put on their green socks, the Major says. On the base, the runways are cracking now, and the public walk their dogs. The old bomb dump is a lake, stocked with fifty-pound carp, huge catfish, and tench. There is a waiting list to join Bassingbourn Coarse Fishing Club, and past the lake a dry ski slope. The old hangars have new uses. One is a practice hall for the band, and in another is the gym. The Major walks me through, past teen-age recruits in green T-shirts learning how to stretch. This was always a place for training, and as the Major drives me across the scarred tarmac there are children everywhere, worrying in lines, trying out the straight-up walk of soldiers.

At lunchtime, the Major leaves me at the control tower and goes to eat at the mess. The tower is a museum now, but the flag on top is the stars and stripes. The RAF left Bassingbourn on 28 September 1942, and the Americans moved in; USAAF 91st Bombardment Group were here until the end of the war. There is a display of log-books and airmen's tunics from the *Memphis Belle*, and photographs of movie stars: Bob Hope in a white suit, James Cagney scowling in a beret and signing the visitors' book. In the museum, the old vol-unteer who looks after the displays asks me stiffly for a donation and says the RAF never used Bassingbourn in anger. I go up the spiral ladder to the second floor. The roof is low, and all is painted green and white, and the windows look out over the cross of runways. There are red flags, and gunshots in the distance, for the trainees are trying manoeuvres in the woods with live ammunition. On the tar-mac, a few men have set up bright plastic baffles against the wind, and they are buzzing model planes above. They come here once a week, to fly their toys, the volunteer tells me, and they pay rent to the Ministry of Defence. The old runways are a playground now, and overhead, a kestrel waits.

In the middle of August 1941, a German Junkers 88 dropped four heavy-explosives and incendiaries on the barracks. Ten airmen were killed, and another twelve injured, and a week later there was another attack at night. On 2 October, four days after my grand-father arrived, an enemy fighter machine-gunned a convoy of trucks, and on the 15th a training Wellington crashed on landing, killing three of the crew. There were no attacks in November, but another Wellington crashed, killing the crew of five, and one night a sergeant was run over by a private car at the edge of the base. The subsequent investigation suggested that he was drunk. In January 1942, a pilot was struck by a propeller, a Wellington crashed on landing, a searchlight at Steeple Morden dazzled a pilot, two Wellingtons crashed into each other, and another rolled off the flare path while landing. It snowed in early February, and there were three separate flying accidents.

My grandfather was there at this time, and these are his students. They bale out on cross-country exercises or forget to lower their landing gear; they land short, collide, and are injured on their motorbikes. They are burned. 'Captain and five other members of the crew were killed,' the station log notes, and later, 'port engine failure' and 'crashed landing in a ploughed field'.

The distance between war and safety narrows, and even as they practise, these students were participating in combat. On their bomb runs they dropped 250 lb sandbags, but on a cloudy night in the middle of April my grandfather took a training crew up in one of the D flight Wellingtons. They lifted off at nine forty-five to jag out over the North Sea, almost as far as the Dutch coast before curving back and landing at Steeple Morden just short of five hours later. There was a big raid this night, 173 planes from airfields up and down Bomber County sent to Hamburg, and my grandfather's crew were on what they called a bullseye run, as decoys for the German coastal radars. This was not really fighting, but it bore the risk. The skies stayed cloudy, and on the night of 25 April my grandfather was on another bullseye, four hours out and back, and on return another crew from Steeple Morden were in trouble and crashed at Waddington aerodrome: three killed, two badly injured.

Training gave no solace from the hardness of this war. In August 1942, the Air Ministry compiled a report on 'Psychological Disorders in Flying Personnel of Bomber Command', and while the report stresses the importance of tour limits and a rest from operations for experienced airmen, it notes also that instructing at an OTU was no escape from combat stress. 'The aircraft are the same, the flying hours are high, there may still be anxiety, especially when dual control is not used, and the preparation for operations is apparent everywhere,' the report concludes, and it was worst for pilots. 'The physical fatigue of flying a heavy bomber is limited to the pilot who, as captain of the aircraft, has an added mental load,' the authors note. An appendix to the report lists 2,989 flying personnel diagnosed with combat stress in 1943, and of these the largest share, at 35 per cent, were pilots. Training is the most stressful duty, and the scene of 36 per cent of cases of stress, followed by night bombing, at 27 per cent of cases. The figures are cold, but they add up to a simple state. Bomber pilots in training duty suffered the most acute condition of combat stress, strain condensed like milk in a tin.

These wartime reports present what now appears a primitive understanding of human psychology. They cite often 'the inherent quality of the man', his temperament and character, as if he had a mechanical inner life built to withstand fear. But so much of the bombing war was premised upon theories of how the mind might react to scenes of destruction. Bomber Command imagined violence before it produced it, and the strategic directives of early spring 1942 narrowed their target to a tiny space. On 14 February, the Deputy Chief of Air Staff instructed the Commander-in-Chief of Bomber Command that 'the primary objective of your operations should now be focused on the morale of the enemy civilian population and in particular, of the industrial workers', and went on to note: 'this is the time of year to get the best effects from concentrated incendiary attacks', as if spring brought out the bombers. 'You are accordingly authorised to employ your effort without restriction,' the directive concludes.

The 14 February directive lists four primary targets – Essen, Duisburg, Düsseldorf and Cologne – and by May 1942 Bomber Command had developed a new idea for bombing. It would send a great stream of bombers, a thousand planes raiding one city at one time.

The target was Cologne, and, for the numbers, the Air Ministry called up every crew it could, from training units and Coastal Command as well as operational squadrons. My grandfather was in the sky on 30 May 1942 as the culmination of a sequence of ideas of what bombing could do and how it could hurt; he was there in order to prove a daydream of destruction. The Wellington R1252 lifted off at eight minutes before eleven, from the satellite station of Steeple Morden.

The history of bombing is a history of imagining destruction. Near the start of the austere four-volume official narrative of the strategic air offensive against Germany, there is an unexpected lyrical pause for, as the authors write: 'In many respects the story is a melancholy one. It is the story not only of what was done, but also of what was done inadequately, and of what was not done at all.' The bombing war can have no simple, linear telling. It is not only a procession of technology, of battles, of victories and loss; it is also a catalogue of failed promises and violent fantasies, and only when we acknowledge the force of things undone, of vows and of imaginings, can we begin to understand the logic of the whole. On 14 September 1939, the Prime Minister stood in the House of Commons and promised: 'Whatever the lengths to which others may go, His Majesty's Government will never resort to the deliberate attack on women, children and other civilians for purposes of mere terrorism.' On 14 February 1942, the Deputy Chief of Air Staff informed Bomber Command that 'the primary object of your operations should now be focused on the morale of the enemy civilian population.' Here is the skeleton of a tragic compromise, grown upon the shifting promises of what this new technology might produce.

Bombing was always psychological warfare, and it was an idea long before it was a practice. Imagination precedes invention: as Sven Lindqvist notes in *A History of Bombing* (2001), 'In his *Prodromo overo Saggio* ("The Aerial Ship") of 1670, Francesco Lana de Terzi already warned of airships that from an appropriate height could drop "artificial fire, bullets, and bombs" at "houses, castles, or cities" without placing themselves in the least danger.' But the imagination never stands alone, and Lindqvist continues: 'Defying his own warning, he himself tried to construct such an airship, built on the vacuum principle.' In the freedom of flight, many saw a weapon. In November 1783, a Prussian military engineer called J. C. G. Heyne witnessed the trial of a hot-air balloon by the Montgolfier brothers in Avignon, and the next year he published a treatise which argued that such a balloon could 'rain down fire and destruction on whole towns with catastrophic results for the inhabitants'.

He saw a balloon above, for twenty-five minutes on a winter afternoon in a field in the south of France, but Heyne conjured instantly the possibility of weaponry, as if violence were the only application for this brave new trick, and again, the fantasy outstrips the fact. In 1842, Tennyson published his prophetic poem *Locksley Hall*, and in it he too looks into what might be. 'I dipt into the future,' he writes:

> far as human eye could see,
> Saw the Vision of the world, and all the wonder that would be;
> Saw the heavens fill with commerce, argosies of magic sails,
> Pilots of the purple twilight, dropping down with costly bales;
> Heard the heavens fill with shouting, and there rain'd a ghastly dew
> From the nations' airy navies grappling in the central blue.

Others were less modest about this ghastly dew dropped by air navies. In Robert W. Coles's fantasy novel *The Struggle for Empire*, published in 1900, the Sirians of planet Kairet bomb London, but the heroic Anglo-Saxons invent a device to bring down Sirian spaceships, and in retaliation bomb the Sirian capital into unconditional surrender. H. G. Wells's *War in the Air* (1908) opens with German airships bombing New York, and all of these violent daydreams predate the first plane flight across the Channel, in June 1909, and then on 1 November 1911 an Italian airman called Giulio Cavotti dropped a hand grenade on rebellious Arabs in Tripoli, and bombing began.

'The popular literature of the late nineteenth century, because of its specific and futuristic elements, had more than a casual relation-ship to the dawn of air power,' argues Lee Kennett in his *History of Strategic Bombing* (1982): 'This sort of literature not only bred in its readers a faith in science and the inevitability of "progress," but it also created a kind of anticipation. When the armed airship did finally appear, it was already familiar to the popular mind.' On the first day of the Second World War, air raid sirens cried out across London, but it was a false alarm. 'Nothing fell in the first air raid except a few women in faints,' runs the wry note in the ethnog-raphy of British social life during the first year of the war, produced by Mass-Observation.

> In the absence of any official explanation of the supposed raids – first real impact of war – people simply invented the news they were not given, in the image of the WAR that had so long been looming in their nightmares. The result was an astonishing proliferation of rumour

the report continues, and because those who cannot have their fears sometimes summon them: 'Nearly every town of any importance was rumoured to have been bombed to ruins during the early days of the war. Planes had been *seen* by hundreds of eye-witnesses fall-ing in flames.' My great-grandparents, along with three and a half million others, left London at the start of the war, but when no raids came that autumn and winter, they returned home. The air raid is always twice. There is the dust and rubble, and wild howling as bombs fall now; and there is the dread of an episode not yet begun.

'To have the heavy bomber,' writes Azar Gat in his 1998 study of early twentieth-century theories of warfare, 'one had first to con-ceive the idea of it.' Poets and science fiction novelists did the work of imagining bombers, and a similar fantastical strain – of quick imagining, guesswork – runs through the development of bombing policy. Perhaps the most influential argument for the possibility of strategic bombing was that of the Italian military theorist and amateur poet Giulio Douhet, who shortly after the first bombing run in Tripoli in 1911 gave a lecture on air power to the Turin polytechnic. He insisted that flight would define future wars, and in his lyrical enthusiasm broke into verse. 'The bent wings / of men are passing,' he declaimed, and on:

> the field machines
> made of stretched hemp-close and light
> wood, which will carry man and his
> dreadful thunderbolt on fragile supports.

By 1921, he had arranged his fantasies into a monograph called *The Command of the Air*. 'To have command of the air means to be in a position to wield offensive power so great it defies human imagination,' he wrote, and only imagination could complete the project. 'Take the centre of a large city and imagine what would happen among the civilian population during a single attack by a single bombing unit,' he instructs his readers, and dizzied by his own daydream he conjures the scene:

> Within a few minutes some 20 tons of high-explosive, incendiary, and gas bombs would rain down. First would come explosions, then fires, then deadly gases floating on the surface and preventing any approach to the stricken area. As the hours passed and night advanced, the fires would spread while the poison gas paralysed all life. By the following day the life of the city would be suspended.

Following the infectious logic of fear, Douhet's fantasy sprawls into a whole imagined world.

Again and again, in the debates over bombing during the decade before the war, there is a moment when one voice says, imagine, and all else falls quiet. At teatime on 21 June 1938, while the RAF were bombing the north-west frontier of India, the MP for Derby, Mr P. J. Noel-Baker, stood in the House of Commons and asked his government to defend the principles of international law against aerial bombing. 'The only way to prevent atrocities from the air is to abolish air warfare and national air forces altogether,' he said. The Prime Minister agreed. Bombing aimed at civilian population is contrary to international law, he allowed, and went on: 'The difficulty arises when one of the forces engaged in aerial warfare, being accused of deliberate bombing of civilians, deny that they were bombing civilians or that it was deliberate, and allege that they were in pursuit of military objectives. Again, what is a military objective?' As he speaks, into his voice creeps the fantastical strain. 'Suppose a church is used as the headquarters of a division,' he asks, and warming to his theme: 'Suppose a man makes a bad shot, which is not at all unlikely when machines are going at over 300 miles an hour and when, as I am informed, in taking aim you have to release the bomb miles away from its objective.' The history of bombing is a series of supposes such as this. Where facts were lacking, outcomes unknown, then fantasies stepped in, to explain, to justify, to invent.

'Suppose a man makes a bad shot,' the Prime Minister mused, but by the spring of 1942 there had been too many bad shots. Science fiction had promised an elegance of massacre. In the anonymous *Gas War of 1940* (1931), 'swarms of dirigibles, each larger than the biggest ocean liner, were clouding the skies of the earth', and drop an invisible gas which kills in three minutes, but the bombers over Germany were often lost and far from target, embarrassed and fallible, and the Butt Report had made this shortfall clear. 'If in 1942, Bomber Command, with its limited and, indeed, diminishing resources, could win some notable victories,' write the authors of the official history of the bombing war: 'then and then only might it be afforded the opportunity of fulfilling its destiny.' The thousand-bomber plan was needed as a show of bombing's promise, and while it had pragmatic ambitions – maximum damage against minimum loss – much of its force was also symbolic, to show this could be done.

The alarms began in Cologne at just after half past midnight, and then the bombs fell for an hour and a half; between the incendiaries and heavy-explosives, the bombers dropped also leaflets, which told of a thousand planes, the magic number, all in the sky. An official report was prepared for the Haus der Technik in Essen in September of that year, and a torn copy is now in the Historisches Archiv at Cologne. It describes a catastrophe in figures: 14,000 people evacuated, and 50,000 homeless; 9,745 apartments destroyed, and 915 shops; but often it turns back to the single totemic number. 'As you know, the English propaganda gave the number of 1,000 planes,' the report notes, but this seems too much, so in the conclusion decides: 'My opinion is that there were approximately . . . planes involved in the attack.' The figure is left blank, as if too many to count. Two days later, the headline of the *Kölner Stadt-Anzeiger* called this the 'night of neverending British terror', and reported that Goebbels, the Minister of Propaganda, had mocked the 'British legend' of a thousand bombers. On the day after the raid, the *Daily Express* in London was consumed by counting. 'The Vengeance Begins!' ran the strap at the top of the front page, and on into an orgy of maths. 'One Bomber Every 6 Seconds, 3,000 tons in 90 minutes,' insisted the headline, above a black box, stretching long down the page, printed with one thousand white stars, eight wide, one hundred and twenty-five deep.

There were not really one thousand planes. Amongst the stream was a Mark I Wellington, W5704, that my grandfather had flown in an operation on Brest in the year before, and this night W5704 was shot down by a night-fighter over the target. My grandfather was in a different plane, but he turned back, and nobody knows how many there were in the skies above Cologne that night. The Operations Record for Bomber Command claims 1,047, but according to the official history 'the total figure, including the four Training Command Wellingtons, amounted to 1,046.' Like so much in bombing, the magic number was a fiction, a fantasy of power and violence, doing its imaginary work.

In 1942 Bomber Command changed the scale by which it measured destruction. A new chill enters its calibrations. In early spring, the British Casualty Survey announced a series of findings from its research into the German bombing of Hull and Birmingham. By weight, it reported, bombing does little physical harm. 'Large towns have a high capacity for absorbing their bombed out population,' it concluded, and 'Other raid effects such as stoppage of water or gas have little effect on the population.' But it found also that 'The factor most affecting the population is the destruction of houses', and added: 'Dwelling houses are destroyed by high explosive bombs and not by fire.' At the end of March, Churchill's scientific adviser, Lord Cherwell, sent a minute to the Prime Minister. 'Investigation seems to show that having one's house demolished is most damaging to morale,' he notes: 'People seem to mind it more than having their friends or even relatives injured.' He is counting physical loss against psychological damage, and is setting policy for the huge raids of the early summer of 1942.

There is imaginative force in a scene of houses falling. 'In succession / Houses rise and fall, crumble, are extended,' wrote T. S. Eliot at the opening of 'East Coker', and:

> Are removed, destroyed, restored, or in their place
> Is an open field, or a factory, or a by-pass.
> Old stone to new building, old timber to new fires,
> Old fires to ashes, and ashes to the earth.

'Houses live and die,' he writes a little later in the same poem. These are not simple buildings. They live, and may pass away; with them resides also the safety of individuals, and this is what Cherwell means by morale. Eliot had long written about urban decay and the inconstant state of the world, and his early poems are full of rotting cities, but this image is particular. In the autumn of 1939, while he was writing 'East Coker', Eliot was living in a cold-water flat at 11 Emperor's Gate in Kensington. He was working as a publisher, at

Faber and Faber in Bloomsbury, but at the weekends and in the evenings he volunteered as an air raid warden. He wore a steel helmet, and an arm band, and practised putting out fires – sand for the phosphorus, a broom for broken glass – and ordering groups of evacuees in the park. He wrote 'East Coker' through the autumn and winter, and it was first published in March 1940. This was a season of expectation in the city, of waiting for the bombs, and for the buildings to fall, and so too was Eliot waiting. His was not yet war poetry.

T. S. Eliot was born in America and lived his life in England, and long after he was celebrated as a poet he worked in the basement office of the foreign accounts department of a London bank. He was handsome; he had bad teeth; he smoked. His umbrellas were made for him, with an unusually large handle, and while he worked at the bank he wore a bowler hat, black coat and striped trousers. In 1925, he left the bank and joined the Board of Directors at the publishing house of Faber and Faber – then Faber and Gwyer – and photographs of him at the time show him wearing a three-piece suit of dark wool. Those who met him often described him, and they always came back to his clothes, to his skin, his fine sharp nose. Virginia Woolf compared him to marble, and an eel, and a poker, and in the end, she said she liked him. His biographer Peter Ackroyd suggests that 'his detachment, of which so many contemporaries wrote, is simply the effect of Eliot looking at himself from the outside, arranging himself with his slow and infrequent gestures as an actor might', and records that he sometimes wore pale-green face powder, to heighten his sickness, to push away the world. He wrote the complex, perfect masterpieces of twentieth-century modernism and rhyming children's verse. 'His manner was vague and aloof, / You would think there was nobody shyer,' he wrote, in 'Mr. Mistoffelees' from *Old Possum's Book of Practical Cats*:

> But his voice has been heard on the roof
> When he was curled up by the fire.
> And he's sometimes been heard by the fire

When he was about on the roof –
(At least we all heard somebody who purred)
Which is incontestable proof
Of his singular magical powers.

In 1948, he won the Nobel Prize for Literature, and he told childish jokes. He liked to drink martinis, and champagne before lunch, and he often appeared larger than his visitors had expected. Late in life, he married his secretary, and they held hands at dinner parties.

Eliot put on war poet like he put on a suit. In the spring of 1940, when the war was going badly for the British and the German army was at the French coast, Eliot was invited to contribute a poem to an exhibition at the Museum of Modern Art in New York. The museum displayed, and then published, a collection of wartime images. There were engravings of the bombed East End of London by the illustrator Edward Ardizzone, and Paul Nash's paintings of aircraft; there were cartoons, from the evening papers, and Eliot wrote a poem about duty and Englishness. 'Defence of the Islands' honours 'those who, in man's newest form of gamble / with death, fight the power of darkness', and ends in the vow:

> to say, to the past and future generations
> of our kin and of our speech, that we took up
> our positions, in obedience to instructions.

This is a strained but proper national hymn, and conscious of the role of work in wartime. Eliot spent the autumn of 1941 editing a collection of Kipling's rousing ballads, which was published that December and which he referred to as his 'war effort'.

This is one version of war poetry, and one version of Eliot: that it was a matter of duty and that he was following orders. The war was an obligation and a passing interruption. After his success as a poet in the early 1920s, Eliot had spent much of the 1930s lecturing and writing plays: the church pageant of *The Rock* in 1934 followed by

Murder in the Cathedral in 1935, and then *The Family Reunion* at the start of 1939. He meant to continue. 'In 1939, if there hadn't been a war I would probably have tried to write another play,' he explained to an interviewer in 1959, but because of the war he returned to poetry. We have seen this pattern before, where a wartime scene troubles a poet into writing, but as so often in the case of Eliot, his version is a little different. In 1935, Eliot had written the long poem 'Burnt Norton', a restless hymn of passing time and memory. When the war came, and Eliot found himself in a bombed city, he added three further parts to this original. 'East Coker' was written at the end of 1939, and published in March 1940; 'The Dry Salvages' was in complete draft by the end of 1940; and 'Little Gidding' was in first draft by July 1941, and then heavily revised in the late summer of 1942. Each of the four dwells upon one of the classical elements – air, earth, water, fire – and taken together, these four poems form Eliot's late masterpiece. They were published as *Four Quartets* in 1943, and it is not necessarily an over-simplification to claim that they exist because of the war and are therefore war poetry; the last of the four, 'Little Gidding', is explicitly concerned with the experience of living in a bombed city. In the *New York Times*, on 16 May 1943, Horace Gregory ended his review: 'for those who wish to take heart as against others who are convinced that poetry was among the early casualties of the present war, I strongly recommend a reading of Mr. T. S. Eliot's "Four Quartets".'

The purest way to approach 'Little Gidding' is to hear Eliot read it, for his voice is crisp as a new rule book and aloud this sounds like what it is, a kind of ritual, a subtle riddle. Aloud, it also at moments sounds like nonsense, and aloud, this is right, for Eliot's subject here is the defeat of any single telling of history. At first, we are in no stable place: in 'England and nowhere', he tells us, and this is 'Never and always', for it is always both, 'both one and many', a place of 'water and fire'. He writes of a journey, and a return, but in a tone of failure, and the narrator is unsure. 'I assumed a double part,' writes Eliot: 'I was still the same, / Knowing myself yet being someone other'.

Yet he, of course, was somewhere. From October 1940, after the Blitz began, Eliot lodged with friends at Shamley Green, near Guildford, for the weekends, but on Tuesday morning he took the train into the city. For two nights a week, Tuesday and Wednesday, he often stayed in Hampstead. It was safer there, in the north of London, but during the days he went into the centre, to the bombed grid of squares around Bloomsbury and the Faber offices on Russell Square; some nights, he slept in a small bedroom at the office. This was his routine during the war, and it places him within the rubble for the worst of the raids, from the autumn of 1940 until the middle of May 1941.

At the start of August 1941, Eliot's friend and editor John Hayward read the first draft of 'Little Gidding'. Helen Gardner, in her critical study of the writing of the *Four Quartets*, quotes a phrase from the draft. 'In the autumn weather / I heard a distant dull deferred report / At which I started,' wrote Eliot, and Hayward was confused. 'I do not get the significance of <u>autumn</u>,' he asked Eliot, who replied, '"Autumn weather" only because it <u>was</u> autumn weather – it is supposed to be an <u>early</u> air raid.' The first raids of the Blitz came in September 1940, and if we are thinking of bombing, then the echo is clear. This was his historical moment, and although Eliot subsequently cut this phrase from the published poem, it is not the only resonance of bombing here. In one particularly opaque passage, Eliot describes 'The death of water and fire', and these two paradoxical elements again begin to resist any real physical landscape. But Helen Gardner offers a simple explanation. 'Anyone who lived through the London raids must link water and fire as equally destructive, remembering the charred and sodden ruins and their smell the morning after as the great hoses played on the flaming and smoking ruins,' she writes, turning a poem's image into a precise report of physical destruction.

'Little Gidding' is Eliot's great poem of bomb damage, and it is no simple act of witness. Eliot was not only working as a publisher, in his top-floor office on Russell Square; for a few hours, two nights each

week, he sat out on the roof as a fire-watcher, looking over the city,
waiting for bombs. From Russell Square, there was heavy damage
just to the east, on Conduit Street and Theobalds Road, and Red Lion
Square was almost completely destroyed. Directly behind his office,
in the east corner of the square, two buildings were hit at the start of
the Blitz, and a little later the Imperial Hotel, in the south-east corner,
received light damage. It is not that Eliot simply saw all this. He
looked, and this whole world of damage gives sense to the troubled,
contradictory surface of 'Little Gidding'. In the poem, Eliot writes:

> Ash on an old man's sleeve
> Is all the ash the burnt roses leave.
> Dust in the air suspended
> Marks the place where a story ended.
> Dust inbreathed was a house –
> The wall, the wainscot and the mouse

riddling in simple rhymes, but this too is a specific moment. In 1968,
an earnest American priest called William Turner Levy published
his reminiscences of an unlikely friendship with Eliot that began
when he was stationed in London at the end of the war, and he
quotes Eliot explaining exactly these lines:

'You see,' Eliot remembered, 'during the Blitz the accumulated
debris was suspended in the London air for hours after a bombing.
Then it would slowly descend and cover one's sleeves and coat with
a fine white ash. I often experienced this effect during long night
hours on the roof.'

Eliot's images in 'Little Gidding' are rooted in the inside-out physics
of bomb damage.

Eliot in the Blitz was fifty-two years old, and after the second year of
the war all men between eighteen and sixty were responsible for

forty-eight hours' duty each month as a fire-watcher. 'Films and books have shown us the devastation caused by bombs,' ran one instructional pamphlet, 'and no one can fail to be stricken with horror at the toll of the dead.' Those with jobs watched their employer's premises; others enrolled in fire-watching parties and walked the streets. As training, they were lectured on the treatment of burns, the 'rescue of insensible persons', and how to cover an incendiary bomb with a sand mat. They were given a whistle, a torch and a respirator. 'Take cover if shrapnel falls but do not go inside,' instructs one handbook dated 14 March 1941: 'You cannot watch from inside a house nor hear clearly.' Falling incendiaries give a white glare and 'a sound like pieces of wood rattling', it continues, and 'if they fall in your area blow your whistle.'

The first duty was to watch, and second to report. The recruitment posters called upon those 'who are capable of accurately receiving and transmitting verbal, written or telephone messages', and all reports must follow the rules set by the Chief Warden at the start of the war. According to *The Method of Reporting Air Raid Damage* of 20 November 1939, the fire-watcher must give the number of the sector, the position of occurrence, and the type of bomb; give approximate number of casualties, the rules insist, and always give a number. 'Try to give a definite figure even if it has to be estimated,' the instructions continue: '*Do not use the word "many".*' They go on:

> In regard to dead persons, if there is the *slightest* possibility that life is not extinct that person must be reported as a casualty. In cases where there is no possible shadow of doubt that life is extinct (e.g., a decapitated person), then the body should be placed to one side, out of sight and covered.

The report must list damage to the mains, the position of unexploded bombs, and the names of blocked roads, and '*If fire, say so* – Always use the word "fire" here, if there is fire. Any amplification should be put under "remarks" (e.g., "Fire spreading rapidly").'

Perhaps Eliot was the worst of fire-watchers. 'Little Gidding' is a great amplification of a fire-watcher's remarks on bomb damage, but it is a ruthlessly unreliable description, at times unimpressed by even the scene before.

> You are not here to verify,
> Instruct yourself, or inform curiosity,
> Or carry report

wrote Eliot, and he has no concern for time and place. 'The timeless moment,' he writes, forgetting every rule in the Chief Warden's method, 'Is England and nowhere'.

But perhaps he was the best. In 'Little Gidding', Eliot is captivated by fire and water and falling ash, all the conditions of ruin, and in the long central scene he goes out 'In the uncertain hour before the morning' only moments after an air raid. This is 'After the dark dove with the flickering tongue / Had passed below the horizon', for the raiders now are leaving, and Eliot describes the scene:

> Between three districts whence the smoke arose
> I met one walking, loitering and hurried
> As if blown towards me like the metal leaves
> Before the urban dawn wind unresisting.
> And as I fixed upon the down-turned face
> That pointed scrutiny with which we challenge
> The first-met stranger in the waning dusk
> I caught the sudden look of some dead master
> Whom I had known, forgotten, half recalled
> Both one and many; in the brown baked features
> The eyes of a familiar compound ghost
> Both intimate and unidentifiable.

He should not use this word 'many', but what he sees in the burnt city is a blend of times and characters, and the man he meets is both long dead and here before him. 'In regard to dead persons, if there is the *slightest* possibility that life is not extinct that person must be reported as a casualty': this was the Chief Warden's instruction and in the air raid Eliot sees a ghost, one whose life is, against all the visible signs, not quite extinct.

Helen Gardner identifies lines and allusions from three dead poets – Dante, W. B. Yeats and Jonathan Swift – making up the compound ghost. He is a mixed, uncertain character, and as they walk he warns Eliot of what may come to him as he ages. Man cannot simply outlive the past, the ghost promises, but rather grows with 'the rending pain of re-enactment/ Of all that you have done, and been.' The old poets are not dead to him, here in the air raid.

Eliot had long written of the unlikely survival of literature; the continuation of culture, in the face of the wreckage of the modern world, is his great theme. In his famous essay 'Tradition and the Individual Talent', first published in 1920, Eliot had established as a literary ideal what he called 'the historical sense'. Great writers are those, he had powerfully argued, who stand as guardians of the past, not from a sense of nostalgic obligation but as the heirs of tradition. 'The historical sense involves a perception, not only of the pastness of the past, but of its presence,' he wrote then, and Eliot in the Blitz is a man immersed in the echoes of old poetry. On 15 April 1942, as president of the Classical Association, he gave the annual address and insisted to his audience that 'the maintenance of classical education is essential to the maintenance of the continuity of English literature', and his repeated ideal of 1942 is what he elsewhere called 'the inherited imagination'. Old poetry can provide a language and a sensibility with which to understand the moment. Writing in the *New English Weekly* in the issue of 21 January 1942, he returned again to this claim. 'For the expression of imaginative reality, for the truths of poetry and religion,' he wrote, 'a man is best equipped when he uses the language of his ancestors.'

One of the great criticisms of the strategic bombing campaigns of the Second World War was that they destroyed cultural monuments:

they tore cathedrals to ruins, turned libraries to ash. The two most powerful photographs of the Blitz in London are both fake, and both present the German raids on London as attacks not upon people but upon traditional English culture. In the first, St Paul's Cathedral rises white above a wild sea of smoke as the city burns. In the second, of the bombed library at Holland House in west London, three men in bowler hats and dark suits lean across rubble to reach out books from the shelves; above, the roof leaks on to the sky. Both say: so much was lost in the bombing, but the Germans have failed because they have left our religious monuments and our thirst for literature intact.

But this same charge can be turned inwards, too, for after May 1941 few German bombs fell in England, and the Allied campaigns grew in scope and weight, night after night across occupied Europe. At the opening of Parliament on 24 November 1943, Lord Cecil, the Secretary of State for Dominion Affairs, reported to the assembled members that Bomber Command had in the previous ten months dropped 130,000 tons of high-explosive and incendiary bombs, of which 85 per cent was on Germany. This was in contrast, he continued, to 37,000 tons for the whole of 1942, and 23,000 for 1941. Such a scale might trouble any stable opinion of the morality of this war, and when in February of the following year the Bishop of Chichester stood in the House of Lords to protest at what he saw as the undue violence of the bombing campaign, he phrased his opposition as a plea for saving cultural monuments. 'Why is there this forgetfulness of the ideals by which our cause is inspired?' he asked, and went on: 'How can the War Cabinet fail to see that this progressive devastation of cities is threatening the roots of civilization?' To conclude, he simply listed works of art and libraries that had been destroyed by bombs dropped in Lübeck, Hamburg and Berlin. A week later, Lord Lang of Lambeth continued the Bishop's appeal. He was speaking, he said, 'to call attention to the importance of preserving objects of historic or cultural value within the theatres of war', and mentioned the paintings by Giotto at Assisi, the Byzantine art of Ravenna, and Venice. Viscount Trenchard responded. 'I suppose he looks upon our airmen,' he began, 'as though they were vandals, as though they were men who wanted to knock down every monument', and soon after he had finished, Lord Lang withdrew his motion. Long after the war, this same charge would haunt the bombers – that they had bombed libraries and churches, the lovely old cities of Dresden and Hanover burned to dust and memory – for it is a powerful way to phrase a criticism. In the 20 July 1941 issue of the *Westfälische Tageszeitung*, a daily newspaper in Münster, the lead editorial ran under the headline 'The British are Culture-Destroyers', and concluded that last week's damage to the cathedral 'is proof of the vandal-like behaviour of the British, who are stupid enough to talk of a crusade for civilization'.

Eliot knew the Bishop of Chichester, George Bell. The Bishop was the most powerful English critic of the Allied strategic bombing offensive, and in speeches and books after the war he returned to the claim that Allied bombing was morally wrong because it had burned down German libraries and museums. In the summer of 1934, the Bishop had commissioned Eliot to write a play for performance in Canterbury Cathedral. Eliot wrote *Murder in the Cathedral*, about St Thomas Becket, and in the early autumn of 1941, while Eliot was revising 'Little Gidding', he travelled to Sweden for a month with the Bishop, to give lectures paid for by the British Council. In the autumn of 1941, as the greatest poet in England was writing his scenes of bomb damage, he was also passing his days and his evenings with a passionate opponent of bombing, for whom the bombs could only ever ruin the monuments of the past.

The paradox of 'Little Gidding' is the paradox of bombing: what we hold on to, through the ruin, may stand up to what we lose. After Eliot died, the poet George Seferis published a memoir of his meetings with the poet, and recalled asking Eliot about his war service. Eliot laughed off the question. 'Oh, I didn't do anything to diminish the results of the raids,' he said. For Eliot, the results of the raids were 'Little Gidding'. The history of bombing is a story of anticipation and delay, time jumbled in the rubble, and the question that remains is what we are willing to hear as war poetry. We have

Eliot on the roof watching for fires; and we have Mr. Mistoffelees, whose 'voice has been heard on the roof / When he was curled up by the fire'. The chronology is off – for Eliot wrote his poems of practical cats before the war began, and they were first published in 1939 – but in the burnt city, simple time fades a little.

Eliot in the Blitz is at the end of a long hidden tradition: a history of poets waiting, imagining and waiting, for the burning city and the flying bomber. The technologies of war may change in time, but our fantasies do not. War poetry begins with the *Iliad*, the great epic of siege, and the soldiers dream of burning a city. Here is Agamemnon in prayer amongst the Greeks on the beach:

> O excellency, O majesty, O Zeus
> Beyond the stormcloud, dwelling in high air,
> Let not the sun go down upon this day
> Into the western gloom, before I tumble
> Priam's blackened rooftree down, exploding
> Fire through his portals!

Priam is the king of Troy, and the Greeks have long been waiting to burn his city. They are certain of this end – 'The day must come when holy Troy / Is given to fire and sword,' Agamemnon later vows – for fire is not only a means of war; it is also the central metaphor for war. Here are the Greeks, massing:

> As in dark forests, measureless along
> The crests of hills, a conflagration soars,
> And the bright red of fire glows for miles,
> Now fiery lights from this great host in bronze
> Played on the earth and flashed high into heaven.

Later, the soldiers fight 'raggedly as fire', leaping upwards like flames, and just as the Greeks long to burn Troy, so do the Trojans long to burn Greek ships.

'The whole of the *Iliad* lies under the shadow of the greatest calamity the human race can experience – the destruction of a city,' wrote Simone Weil, in Marseilles in the summer of 1940. She had seen Paris fall to the Germans, and she was on her way to London, where she would see the ruined city, and in the *Iliad* she found predicted this new landscape of war. Yet Troy never burns in the *Iliad*. This promised ending is deferred, and while we see that it is inevitable, we are never told of it. It was perhaps too terrible for Homer to imagine, and Virgil picked up the story 800 years later. In the second book of the *Aeneid*, Aeneas, who has fled from Troy, tells his escape from the burning city, and again insists that such horrors are beyond report. 'Who could unfold the horrors of that night?' he demands: 'Who could speak of such slaughter? Who could weep tears to match that suffering? It was the fall of an ancient city that had long ruled an empire. The bodies of the dead lay all through its streets and houses and the sacred shrines of its gods.' The burned city is the worst of things.

The poets were always drawn to the fire, for its readiness as a flickering metaphor for war. 'O for a muse of fire,' longed Shakespeare at the start of his greatest dramatic consideration of the glamour of war, and King Henry later stands at the gates of a city that will not surrender.

> For as I am a soldier,
> A name that in my thoughts becomes me best,
> If I begin the batt'ry once again
> I will not leave the half-achieved Harfleur,
> Till in her ashes she lie buried

he vows, and goes on to demand:

> What is it then to me if impious war
> Arrayed in flames like to the prince of fiends
> Do with his smirched complexion all fell feats
> Enlinked to waste and desolation?

The threat is to burn a city, but as in the *Iliad*, it is no more than a promise, and faced with such an image the Governor calls down from the walls. 'Dread King, / We yield our town and lives to thy soft mercy,' he says: 'Enter our gates, dispose of us and ours, / For we no longer are defensible.' The city shall not be burned.

At eight minutes before eleven, my grandfather takes off from the satellite station of Steeple Morden. He is going to bomb Cologne, but in twenty minutes he turns back.

Chapter 5. The Most Beautiful City in the World

31 May 1942

The day after the thousand-bomber raid, they came again to Cologne. Sirens sang up at five minutes before one, and for fifteen minutes British planes flew over; and then again that night, for an hour and a half. The following morning, Wellingtons were above the city at just after ten, and at half past eight in the evening, and for three hours at midnight. The next day they came at seven and at twelve and at two. There were ten air raid alarms in Cologne in the seventy-two hours following the raid of 30 May 1942 and not a single bomb was dropped for the bombers now were tourists, come to inspect the damage. Six hundred acres of the city were in ruin, concluded the reconnaissance report, and added: 'There is, however, no considerable area which is free from incidents.'

The war was changing. At Bassingbourn, the station log records a new schedule of 'night flying suppers'. From 31 May, it instructs that on nights when there are operations 'all personnel, officers, NCOs, and airmen to be served in future in the airmen's mess.' When they are bombing, the officers and men will eat together, and on 1 June my grandfather is pilot of the same plane, with the same crew – except the wireless operator – on the second thousand-bomber raid. They bomb Essen at a quarter past one, and report fires in the target area, but the flash in the camera slung under the plane fails, so they cannot take a picture. The night was cloudy, and the planes scattered, causing little damage to the town. Two nights later, he is out on a bullseye, getting home at half past two, but this is the end of the full-moon period and operations stand down. At six o'clock that night, there is a garden party at Kneesworth Hall for aircrew who participated in the two thousand-bomber raids, to toast what they have done.

The most enduring and least verifiable myth about my grandfather is that one night during the Blitz he drove into London, simply to see. When I went to speak with her, many years later, I asked my great-aunt about this story, and she said that she and my grand-father were once caught by a raid on the Euston Road. Her version has the calm of truth, a detail and a witness, but it lacks the essential element of the other. If he chose to be there, then perhaps this was a man who considered what he was doing and who once invited another perspective. My father holds on to this story for it makes his father a good man: his morality shown in the act of going to see.

If he was there, out in the wild circus for a night, then he was part of a great tradition that runs thick through the history of bombing: of those thrilled by this as a show. In the bombing war there are not simply soldiers but other roles too, in the whole of the drama, for bombing comes alive only in the eyes of an audience. In late November 1939, following a German raid on the east coast, the Regional Commissioner for Defence, Sir Auckland Gedden, issued a public warning. 'If you hear anti-aircraft fire or see an air battle going on when the warning sirens have not been sounded, there is risk of injury from falling fragments of anti-aircraft shells or machine-gun bullets,' the warning instructs: 'It is foolhardy, and not heroic, to stand in the streets and watch the combat.' But everyone looked, regardless, mesmerized. The Blitz began at teatime on a Saturday, and the next day the *Observer* reported:

> Despite the boom of AA guns and the drumming of machine-gun fire London remained calm, and thousands at football matches and greyhound races treated the desperate fight being waged in the air as a spectacle: 'That was a near shave' was the comment of one man among several hundred at the greyhound track where 3 bombs fell, one outside the ground, one behind the stand and one right on the track. Four thousand people at a football match had a grandstand view of one air battle. They forgot the risk of falling shrapnel and cheered when one plane fell in flames.

As the summer gave way to autumn, and the raids went on, posters appeared in bus shelters and on the tiled walls of underground stations. 'In a raid – Don't stand and stare at the sky,' they instructed: 'Take cover at once.' But there was a great drama above, and only a fool would turn away.

The poet and critic A. Alvarez was a child in Hampstead during the Blitz, and writes with a mix of nostalgia and precision of:

> air-raid sirens wailing, the steady rise and fall of the bomber engines (the radio newsreaders talked about 'waves of bombers', and that was how they sounded), bombs whistling (you learned from their sound to judge their closeness with great precision), the thump of anti-aircraft batteries on Primrose Hill, planes pinned against the night sky in a latticework of searchlights, the eerie glow over London the night the City caught fire.

'I watched it from the night-nursery window until my distraught mother found me and hustled me downstairs,' he goes on, and in the days he went out and 'explored the shells of bombed-out houses, looking for trouble but pretending we were looking for treasure'. 'It was more than exciting,' he writes: 'It was also beautiful.' Writers often reach for this particular word in the bombed city. The American journalist Ernie Pyle was in London during the great raid of 29 December 1940, and he 'gathered a couple of friends and went to a high, darkened balcony that gave us a view of one-third of the entire circle of London'. They did not want to miss a glimpse, and through all the 'boom, crump, crump of heavy bombs at their work' he cannot keep from his voice a tone of wonder. 'There was something inspiring in the savagery of it,' he writes, and in the end 'this was the most beautiful sight I have ever seen.'

Those in the city watched; and those in the suburbs took the train in. In January 1941 Rebecca West wrote 'A Day in Town', a short essay for the *New Yorker* in which she describes her visit to London on the day after an air raid. She has errands to run, black-out lampshades to buy and vegetables to deliver to her sister, but amongst her daily chores are sirens and unexploded bombs. In a taxi, she writes, 'I made myself dizzy by swivelling round to look out of the back window to see, against the blue sky, the trails of exhaust fumes which marked a fight between a German and an English plane', and she notes how 'cheerful' the train station was looking. 'This was because all the smoke-dimmed glass had gone,' she explains, 'and the sunshine was pouring in through the iron ribs.' With repetition, this pleasure can pass. West notes that 'everyone wore the expression characteristic of people in a raided town', and by the spring Blitz tourists were a cliché and a nuisance. The *Daily Express* of Monday, 12 May 1941, the day after the last raid, described them: 'Being Sunday and a day of rest thousands of people had nothing to do. So they came in their droves to look at the seared ruins, to block the streets, to trample on hoses, to hold up fire engines, to gawp at weary, blistered firemen.'

Like rare birds, the bombers too were studied, tracked; their curious migrations were the subject of breathless magazine articles, splashy documentaries, silver-tint fashion shoots. In early 1942, the Ministry of Information in London hired the glamour photographer Cecil Beaton, known for his work in *Vogue*, to record life among the bomber crews. 'The motive of their existence carries them to a skyline to which we cannot follow them,' writes Beaton in the flowery text which accompanies the collection, *Winged Squadrons*. Half in love with the handsome young men, clean-shaven and slicked-back, smiling in front of their planes, Beaton continues: 'They possess the secret ecstasy of the mystic.' When the US Air Force started bombing from British airfields in the summer of 1942, they were joined by Lieutenant Clark Gable. Gable was the most famous movie star in the world, and *Gone with the Wind* was playing to full cinemas across London. Handsome and avuncular, with a tender streak and a thin moustache, Gable was the perfect example of American force; he had been commissioned by the 351st Bombardment Group to film a documentary, and *Combat America* follows a bombing crew across the Atlantic and out on the raids of the early summer of 1943, on Bremen and Saint-Nazaire. On the night of 17 January 1943, the journalist Richard Dimbleby flew in a 106 Squadron Lancaster on a raid on Berlin, and recorded a live report, which was broadcast on the BBC the next day. At the end of that year, the American journalist Edward R. Murrow went too. 'Last night, some of the young gentlemen of the RAF took me to Berlin,' begins his account, and with a nervy cool he describes the briefing and the crew on their way into the plane, the lift-off 'smooth as silk', the searchlights and finally the 'sullen, obscene glare' of Berlin below.

Some of this rush of attention may be explained away as publicity for the war effort, and some as human curiosity in the face of violence, but taken together these stories hint at a larger paradox of the bombing enterprise. Just as journalists accompanied the bombers on their raids, and just as visitors to the cities marvelled at their work, so the bombers too were tourists. At the end of March 1942 Bomber Command destroyed Lübeck, burning the old town in a single night, and in retaliation Hitler ordered raids on five historic English cities: Exeter, Bath, Norwich, York and Canterbury. This was a gesture. The cities were ancient and of no military importance, so largely undefended, and they were evenly scattered across England. The raids began in late April and lasted until the start of June, and they took their nickname from a widely reported boast by an official for the Information and Press Division of the German foreign office. 'The Luftwaffe,' he vowed, 'will go for every building which is marked with three stars in Baedeker.'

Baedeker was the name of the great nineteenth-century set of guide-books to Europe. Their publisher was German, but they were hugely popular in England, and the little red volumes came to represent a kind of well-toned cultural travel. The phrase and its thuggish promise was a gift to English propagandists, as easy proof of German vandalism. 'The phrase "Baedeker attacks" is playing an important role in English commentaries,' noted Goebbels in his diary on 2 May 1942: 'Unfortunately, one of the gentlemen in our own Foreign Office invented this phrase and thereby did us tremendous damage. I censured this in the sharpest terms and took measures to prevent the repetition of such folly.' But the nickname was contagious. In the

RAF museum at Hendon is the logbook of a bomber pilot from the closing months of the war. In May and June of 1945, as ground defences collapsed and Germany surrendered, he flew a series of tours over German industrial cities. The entry for 2 June 1945 runs: 'Southwold – Wesel – Osnabruck – Bremen – Hamburg – Hanover – Bielefeld – Hamm – Dortmund – Duisburg – Westkapelle – Base.' In the margin by this extraordinary itinerary he has noted 'to view damage', and then the comment 'Baedeker Op'.

Guide-books tell us what to look for; they tell us what to see. In January 1943 the Ministry of Economic Warfare in London issued a 'Guide to the Economic Importance of German Towns and Cities'. The folder lists urban areas with a population of 15,000 and over, and gives map references, distances from London, and a brief account of the terrain. Cologne 'is the centre of trade, traffic and commerce in the Rhine Province' and 'it handles the corn, wine and timber which comes from the upper Rhine districts.' Dortmund has cereal storehouses, and in Kassel they make aircraft fuselages, and weave sailcloth for tents and uniforms; Duisburg has hard coal, and the world's largest inland port. The desirability of each target is indicated by a number – 1, 2 or 3 – and inevitably, this volume came to be known as 'The Bomber's Baedeker'.

Like all guides, the Bomber's Baedeker lists curiosities and recommends marvels. In Kiel you will find 'the largest naval arsenal in Germany. It includes a floating dock lying outside the Harbour and has been considerably extended recently', and the sights in town include also the lock gates at the eastern end of the canal and the 55,000 kW Kiel-Wik power station, adjacent to the municipal gasworks. Its twin, the last English edition of the Baedeker guide to Germany to appear before the war, was published in 1936, and it too reads as military intelligence:

> *Essen*, the centre for the Ruhr coalfield, can boast one of the oldest churches in Germany; *Dortmund* likewise has medieval churches; *Düsseldorf*, an elegant and art-loving city, has diverse attractions in

the form of museums, picture galleries, parks, and pleasure resorts; the docks of *Duisburg* are of an astounding extent for an inland town; while the double town of *Wuppertal* (Eberfeld and Barmen) has a unique suspension railway constructed over the river Wupper.

My grandfather visited each of these cities, for their astounding docks and their coalfields, because the Ruhr was the heart of the German war economy; the aircrews called it 'happy valley', and they bombed it night after night.

Today, the 1936 English Baedeker to Germany is a lonely work. It may as well be a guide to the moon, with its promise of a slow afternoon of walking and sight-seeing and its fiction that the English could find peace in Germany. In Cologne, in the summer, there are open-air restaurants, and concerts in the Botanical Gardens, and in Münster is a shaded promenade along the town walls. 'The RHINE VALLEY is a classical touring region,' it beckons, 'a joyous wine-district that combines lovely scenery with architectural master-pieces and historic memories.' The Rhine is the loveliest river in Germany, but Hamburg on the Elbe has fine quays where steamers bob, and there are Rembrandts in the museum. On the east side of Altona, next to Hamburg, is the Tierpark, 'a famous menagerie, opened in 1907 by Karl Hagenbeck (d. 1913), the dealer in wild animals'. Should you see something you like, the guide encourages, 'all the animals are for sale', and the menagerie is only half an hour, on the number 16 tram, from Adolf-Hitler-Platz.

Hamburg was the first city my grandfather bombed, but he had been there with my grandmother in the years before the war. It was a fond memory. They had fun there, by the quays and in the museum, and perhaps, in this other life when they were tourists, they took the number 16 tram from Adolf-Hitler-Platz out to the menagerie and they laughed, for all the animals were for sale.

Outside St Maria im Kapitol, a woman in an ill-fitting blue wimple, with white stockings under her sandals, is waiting for the tour group. She has put her book away in her white rucksack, and she loiters on a bench. She is Plectrudis, the widow of Pepin, and at the end of the seventh century she gave the money that built the church, and today she has been hired by the city council to tell a little history. Some tourists prefer the other characters, she tells me and my father, because the other characters do dialogues, but she only has a monologue. We ask about the war. In the war, she says, people hid from the bombs here. Inside, a princess in a purple headdress harangues a servant, and blond bored children kick a football in the cloister. Inside, there is a photograph of this church in rubble.

We arrived in Cologne on the day of the European Championship final. Germany is playing Spain so the kids are in flags, and every now and then, a screech of trumpet from another street. In the flea market there are fake Bauhaus lamps and old copies of *Playboy* and the evening news from 1942, all wrapped in plastic. The sky is clear blue, late-afternoon hangover weather, and in the cool churches the new bricks are speckly on the old, outbreaks like measles. We try to tell one from the other, to read the rash of what was repaired. Later in the day, I climb 509 steps up the spire of the cathedral, and at the top there are couples taking photographs. Having climbed all this way, nobody knows what it is proper to say. One American says to another, it gets hilly over there, and points. There are warehouses, white houses, the river curving through, and in the square a man balances two green bottles on a stick from his tongue.

I wanted to know about the raids so in the city archive I ordered photographs, like a tourist who travels through his camera. In black-and-white squares were the scenes of the old city and the stages of its end. Here are often prams, used now to ferry clothes, and there is furniture in the streets. The bridge is in the river, and the walls are down and the houses inside out. In the bombing of Cologne, the world turned upside down.

Some nights, my grandfather dreamed he was in Cologne. He had been here on his second operation, when the alarms began soon after midnight; this night, 17 May 1941, the city archive records two heavy-explosives and forty-four incendiaries on the Atlantik rubberworks in Bramsfeld, twelve kilometres north-west of the old city, where doors and windows blew out and stocks of oil and fabric burned. A week later he was here again, and that night there were bombs on the Rheinisch-Westfälische generators at Knapsack, west of the city, and a coal plant at Brühl to the south. But in his private logbook, and confirmed by the raid reports of his squadron, he notes that he has bombed Cologne on the nights of 21 June 1941, and 30 June, and 10 July, and in the records of the Stadt Köln Historisches Archiv there are alarms on each of these nights but not a single bomb dropped.

One old man I met told me that in the early years of bombing, he watched the raids with his schoolfriends. When they caught a bomber in the searchlights it was beautiful, he said, and the next day they played a game with only one rule. The winner was he who found the biggest piece of shrapnel in the street. In the summer of 1941 these were only skirmishes in the skies over the city, and they seemed no harm. Herr Boll has a beard like Abraham Lincoln, and red cheeks. He looks like a garden gnome or your best friend's grandfather, and 'skirmish' was the word he used but my pretty blonde interpreter translated it as 'foreplay'. She is twenty-six years old and like many educated Germans of her generation still living at home while in the final stages of an interminable university degree, and so the phrase may have shown more of her than the war but for a moment it caught with some precision the way they remember the early raids in old Cologne. They were sexy, and fun, and just beyond the ordinary.

At first, the city was prepared. In the archives I had read about the emergency decree passed in September 1940 to build air raid shelters in eighty-two German cities, and by May 1942 there were 500 shelters in Cologne, with space for 75,000 people. There were twenty-five bunkers too, and fourteen auxiliary hospitals, and twenty-seven first aid stations. The Luftschutzpolizei, the air defence police, numbered 4,000 men. The old man told me that his family left a packed suitcase by the door at night, ready for a trip to the shelter, and sometimes they listened to the German language service of the BBC. This was forbidden, but he laughs now and chants the old announcement, 'Hier ist London.'

We were sitting in the small dining room of his terraced house in the suburbs. There was a round table, with four chairs and a thick tablecloth, and although I was only speaking through an interpreter and she sat to his left, and she asked the questions, he never looked away from me as he answered. His wife approached slowly in her wheelchair and stopped at my left, and I asked what the city looked like at the end. At the end, he said, you could not walk in the streets. It took two hours to walk the same route that had taken twenty minutes before, and as I looked up from my notes I saw that across the table he was crying.

All changed with the *Grossangriff*, the big raid; even in German they sometimes call it 'thousand-bomber'. This was a different scale of wreckage. The police reports in the archive number bombs and casualties, and in the early raids of May and June 1941 the worst nights are those of one or two thousand incendiaries, ten or one hundred heavy-explosives, eleven or eighteen killed. On the night of 30 May 1942 there were close to 900 heavy-explosives, 110,000 incendiaries and perhaps 400 dead. The highest casualties were on 28 June 1943, with almost 4,000 killed and 15,000 wounded. The heaviest night was 29 October 1944, when they counted 4,000 heavy-explosives and over 200,000 incendiaries.

A city dies in phases. According to the 'Cologne Field Report' issued by the United States Strategic Bombing Survey after the war, the city administration stopped repairing damaged buildings in December 1943. The survey quotes a report by the price control agency from February 1944. 'It must unfortunately be stated that *money as a medium of exchange* is limited to a smaller sector of the economy,' the report observes, and goes on to describe how barter has replaced payment. 'In the Cologne district,' it concludes, 'where the appearance of enemy planes shows the population almost every night the way of all flesh, an exact legal price determination does not play the role it used to.' By October 1944, the firefighters had given up. The survey explains: 'most of the City was in ruins and what happened after that regarding damage and devastation did not matter.' There were mass evacuations at the end of that year, and the old man I was visiting went to stay with his cousins near Bonn.

In its ending, the city transforms: it is complete in damage. 'In the heavy air attacks a condition arose which had not been envisaged,' notes the USSBS report on the state of the city after the summer of 1942: 'hundreds of individual fires coalesced into a conflagration area.' The continuous bombing overwhelmed the careful schemes of German civilian defence. 'No plan, regardless of how scientifically and thoroughly devised it may be, will work effectively in actual practice and under all conditions, particularly when subject to extraordinary stress far beyond any possibilities envisaged by its authors,' continues the survey, and concludes: 'No system for civilian protection yet devised appears adequate in total warfare.' In Cologne, the bombers at last achieved and then exceeded their old fiction of total warfare, of a battle won only from above. This was, in the phrase of the report, 'totally unexpected chaos created by unprecedented bombings'. Cologne was the city where bombing outstripped the imagination.

Cologne was perfect ruin, and what survived, like the front of the great cathedral, stood only to mark the loss. The American First and Ninth Armies entered the city on 6 March, and with them came journalists, and they marvelled. Janet Flanner, reporting for the *New Yorker* under the pen-name 'Genet', called Cologne 'a model of destruction', and she was shocked at the achievement. 'Cologne lies recumbent,' she wrote, 'without beauty, shapeless in the rubble and loneliness of complete physical defeat.' The Australian journalist Alan Moorehead found the city at the limit of imagination. 'There was something awesome about the ruins of Cologne,' he wrote, 'something the mind was unwilling to grasp, and the cathedral spires still soaring miraculously to the sky only made the *debacle* below more difficult to accept and comprehend.' He was covering the war for the *Daily Express* in London and this was, he wrote, the opposite of a city, for:

> A city is a place on a map, and here, over a great area, there was no plan. A city means movement and noise and people; not silence and emptiness and stillness, a kind of cemetery stillness. A city is life, and when you find instead the negation of life the effect is redoubled.

In this place of total loss, it is not enough to report, and so Moorehead starts immediately to imagine, to invent a story of the cause. 'Jumping from stone to stone over the guts of shops and office blocks in Cologne,' he writes, 'one tried to picture the immense play of light and explosion in the raids, the fantastic courage which had put a calm clear brain into the head of the master-bomber in the midst of it all, and then – then this curiously dead result.' But then, like Virginia Woolf in London, he is hungry in the bombed city, and so:

> We went down to the river bank and looked across the broken gird-ers of the bridge at the other bank where the German soldiers were watching us, but no one fired. We ate a cold chicken on the Cathedral steps. All that was left of the building opposite was the sign '4711' – the name of the finest Eau de Cologne. Two drunks lurched by. All around us, acre after acre, the rubble lay in the morning sunshine, so real and solid that it seemed that Cologne had always been like that, and that there was no sense or pattern any more in anything.

This is too much to watch for long. 'We were glad to leave,' he ends.

Alan Moorehead is my grandfather: my mother's father. One day in the early spring of 1945 one of my grandfathers sat and looked and imagined the work of the other. Bombing builds an invisible city, from the ruin of the past and the play of the imagination, and the invisible city is always double. Half belongs to the bombers, and half to the bombed; half to the present, and half to the past.

The old man I went to speak with in the summer of 2008 returned to Cologne in May 1945. The only currency was cigarettes, and he helped to clear the stones from the streets. In the Neumarkt there were ten metres of rubble. He carted the stones outside the city and left them there in mounds, which are now covered with grass, he says, and my interpreter gasps, for she grew up next to one of those hills, and she never knew what it was. I came to Cologne on the day of the European Championship final, and I watched the game in a bar that night, and Germany lost to Spain, but the old man told me that after the war the British soldiers challenged the locals to a football match in the Müngersdorf stadium to the west of the city, and he tells me now that Germany won 12–0.

At the close of 1945 the naturalist R. S. Fitter published a study of the wildlife of London. He had begun his research a decade earlier, in the mid-1930s, and his story opens with the ancient rock platform laid down beneath the city several hundred million years ago. He tells of successive chalk basins and gravel pits, then topped with clay, and laid on to these the cycles of plant and animal life, each generation reconsidering the one before. 'Not the least interesting part of the story is the high degree of adaptation which the animals and plants of the lower Thames valley have shown to the immense changes wrought by man,' he writes, and as through the centuries we come to 1940 and 1941 and a modern city under the bombs, here too he describes the natural world as a force of constant improvisation. *London's Natural History* has a fluid sense of place, and shows the Blitz to be one further episode in a deeper tradition.

'The outstanding effect of the 1939 war is the creation of large areas of waste ground in the centre of the built-up area,' writes Fitter, 'which many plants, notably the rose-bay willow-herb, have rapidly colonised.' This plant was previously found only in gravel banks and woodlands, and by the middle of the nineteenth century was therefore rare in London; but it is curiously well adapted to modern aerial warfare given, Fitter explains, 'a liking for plenty of light, which of course it gets on the open blitzed sites, combined with a tolerance for soil that has been subjected to heat'. The willow-herb was not alone in finding the bombed city suited to its desires. Since the 1920s, breeding pairs of black redstarts were recorded in the empty areas around the hospitals and museums of central London. According to the *Handbook of the Birds of Europe, the Middle East and North Africa* (1988), this species 'favours rocky, stony, boulder-strewn or craggy terrain, including cliffs . . . warehouses, large public holdings and especially churches with towers, provided there is immediate access to open ground', and the Blitz filled London with precisely this landscape. Fitter observes a 'remarkable spread' of black redstarts after 1941, and adds: 'Since 1942 all the nesting sites of this species that have been located in London have been in crannies created by the bombing.'

In the history of bombing, as it has been told, perhaps too much weight has been placed on what was lost; and not enough on what was found. After the raids, there are reconciliations and compensations, unexpected and wondrous. At the end of *London's Natural History* Fitter includes a list of 126 species of flowering plants and ferns recorded on bombed sites: the bulbous buttercup and the field poppy, the mouse-ear chickweed and the dwarf mallow, annual mercury and great snapdragons all found new habitat in the ruins. In such profusion, you might be forgiven for forgetting that this was the centre of a great urban sprawl, and Fitter notes: 'Wheatears have sometimes mistaken the brick-strewn surface of bombed sites for the rocky and stony places they often frequent in their breeding quarters.' The wheatears and the black redstarts, like Fitter himself, found the evidence of a continuous natural history in the occasions of destruction, as across the bombed city the air raids provoked growth. 'Air damage to the herbarium in the Natural History Museum meant that certain seeds became damp, including mimosa brought from China in 1793,' writes Peter Ackroyd in his biography of London: 'After their trance of 147 years, they began to grow again.'

Bombing tricked the wheatears into believing they were else-where, and for people too it shifted their relationship with place. Issued after the war, report 64b of the United States Strategic Bombing Survey summarizes the findings, by the survey teams, of 'The Effects of Strategic Bombing on German Morale'. 'Bombing seriously depressed the morale of German civilians,' it concludes, but the pattern was unexpected. 'The biggest drop in morale was apparent in a comparison between unbombed towns and the only lightly bombed towns,' it notes, and continues:

The morale in towns subjected to the heaviest bombing was no worse than that in towns of the same size receiving much lighter bomb loads. Morale was just as poor in towns with a moderate proportion of homes destroyed as in those with a high proportion of homes destroyed.

The effect of bombing has little to do with weight or scale of bombs dropped; a light raid may do as acute psychological damage as a heavy one, for even one bomb can promise more. 'The maximum morale effect of dropping a given tonnage of bombs on Germany would have been attained by lighter raids as widely distributed as possible, rather than by concentrated heavy bombing in limited areas,' the report ends, as a note for future policy. A single raid transforms the city for it establishes the vulnerability of those beneath; and even a single man on a single night in a single raid may see that he, too, is prey to war.

Yet he may learn on this same occasion a longer lesson. As Fitter noted, 'the sparrows and owls in Kensington were very restless for an hour or so before the earlier raids, but afterwards became accustomed to them', and perhaps the worst of bombing is the worry of raids to come. In London the black-out began at sunset on 1 September 1939, and the rate of car accidents rose sharply. At Covent Garden the opera closed, and at the Zoo the keepers shot the manatees and fed chloroform to the poisonous snakes. One million burial forms were issued to council authorities, and the department store John Lewis announced a special line of air raid suits, 'warm material and zippered throughout'. On 5 October, the *Evening Standard* ran a short article on new inventions, including 'a small lamp which can be attached to an electric razor and which throws a spot light on the face', and in November the *Daily Express* advised readers to keep pheasants in their gardens as an early air raid warning. There were rumours of German carbon monoxide gas, against which no mask held.

In time, the sparrows and the owls of London found a different peace; the rose-bay willow-herb crept in, and the black redstarts nested. Sparrows, Fitter observed, 'have been presented with many suitable new nesting sites, and an observer at Watford in 1940 found that they were quick to explore the new nooks and crannies in a bombed house'. Londoners had long been imagining the raids, and in doing so made them familiar, so when the German bombers finally came after the first year of war, the city was ready. 'The stimuli presented by a heavy air-raid are more intense and terrifying than civilised human beings normally experience,' wrote Dr P. F. Vernon of the University of Glasgow in his article 'The Psychological Effects of Air Raids', published in *The Journal of Abnormal and Social Psychology* in October 1941. Yet he observed few cases of neurosis and no new type of 'air raid neurosis' amongst his subjects. 'The extent to which people have become habituated to conditions and to noises which were almost unthinkable a year ago still strikes me as extraordinary,' he admitted.

In this new habitat, where each night fell with the promise of trauma, what was imagined could sometimes seem more real than what was present. Those inside the bombed cities fantasized themselves into the centre of this new drama. As Dr Vernon observed:

A certain amount of egocentricity is apparent in people's accounts of raids. Any raider within two miles or so at night is often said to have been heard passing directly overhead. Typical also is the statement: 'Bombs fell in an ever-narrowing circle round us from 10 pm to 4 am.'

He goes on to list the kinds of 'irrational thinking' that were common during an air raid. 'Two other tendencies noted by informants are, first, to keep quiet in a house when planes seem to be overhead, lest one attracts their attention,' he notes, and 'secondly, on moonlight nights out of doors to walk in the shadows lest the raiders see one.' The raid itself, in this delusion, turns upon the single spectator, as if the bombers were there for the story he could later tell.

The bombed cities were full of such heightened imagining. As those inside them watched the raids, and waited, they sought too to make sense of their experiences, and they did so in the oldest way of all: by fashioning the rough fragments of daily life into stories, into elegant structures of expectation and resolution. These are the beginnings of an aesthetic understanding of bombing: an appreciation that this war was a subject for art. The journalist and illustrator Negley Farson was in London for the start of the Blitz, and drew the scenes of the city before him. As he explains at the start of his collection *Bomber's Moon* (1941), he began to sketch the Blitz 'after a week of heavy bombing', at the suggestion of a friend: 'The skyline of London was bound to be altered, he said: so why not make a picture of it?' He wandered the city, recording anecdotes – more than 2,000 sets of bones were removed from the crypt of St Martin-in-the-Fields to clear space for an air raid shelter – and childlike pencil scenes. 'This picture does not represent any specific locality,' he captions one drawing, and by another: 'London, when you can see its skyline at all, seems particularly beautiful under the blackout.'

The city was waiting for its transformation. In his journal on 30 September 1939 the poet Stephen Spender noted that 'the sandbags on the pavements, the strips of paper on the windows, the balloons in the air, are sufficiently new in the bright sunlight to be interesting and almost gay', and he was struck that night by how all the elements composed themselves into a scene. 'The moon shines above the London streets during the blackouts like an island in the sky,' he wrote, and 'The streets become rivers of light. The houses become feathery, soft, undefined, aspiring, so that any part of this town might be the most beautiful city in the world, sleeping amongst silt and water.' In the promise of bombs and in their falling, the artists and writers of London saw the unfurling of a great subject. The burning city offered itself to the eyes of passing artists: it was not quite a real place, for it was imagined before it came, and even as it was new it soon curved and fell into the most expected of terms. Again and again, writers reached for an old vocabulary. They saw this scene as 'beautiful', the most predictable praise of all.

The bombed city was an instant cliché. In May 1941, as the Blitz was ending, Cecil Beaton published a collection of photographs. *History Under Fire* presents visions of rubble and ruins, of damage to old buildings and churches, and the accompanying text by James Pope-Hennessey compares the air raids to the Great Fire of London of 1666. There is, Pope-Hennessey saw, 'a kind of continuity' in the loss, as if new technology were only completing an older pattern. The act of photographing the ruins is the work of making it familiar. In December 1944, after the V-bomb raids, Beaton was again walking through the streets of London, looking for images, and was confronted by a promising scene.

Near the cathedral is a shop that has been burnt unrecognisably; in fact, all that remains is an arch that looks like a vista in the ruins of Rome. Through the arch could be seen, rising mysteriously from the splintered masonry and smoke, the twin towers of the cathedral. It was necessary to squat to get the archway framing the picture. I squatted

he wrote in his diary. He was keen to compose this scene right, the symmetry of ruin and frame, but even as he begins to take the picture he sees he is not alone. The diary continues:

A Press photographer watched me and, when I gave him a surly look, slunk away. When I returned from photographing another church, he was back, squatting and clicking in the same spot as I had been. Returning from lunch with my publisher, my morning's pictures still undeveloped in my overcoat pocket, I found the Press photographer's picture was already on the front page of the *Evening News*.

The bombed city offered the satisfaction of predictable coverage. Just as London came to look like ancient Rome, so every image of ruin is a quotation, a rough copy of one before.

A cliché is old form fitted to new experience, and so Beaton and Pope-Hennessey were creating clichés as they walked. Like the sparrows and the owls, they were rendering the damage familiar; like the wheatears and the black redstarts, they saw in the breaks an older and natural pattern. Earlier in his diary Beaton notes that 'this desolation is full of vitality', and the particular habit of finding the ruined city alive and traditional instead of bare and new is shared by many visual artists of bombed London. In August 1940 the War Artists Committee commissioned Graham Sutherland to paint 'pictures of damage which may be caused by enemy action'. He started in Cardiff and Swansea, and at the start of 1941 he came to London; he walked around the city, carrying a sketchbook and coloured chalks, and in the ruins he too found unexpected echoes and patterns. 'I will never forget those extraordinary first encounters,' he recalled, in an article in the *Sunday Telegraph Magazine* in 1971: 'the silence, the absolute dead silence, except every now and then a thin tinkling of falling glass – a noise which reminded me of some of the music of Debussy.' Elsewhere, a collapsing lift shaft 'suggested a wounded tiger in a painting by Delacroix', and 'a mattress that had been blown out of a house into the middle of the street looked more like a body.' In one abandoned factory he saw 'machines, their entrails hanging through the floors, but looking extraordinarily beautiful at the same time'.

Sutherland saw the ruined city as organic – a place of entrails, a body, a tiger – and simultaneously as a place of art. It was, he thought, a beautiful scene, sounding like Debussy, looking like

Delacroix, and when he came to draw it, in charcoal and in crayon, he showed this world as formal. Sutherland's drawings of the East End of London and Henry Moore's famous sketches of the Underground share a common structure: in each, the line of sight disappears down the centre of a carefully framed image, and in each are almost straight lines reaching into the distance. These could be lines of bodies sleeping in an underground tunnel, or a street of bombed houses, and while this is a simple painter's trick of perspective it lends the ruined city a curious elegance. The images are as carefully structured as Renaissance Italian art, and the perfect triangles running from the centre are the wings of angels, reaching out.

The bombed landscape is also a natural landscape, and it is most a part of the natural world in its patterns and cycles, its insistence upon a rhythm of survival and adaptation. What they saw, the war artists and the wheatears, is the invisible city that the bombers uncovered just beneath the accustomed world. This invisible city takes as its architecture a sequence of correspondences and continuities, between natural and urban structures, between the past and the present, between the imagined and the real. The bombing war dissolved the traditional distance between the battle front and home; it flattens the world with the promise of ruin, and all are now joined in its imagining, the painters and the poets, the black redstarts and the rose-bay willow-herb, the bombers and the bombed.

The greatest fictions of this invisible city are Churchill's wartime speeches. They too refer to natural forces, to the British spirit; they too see that which is continuous in that which is broken. They too are built on the steady rhythms of perfect doubles. On 27 April 1941, in the closing weeks of the Blitz – but of course you could not have known this then – the Prime Minister broadcast an address to the nation. London, Swansea, Bristol, Cardiff and cities across the north were in ruins. 'I was asked last week whether I was aware of some uneasiness which it was said existed in the country on account of the gravity, as it was described, of the war situation,' he began, and like so many others, he decided to go for a walk. 'I thought it would be a good thing to go and see for myself what this uneasiness amounted to,' he explained, 'and I went to some of the places where the poorest people had got it worst.'

A single man goes out into the bombed city, because he wants to see what is there, but before him the ruins melt into patterns and he stands among things invisible. He is not blind to the damage, but in the unexpected light, this is not all. 'It is quite true that I have seen many painful scenes of havoc, and of fine buildings and acres of cottage homes blasted into rubble-heaps of ruin,' Churchill said:

> But it is just in those very places where the malice of the savage enemy has done its worst, and where the ordeal of the men, women and children has been most severe, that I found their morale most high and splendid. Indeed I felt encompassed by an exaltation of spirit in the people which seemed to lift mankind and its troubles above the level of material facts into that joyous serenity we think belongs to a better world than this.

Out in the invisible city, the longer history is shown, and the rubble is no occasion for grief.

When the bombs came, Stephen Spender was elated. This was the third week of February 1944, so late in the war, and he had already imagined their falling, here on his sloping street in Hampstead, and then this night they came. 'The noise of the bomb was like that of a train emerging from a tunnel,' he wrote later, in an autobiography, and 'when it rushed out of the tunnel of the darkness I had what I supposed to be my last thoughts: "This is something I have all my life been waiting for".' Now he was awake. 'I wanted to go out and see where the bomb had fallen. It was on a building a hundred yards from our house. Owing to the darkness, and still more to the great cloud of dust caused by the explosion, I could see nothing.

This left me unsatisfied,' he wrote, but there were more bombs falling to the south and the west, and he continued: 'I still wanted to see some tangible result of the raid, so I decided to walk to the nearest fire.' Spender was living with his wife in the upstairs flat of a square, dark brick house on Maresfield Gardens, and now he closed the front door behind him and turned left. At the end of the street, he cut steeply down Trinity Walk to the Finchley Road, and crossed over. He is walking towards Kilburn and the fires.

Spender had missed much of the war. He was a week shy of his thirty-fifth birthday today, and ten years earlier T. S. Eliot had described him as the lyric poet of his generation. He travelled, during the 1930s; he published a book of short stories, *The Burning Cactus*, and a political manifesto, *Forward from Liberalism*. As the war began, he was finishing a novel, and translating Rilke, and helping to edit the new magazine *Horizon*. In the early summer of 1940, under the threat of raids, *Horizon*'s editors relocated their office to a cottage at Thurlestone Sands, near Salcombe in Devon, and here Spender wrote a poem about watching bombers from a distance.

> Above the dead flat sea
> And watching rocks of black coast
> Across the bay, the high
> Searchlights probe the centre of the sky

begins 'The Air Raid across the Bay', and the distance is both imaginative and physical. The poem finds bombing to be an idea only, a faraway abstraction: the searchlights are 'triangles and parallels / Of experimental theorems', and as bombs drop 'a thudding falls from remote cones / And pink sequins wink from a shot-silk screen'. As the summer ended, *Horizon* moved back to London, but Spender stayed on in Devon, teaching at a school.

It was in poetry that Spender first approached the bombs. He returned to London in January 1941 and wrote an awkwardly rhyming poem about the Blitz-damaged city he found, where:

> the inside-turned-outside faces the street.
> Rubble decently buries the dead human meat.
> Piled above it, a bath, wardrobe, books, telephone
> Though all who could answer its ringing are gone.

In the spring, he tried to enlist, but failed his medical; in September, he joined the National Fire Service, and for the next three years this was his war. He wore blue dungarees, his biographer John Sutherland records, and since the Blitz was now ended there was little for a fireman to do. 'My life seems completely wasted at present,' he told a friend. 'The entire effort is to put myself / Outside the ordinary range / Of what are called statistics,' he wrote in 'Thoughts during an Air Raid', published in 1942, and the only raids in this time were imaginary. 'Yet supposing that a bomb should dive / Its nose right through this bed, with me upon it?' the poem continues: 'The thought is obscene.'

The music of the bombing war is a broken fugue, jagged and lively, and if these stories bear telling it is because in each repetition there are variations too, elaborations on the minor theme. All is old; all is new. Spender knew there must be a poetry for the bombed city before he found it, and his early air raid poems are feints at a possible subject. Each year during the war he wrote for *Horizon* a round-up of the previous year's poetry, and in his study of 1943, published in March 1944, he noted: 'War poetry and poetry of violence is particularly difficult to write because the images the poet uses mean either too much to the reader, or too little.' Bombing raises the problems of distance and scale, he goes on, for 'A bomb means either the bomb which fell next door, in which case the reader ceases to think the poem, and thinks his own experience, or else it means the thousand tons rained last night on Berlin, which are beyond our comprehension.' The poet of bombing must juggle proximity and distance; he cannot stay at home and wait yet nor can he tell the whole of the raid. But if it comes to him, one winter night, then his duty is clear. In his book *Life and the Poet*, published in March 1942, Spender had described the poet as 'the man who lands on the moon, steps out of his rocket, and stares at the unexperienced landscape for the first time', and there is some urgency here, for he must be first. Stephen Spender crosses the Finchley Road, towards the red-brick terraces of Broadhurst Gardens. The worn Victorian fronts have dates, 1890, 1894, carved on whiter blocks, but this is 1944, and as he walks downhill, he can smell the smoke.

He compared it, later, to an illustration of the inferno. His wife had given him an edition of Dante with Botticelli's engravings of heaven and hell as a wedding present, three years before, and now as he looked down the hill he saw the city 'black and calm, with a few isolated fires rising up from scattered areas, like tongues of flame fallen from the heavens upon a darkening view of Florence, in some late morbid visioning of Botticelli'. But as he descended to the smoke, 'I was lost in a maze of streets whose stuffy, foggy blackness seemed to curtain away the light of the fire.' He pauses. On the corner of Broadhurst Gardens and Abbey Road is the church, and Spender is approaching the fires, now, but in his description of the scene he is also moving away. Over the train tracks, at the end of Kilburn Priory, a corner of two streets is a crater, and to the right by the station a whole row of houses has fallen, but the great scene that strikes him now is not new damage but a vision of London's history.

As he walked he passed low brick houses, terraced at his sides, 'with their steep roofs and slummy walls, crouched like indestructible, imbecile peasants under the flogging night', and here in the ruins of Kilburn he saw:

the immense force of poverty which has produced the narrow, yet intense, visions of Cockneys living in other times, with their home-made poetic philosophies – William Blake at Lambeth, Keats and Leigh Hunt at Hampstead, all the Cockney characters of Dickens, dancing in the roads, sniffing and snivelling as they ran.

Here, in the centre of the damage, he quotes Blake: 'Then naked and white, all their bags left behind, / They rise upon clouds and sport in the wind'. He returned home at dawn, wiped the plaster from the kitchen table, and wrote the first draft of his poem 'Rejoice in the Abyss', about surviving the blast and going for a walk in the ruins.

This is a strange war poetry, for it does not describe a place. I know the street names, for on a clean cold day at the start of 2009 I walked his same route, with a copy of the London County Council Bomb Damage Maps. The bomb maps were painted by hand, and they code ruin by colour. Black is 'total destruction', purple 'damaged beyond repair', and dark red 'seriously damaged'. They fade to lesser loss, in orange and yellow, but Spender is not so certainly visual. 'The great pulsation passed,' begins his poem:

> Glass lay round me.
> Resurrected from dust, I walked
> Along streets of slate-jabbering houses,
> A prophet seeking tongues of flame.

He tells of the 'acrid cloud' and 'Sulphurous nether hell' of the scene, but he sees here a parade as 'The dead of all pasts float on one calm tide / Among the foam of stars' above him. The streets are 'aflame with London prophets', he writes:

> Saints of Covent Garden, Parliament Hill Fields,
> Hampstead, Hyde Park Corner, Saint John's Wood,
> Who cried in cockney fanatic voices:
> 'In the midst of Life is Death!'

They are naming London but are apart from it, as if this bombed world were only a preparation for the next.

Spender had long been thinking of bombing and poetry, of the challenges and promises raised by the meeting of the two, and so when the bombs came, they arrived to him as a poem, rejoicing in the voices of Keats and Blake. One walk out in the bombed city was not enough, however, and on 6 July 1945 Spender went to Germany. He was employed by the Allied Control Commission to report on the intellectual and cultural life of German universities, and to find what survived the war. He spent two months there, touring Bonn and Cologne, and in the autumn he returned to see Berlin. In 1946, he published his diaries of this time as *European Witness*.

In Hamm, the bombed city 'had the simplicity of a caricaturist's cartoon done in charcoal', and in Bonn he saw a burned-out tank surrounded by 'shells the shape of Rhine wine bottles'. Cologne was 'broken like a trayload of crockery', and in Düsseldorf a fire engine was 'like a large long insect with withered spindle legs'. The poet is a spaceman, Spender had written, who steps out of his rocket on to the new surface of the moon, and his duty is to report back to those on earth. 'The voyager is the link between them and something strange,' he wrote: 'They experience its strangeness through his power of invoking familiarity', and in *European Witness* we see the strain of composition, as the spaceman-poet finds the common images to render this exotic landscape. Most often, like those before him, he returns to an organic vocabulary, as if this too were natural. In Cologne, 'One passes through street after street of houses whose windows look hollow and blackened – like the open mouths of a charred corpse,' he wrote, and again: 'the great city looks like a corpse and stinks like one also.' At Wuppertal, the tram lines were 'curled up like celery stalks', and in Berlin 'the centre is broken and blackened, like the centre of a leaf which is brown and torn.'

The bombed city must be imagined. 'In the destroyed German towns one often feels haunted by the ghost of a tremendous noise,' wrote Spender in Cologne: 'It is impossible not to imagine the rocking explosions, the hammering of the sky upon the earth, which must have caused all this.' He cannot see them, but the bombed city is composed of things invisible, and so the bombers too are present for Spender, whistling overhead. 'I saw them gleam above the town like diamond bolts,' he wrote in a poem shortly after his return from Germany: 'Conjoining invisible struts of wire, / Carrying through the sky their squadrons' cage / Woven by instincts delicate as a shoal of flashing fish.'

'Responsibility: The Pilots Who Destroyed Germany, Spring 1945' is Spender's great air raid poem, and it presents poet and bomber as joined in a common action. The witnesses in the cities are not simply separate from the war around and above them. 'The conception of guilt cannot be isolated,' Spender wrote in *European Witness*, in his discussion of the war crimes of Germans. 'Everyone is to some extent guilty for the crimes of everyone else, because everyone is to some extent responsible for the conditions which produce those crimes,' he continued, and in the poem he confesses:

> Oh, that April morning they carried my will
> Exalted expanding singing in their aerial cage.
> They carried my will. They dropped it on a German town.
> My will exploded. Tall buildings fell down.

Poets and pilots imagine the bombed city, and in imagining they bring it into being; and so they share some complicity for the damage. Spender had waited for the bombs, and when they came he welcomed them, and now in writing he 'Assumes their guilt, honours, repents, prays for them'.

Again and again, in the poetry of this war, we find the new landscape of a bombed city; again and again, in the new landscape of this war, we find a poet going out for a walk in the rubble. One night of the war, my grandfather drove into an air raid, to see what he had done. He is thinking, now, of his own work; he is considering his guilt. I do not know when this was, for he too has the capacity to vanish at times, and at the centre of his war there is a great disappearance. In May 1942, he flew for almost thirty-three hours by day, and eight by night, as Pilot Instructor with D flight at RAF Bassingbourn; in June, when he was promoted to Acting Flight Lieutenant, he flew a further thirty hours by day and eight by night, and ten more on operations. On 1 June, he flew with the second thousand-bomber raid on Essen, and on 25 June he was pilot amongst 960 planes bombing Bremen. He is instructing, at night, for the first two weeks of July, but on 16 July he is again promoted, to Acting Squadron Leader, and he becomes Chief Ground Instructor for 11 OTU.

Until now, I have followed him through his little red logbook and through the operations records for 11 OTU, and from this skeleton I can trace out the wider war, finding his raids and movements echoed in the larger narrative of the great strategic offensive. But on 12 July 1942, at a moment when the RAF is at last starting to win this war, his private logbook pauses; and after 16 July, he vanishes from the squadron record. He is not wholly gone. On 27 August 1942, he records a short flight in a training plane: '(Tutor) K3277 (W/C Maling) 55 minutes,' runs the note on a spare page in his logbook. On 6 January 1943, Squadron Leader J. E. Swift is mentioned in dispatches, along with seventeen others. But apart from these two flashes, there are no surviving records of his location or duties for eight months until March 1943, shortly before he is transferred to 83 Squadron at Wyton.

Chapter 6. The Sadness of Soldiers

2 May 1943

'You would like daddy's new aeroplane,' my grandfather wrote to my father on 22 May 1943, 'it is bigger than the old one.' 'I like this place,' he told his parents. The food was good – 'early morning tea & a glass of real cows milk at lunchtime' – and 'The aircraft are superb.' He missed my grandmother, but was happy to find a wireless set in his new room, and most of all, there were the planes. On the reverse of the note to my father, in clumsy pencil, he added a drawing: a long thin bomber, four engines, with an arrow marking 'Daddy' by the cockpit, and beneath, 'Bombs for the nasty Germans'.

My grandfather drove to RAF Wyton in Cambridgeshire on 2 May 1943, and at 1800 hours that evening Bomber Command reported their operational strength to the Air Ministry in London. They had now a total of 728 ready crews, including 129 Wellingtons and 250 Lancasters. The next day is his first flight in a Lancaster. He is up for just over two hours, to Bramcote and back, and the day after he is out in the afternoon, and at half past ten that night he takes off on his first operation in more than ten months. At nine and a half minutes past one on the morning of 5 May 1943, from an altitude of 18,000 feet and in conditions of heavy flak, the crew drop red marker flares for the main force of bombers who are behind. It was a clear dark night at Dortmund, and the crews can see the fires as they fly over the Dutch coast at dawn. He lands at Wyton at a quarter to five. His war has begun again.

The Lancaster is not a perfect plane. It is slow to fuel, and the worst of the heavy bombers to jump from in case of trouble, for the escape hatch is too narrow. But it flies faster and further than the Wellington, and it lifts at 100 miles per hour with a bubbling cry of four Rolls-Royce Merlin engines. I have seen old men weep when they describe the sound of these engines and I have stood on the crackling tarmac of an old bomber field with children waving up at the Lancaster rolling past, and if there is any glamour to war then it lives in this machine. It has oddly slender wings. All my grand-father's earlier operations were in Wellingtons, and where the Wellington carries an internal bomb load of 4,500 lb, the Lancaster bombs up at three times as much. It is wide and it is tall and after three years of war and 160 combat hours he is excited. On the first day, he writes 'Lanc' in his logbook, and he draws it for his son.

At Wyton, my grandfather joined 83 Squadron. The first Bomber Command sortie of the war flew from here, a photoreconnaissance raid over the north-west German coast at the start of September 1939, and a side-note in the squadron record for 10 February 1943 suggests how 83 considered themselves. 'This (with all due credit to other squadrons) the best squadron in Bomber Command,' runs the note, so polite in its boast. In August 1942, 83 Squadron re-formed at Wyton as part of a new and separate force within Bomber Command. They were called the Pathfinders, and their only insignia was a small brass eagle, worn on the left breast pocket.

The Pathfinders were markers. They flew ahead of the main bombing force, in radar-equipped Lancasters and little Mosquitoes, carrying bundles of flares. First were the blind markers, flying at sixteen or eighteen thousand feet, who dropped green candles using radar to light up the area; then the primary visual markers, who used their bombsights to mark the target in red. Beneath, in the German cities, the children called these Christmas trees, this tumble of green and red, and the Pathfinders waited through the bombing, circling over the target, to direct the attack and if needed to drop more flares. They were the first in and the last out, and as strategy this relies on the willingness of small groups of men to behave beyond the logic of fear or self-regard. In joining, an airman agreed to a longer tour of operations, now forty-five sorties: he might be selected from training, or during his first tour; he might be recruited from instructing at an OTU. But he had to be invited, and he had to go voluntarily, and part of the thrill was the knowledge that the Pathfinders only wanted the best. 'I like this place,' wrote my grandfather, in his first letter home, 'I found a number of people here I knew.'

'The contribution of a Pathfinder, in the same terms of intensity and duration of danger – and indeed of responsibility – was at least twice that of other Bomber Command units,' wrote Don Bennett, the commanding officer and founder of the force, in his autobiography. Bennett never drank; he could fly any plane. He was a thin-lipped Australian with ten thousand hours of flying time before he joined the Pathfinders, for he had spent the first years of the war bringing American bombers across Canada to the UK. On operations, he accompanied his crews in an unmarked plane because he had been forbidden to do so. We meet these leaders from time to time in epic. According to Livy, Hannibal was impervious to hot and cold, and led elephants over the Alps; Bennett, they say, had no personal feelings, and when his plane was shot down in a raid and crashed in Norway early in the war, he simply made his way home. He was, in the old forces phrase, a very press-on type. There will only be posthumous VCs in my squadrons, he said. The Victoria Cross is the highest military medal, for exceptional bravery, and Bennett held every heroism short of death to be a day's work.

The cult of Bennett tells much of the Pathfinder ideal. The bombing war was full of myths, but where in the early years, in 1940 and 1941, they were chancy stories of a flimsy heroism, by the end of 1942 these turn to myths of efficiency, to the chronicle of a war about to be won. As Bennett explained in his autobiography, in the curiously elaborate prose of a man indifferent to elegance in language: 'At the beginning of 1943, the mighty sword of Bomber Command was veritably poised for the attack.' In January, in the Pacific, the Japanese were evacuating Guadalcanal. Rommel surrendered in North Africa, and in the east the German army was trapped in the snow at Stalingrad. On 14 January, Churchill and Roosevelt met in Casablanca to co-ordinate their joint war policy. On 16 January, Bomber Command was over Berlin; this was the first heavy raid on the city for more than a year, and the first time that the Pathfinders used ground markers to indicate the target. On 27 January, the US Eighth Air Force bombed Germany for the first time, and four days later the German army surrendered at Stalingrad. On 5 March, Bomber Command renewed its heavy raids on the Ruhr, beginning with the Krupp works at Essen, and on 22 March my grandfather's logbook resumes. He is up in a training Oxford, and he notes 'Fig 8', the trick of a circus flyer, as if he were only playing.

My grandfather first wrote from Wyton, to his parents, a week after his arrival. 'Sorry to have been such a time writing,' he began, 'but I have been busy settling in & getting to know what it is about.' On 3 May he is flying in the new plane and the next day there is a night practice run and then up on operations, on Dortmund. He flies this first time as an observer with a decorated Pathfinder crew, in Lancaster W4982, and is back at dawn. 5 May is cloudy, so operations stand down, but according to the squadron record: 'S/Ldr Swift carried out two hours local flying with circuits and landings and a certain amount of "Y" training.' He is again in the same plane; he is becoming accustomed. 'Y' is RAF code for the primitive radar system also known as H2S. The crews called it 'magic eye', and in his history of the Pathfinders, John Maynard describes it: 'A rotating scanner mounted in a perspex blister under the bomber's rear fuselage transmitted radar signals to the ground over which the aircraft was flying, and the returning echoes were displayed on a cathode-ray tube on board.' In retrospect, it was a humble innovation, and its major flaw was that it emitted a signal that German night-fighter crews could track, but in early 1943 this was still a breakthrough. There is an interview with Bennett in the sound archive of the Imperial War Museum in London. 'We could paint a map of the ground below us from 20,000 feet through cloud,' he says, boasting with Australian calm: 'Never been dreamt of before.'

With devices such as this, dreamed and tested, the war was won. Operations stood down on 7 May for four days, but my grandfather flew two-hour trials in three different Lancasters and then at one minute before midnight on 12 May he lifted off again as observer with the same crew. This time, the Lancaster 4904 dropped green target indicators at three minutes past two, over the town centre of

Duisburg, and half an hour later when the main force passed over there were fires across forty-eight acres. The reconnaissance report the next day noted 'very considerable damage' to the town, including four factories, an oil refinery, and the docks. 'Altogether,' concludes the report, 'over 2,000 houses or other buildings are seen to have been destroyed by fire or H.E. [Heavy Explosive] or rendered uninhabitable.'

He landed at just after four on the morning of 13 May. He will fly a cross-country practice the following night, again in a Lancaster, again trying the new H2S technology, but now operations stand down, and there is a great innovation here, but it is invisible unless we follow the rhythms of the bombing war. The full moon was 19 May, and bombers used the moon. They needed its light, and on a clear night they called it the bomber's moon, but now all combat Lancasters are held on the ground for the ten-day full-moon period. This is not due to the weather. On 16 May, the scheduled squadron cricket match takes place at Wyton, A Flight against B, and still operations wait. By 20 May, there is some impatience. 'Yet another stand down,' runs a note in the squadron log, and on 22 May: 'Still no operations.' They are waiting, now, for the ending of the full moon, and only on 25 May, after the skies are again dark, do Lancasters raid Germany once more. The reason for their delay is simple. With H2S, they no longer need the moon, for they can see the ground beneath lit up on a hazy cathode-ray screen inside the plane. On 12 May 1943, the bombers abandoned the moon and began to bomb on the nights they chose.

The bombing war was turning here, in the early spring of 1943, and my grandfather's days were turning with it, but this was not a wholly easy time. 'It is a perfect day & I only wish that I were in Bolney now sitting with you under the tree eating strawbugs & cream,' he wrote to my grandmother on 16 May, and 'There is very little noos of any sort.' This was not quite true. 'I am to do a spot of flying tonight,' he had mentioned earlier in the letter, and that night he was out for over six hours on a bullseye run up the North Sea, and he was not well: 'My cold & throat were badish this morning.'

At the end of this letter, he adds what I can only read now as a strange and vulnerable joke, but it was probably not meant this way. 'I am still holding my own against the cold & throat although fighting great odds of course,' he wrote, and for all his upbeat wishfulness – 'The time is passing quite quickly still' – he was, like all the Pathfinders, like all the bombers, faced with terrible odds. Many years after he wrote this I will go to RAF Wyton with my father, and we will pause by a plaque on the wall of the old base which says that 3,618 of the Pathfinder Force were killed in action. But now he is keeping the strain from his letters, like the Lancasters grounded under the full moon. On 20 May, he writes again to my grandmother, thanking her for a parcel, and perhaps today he has less to say, for he is waiting for a night cross-country in a new Lancaster with a new crew but he cannot mention this, and so he simply tells a few anecdotes. He writes:

Yesterday morning I went into Huntingdon just before lunch & did a lot of shopping buying throat & cold things – tooth brush & powder aspirins, paper & envelopes pint of beer – watch glass all in ¾ hr. Not bad, I think. Last night I went into St Ives for a drink with Walt Shaw & succeeded in making my throat sore again. I manage to keep off smoking during the day but find it very difficult at night.

In the third week of May 1943, as the Pathfinder Force was reinventing bombing strategy, my grandfather was trying and failing to quit smoking.

All I know of the strain of war I have read in books, but the closest I have come to touching my grandfather was in the winter a year ago, when I went to my father's house in Wales and one night as we were talking he told me that he had kept his father's dress tunic. It sat in my grandmother's house until she died, and now he gets it for me from the cupboard. It is small, and its thick blue-grey wool is tight with age, and I worry as I stretch to put it on that I will tear it. Because it is not mine, and because I do not know what else to do, I put my hands in the pockets, by the sides, and then I reach through the breast pocket and here is a burned cigarette filter furled in the lining. A man who hides a cigarette butt in his pocket is a man who was trying to stop.

In the summer of 2008, on the hottest day of the year, my father and I drove to RAF Wyton. Like all bases it is low, with squat brick buildings, but on the gate there are men with guns in the sunlight, and, inside, places we could not go with our temporary yellow passes. The terror alert was heightened, and we did not stay long. The Pathfinder museum fills the old chapel, and there are the usual uniforms, anecdotes of lucky scrapes, and rotting kit; there are plastic-wrapped photographs, posed during a royal visit, and an engine or two, smashed flat, pulled from a field somewhere. In one glass case is a pile of postcards sent from POWs, written in pencil. 'Hello Geoff,' begins one: 'Hope you have not given up on me.' Beneath, heavy like an old crab, a box of dials is an H2S machine. This was the first of the terrain-following radars, the Scottish technician tells us, but it is black and ancient now. He takes us into the main office building, where Pathfinder HQ was, and where once they plotted the raids, and there are framed prints on the walls, the same sad oil reproductions I have seen in hotels and hallways up and down Bomber County. The ops clock, with blue, yellow, red markings, is stopped at half past two. Theirs was a horrendous job, says the Scottish technician, but he is late for his lunch, and we do not want to keep him. Around the base there are alpacas in the orchards, and wheatfields, and hangars peeking over hedges. This is a tomb, and soon we leave.

A week after returning from Wyton, I went to lunch at the RAF Club on Piccadilly. It is a tall white stone building with a pale-blue flag, and the crest of the RAF, and the Squadron Leader is waiting in a tweed jacket. He leads me down to the pub in the basement. Here all is dark wood and shiny brass, caricatures on the walls, and at the bar the Squadron Leader orders two pints of Bombardier ale.

We have a couple of omelettes too, with chips; they serve the kind of meals here that gave English food a bad name, scampi, prawn cocktail, steak and kidney pudding.

As we eat, I ask him why, after completing a first tour, my grandfather would have chosen to go back. There's something unique about an operational squadron, he says: in a training unit, you are teaching others to fly in a clapped-out Wellington. But this is not enough, so I take out and show him my grandfather's military record, Air Ministry form 1406. This tells the movements and the postings of his career, from education and civilian occupation to his arrival at 83 Squadron on 2 May 1943 as Acting Squadron Leader. It is the document I began with; it is his biography in code.

I have always read the Air Ministry form as a map, as a series of instructions for journeys, but here in the basement of the RAF Club the Squadron Leader sees a portrait: an account of character. He must have been smart-looking, always on parade on time, never stayed out all night, says the Squadron Leader: he was a busy young man, and exactly the type they were looking for. He had the initiative to have got on with this before, to have started flying with the Civil Air Guard, and then when he came to Service Flying Training he was only there for three months. He had done well, says the Squadron Leader. He didn't mess about, and this is the type to be a bomber pilot: methodical, determined, calm, and he repeats this word, calm. These are the qualities of a good bomber pilot, he tells me, and these are the qualities that might lead a man back. The Squadron Leader was a bomber pilot, and as he tells me the temperament of my grandfather – unruffled, he says, able to take it, aircraft problems, in his stride – he is telling me of a man like himself. The Air Ministry form is a mirror now in which he sees an ideal he has lived by, but the last page is stamped 'NON-EFFECTIVE'. It's a cold assessment, isn't it, he says, for this is also his biography in the boxes and abbreviations of my grandfather's career.

Late in the afternoon of 25 May 1943, my grandfather wrote to my grandmother. He asked after my father, who had toothache, and as so often before, he apologized. 'I shall not be able to phone you tonight I fear,' he wrote, and signed off: 'Must leave you my pet & go to my balloon.' Tonight is his first operation with his new crew, as pilot, in a new plane. They were less experienced than him, so they were nervous, but they fly a practice run for forty minutes that afternoon. At sixteen minutes past eleven that night the Lancaster lifts again, bombed up with one 4,000 lb heavy-explosive and twelve smaller bombs. Because they are a new crew, they are not marking tonight, and when they reach Düsseldorf not long before 0200 there is thick cloud and they can hardly see the flares. They bomb from 20,000 feet and are home at 0400.

The raid was not a success, but by now in the bombing war even the bad nights were a punishment for those below. According to the reconnaissance survey:

> Damage is seen to be widespread and severe, the greatest concentration, mainly caused by fire, being in the centre of the old town . . . Industrial damage is estimated at over 45 acres of devastation, including 28 factories, of which two (the Dortmund Union and the Hoesch Iron and Steelworks) are of the first priority.

There is no way to read these records and not conclude that by the last week of May 1943 Bomber Command was winning the war. The 'War Room Monthly Summary', now in the National Archives, tells the same. The day before his raid on Düsseldorf, it notes two firsts: '(i) The total sorties flown on Bomb Raids to all targets and (ii) The tonnage dropped on Germany both passed the 100,000 mark.' In Berlin, on the same day, the Nazi Minister of Propaganda, Josef Goebbels, wrote in his diary: 'One can only repeat about air warfare: we are in a position of almost helpless inferiority and must grin and bear it as we take the blows from the English and Americans.' Those who would memorialize the bombers founder here in the last week of May 1943, for the scale of damage runs to a nightmare, and we are not at the end.

The question of why is the moral question: of why the bombers went on. War poetry begins with the *Iliad*, and before the final battle Andromakhe comes to her husband Hektor. 'Lover none but you,' she begs: 'Be merciful! Stay here upon the tower! / Do not bereave your child and widow me!' Already in his helmet, he answers:

> Lady, these many things have beset my mind
> no less than yours. But I should die of shame
> before our Trojan men and noblewomen
> if like a coward I avoided battle,
> nor am I moved to.

In speaking he reaches to take his son up in his arms and goes on:

> Unquiet soul, do not be too distressed
> by thoughts of me. You know no man dispatches me
> into the undergloom against my fate;
> no mortal, either, can escape his fate,
> coward or brave man, once he comes to be.

In his home they start to mourn him now. He is telling us here that war might generate a necessity of its own, apart from daily concern, and in this austerity is no space for human motive. 'These many things have beset my mind,' Hektor tells his wife, but fear or doubt remain unvoiced. Beyond character is a sea of only force, of violence as its own perfection, and it is calling now. 'My spear is mad for battle,' declares Diomedes, not long after. A man turns away from his wife and child; a man goes out to war.

Writing at the end of the First World War, Sigmund Freud addressed this same puzzle. He finds himself, he writes, confronted by 'the disappointment that this war has called forth and the altered attitude towards death to which it, in common with other wars, forces us'. In the performance of war, in 'the brutal behaviour of individuals of the highest culture of whom one would not have believed any such thing possible', we appear no longer constrained by a decent fear of death. In times of peace, he writes:

> We do not dare to contemplate a number of undertakings that are dangerous but really indispensable, such as aeroplane flights, expeditions to distant countries, and experiments with explosive substances. We are paralysed by the thought of who is to replace the son to his mother, the husband to his wife, or the father to his children, should an accident occur.

Each of Freud's fears is fulfilled by the bomber who flies to foreign countries with high explosives, and who leaves behind a wife and children to return to a war he knows to be dangerous; and it is not that this is simply cruel but more it is not rational. But now, writes Freud, 'the war must brush aside this conventional treatment of death', and 'Death is no longer to be denied; we are compelled to believe in it.' 'No man dispatches me / into the undergloom against my fate,' says Hektor. Both understand our choices as not wholly our own, even in our wildest circumstance; in war that which should be avoided – 'Do not bereave your child and widow me,' she pleads, again – here becomes natural, even inevitable. There is something different about an operational squadron, the Squadron Leader told me.

The laws of war – a loose network of rulings, hopes, warnings – are the human attempt to constrain precisely this impulse. They seek to place war back inside the logic of human evaluation: they insist that wars arise when single agents decide and act upon their decisions, and that these choices are therefore subject to judgement. When historians and philosophers have come to judge the strategic bombing offensive of the Second World War, they have like Freud been disappointed. 'Atrocities pure and simple,' writes Michael Bess in *Choices Under Fire* (2006), and the political philosopher Michael Walzer agrees: his *Just and Unjust Wars* (1977) concludes that the Allied bombing war was 'an entirely indefensible activity'. The clearest and most thorough moral criticism of the bombers is set out by the philosopher A. C. Grayling in *Among the Dead Cities* (2006), and he insists that the bombing offensive was a 'moral crime' comparable to the terrorist attacks on the World Trade Center in New York in September 2001. The most extreme case against the bombers is presented by Eric Markusen and David Kopf in their book *The Holocaust and Strategic Bombing* (1995), which presents the Allied bombing offensive as 'genocidal' and comparable to the Nazi persecution of Jews.

This judgement is chronological: the moral critics of bombing tell a story of decline into barbarity. In April 1900 the United States ratified the Hague Convention, and under the terms of section 4 agreed 'to prohibit, for a term of five years, the launching of projectiles and explosives from balloons, or by other new methods of similar nature'. The law is bound by time: for five years only, and it is meaningful for only so long as balloons are new. It was renewed in 1907 but not again, and by the outbreak of the Second World War there was no global law restricting the use of bombing in wartime.

'Must leave you my pet & go to my balloon,' wrote my grandfather on 25 May 1943, and the trouble is precisely that he was not going to a balloon but to a Lancaster bombed up with 12,000 lb of explosives, in a stream this night of 759 heavy bombers all heading to Düsseldorf. On 21 January 1943, a combined directive to the commanders of the RAF and the United States Army Air Force had instructed: 'Your primary object will be the progressive destruction and dislocation of the German military, industrial and economic system, and the undermining of the morale of the German people to a point where their capacity for armed resistance is fatally weakened', and on 5 March 1943 what military historians call 'the Battle of the Ruhr' began, with a raid on Essen. This campaign was to last almost five months, and its scale and ferocity are new to the bombing war. On 10 June 1943, the Assistant Chief of the Air Staff confirmed the 21 January directive, and further defined the strategy. The primary targets now are 'the destruction of German air-frame, engine and component factories and the ball-bearing industry on which the strength of the German fighter force depend', but listed second is 'the general disorganisation of those industrial areas associated with the above industries'. The industrial region of the Ruhr was now the target of what has become known as 'area bombing'.

Critics name specific cities as the scene of the crime. 'Starting in 1943,' writes Michael Bess, 'the air war in Europe began – gradually, but unmistakably – to undergo a qualitative shift', and he gives a date: 'The first clear sign of this transformed reality came during the night of July 27, 1943, when 787 British bombers passed in a steady stream over the northern German city of Hamburg, dropping a carefully calibrated mix of incendiary bombs and high explosives.' A. C. Grayling too begins his account of the bombing war here: the late July raid on Hamburg was 'something new and terrible even by the standards of industrialised violence so far experienced in the Second World War'.

From here, the moral critics of bombing follow a clear itinerary: from 45,000 dead in Hamburg to Berlin in early February 1945 and 25,000 dead, and two weeks later a combined bomber force of 1,200 British and American planes burned down Dresden, killing 60,000. On 9 March 1945, narrates Bess, '334 B-29 bombers went in over Tokyo, laying down incendiaries in a dense grid pattern that rapidly turned the city center into a superheated furnace. Between 90,000 and 100,000 died on the ground, the majority of them noncombatants.'

Each of these counts is speculative, uncertain, contested; but I am taking here the figures offered by Bess and Grayling for some of the work of moral judgement resides in numbering the dead. In counting, the critics of bombing seek to establish the redundancy of this war: its savage excess. For there is no simple legal statute by which the bombers may be judged, but in the laws of war are two abstract principles used to try the campaign. The first is discrimination, and I quote Article 51 of the 1977 protocols to the Geneva Convention, but the same principle dates back to at least St Thomas Aquinas's thirteenth-century *Summa Theologica*, which discusses what a Christian may and may not do in war. The principle of discrimination holds that 'Indiscriminate attacks are prohibited', and we may not treat 'as a single military objective a number of clearly separated and distinct military objectives located in a city, town, village or other area containing a similar concentration of civilians or civilian objects'.

The second principle is proportionality. Loss of civilian life may be inevitable, but is not permitted if it 'would be excessive to the concrete and direct military advantage anticipated'. For as long, that is, as the bombing offensive was a deciding factor in victory, then it is justifiable; but once we pass the point at which Allied victory was certain, then their conduct comes under new scrutiny, for they are without the justification of a necessary atrocity. 'After the immediate threat posed by Hitler's early victories had passed,' writes Michael Walzer, then large-scale bombing 'was an entirely indefensible activity'. For Grayling, the late bombing of the war has 'an intensified moral questionability, partly because victory was no longer genuinely doubtful'.

The twist here is that those who would condemn the morality of the strategic bombing offensive also question its efficacy: for if it was cruel but necessary for victory, then it could be defended as proportional. Its consequences shift its moral standing. For Bess, the late campaigns 'seemed to be wasting precious resources of men and materiel on a fairly ineffectual project', and according to Grayling: 'Almost every authority on the subject of Bomber Command's area-bombing campaign agrees that it was a failure – a failure in military terms, that is.' In footnotes they cite the bombing surveys conducted by the British and American governments after the war, which concluded: 'the area attacks against German cities paradoxically reveal themselves as an inconclusive offensive.'

This is one story of the bombing war: of an unnecessary, and therefore unjustifiable, campaign. It is not the only story. The historian Richard Overy, in *Why the Allies Won* (1995), insists upon the value of the strategic offensive. 'For all the arguments over the morality or operational effectiveness of the bombing campaigns,' he writes, 'the air offensive was one of the decisive elements in Allied victory', and the most recent and serious account of the German war economy agrees. In *The Wages of Destruction* (2007), Adam Tooze details the disastrous impact upon the German steel industry – and therefore the manufacture of armaments – of the bombing, and specifies the raids of the early spring of 1943 as the essential period. 'Reading contemporary sources, there can be no doubt that the Battle of the Ruhr marked a turning-point in the history of the German war economy, which has been grossly underestimated by post-war accounts,' he argues, and goes on to dismiss much of the previous historical and economic analysis of the impact of bombing. 'For lack of sustained attention to contemporary evidence from inside the German war economy rather than post-war accounts, the entire literature underestimates the importance of the Ruhr battle,' he writes.

The moral arguments bring us back to the early summer of 1943, to a season when the new technologies of war allow the bombers a sudden, terrible power; to the weeks when they are both winning the war and going too far. Grayling writes that the devastation of Hamburg in the last week of July 1943 'was the real beginning of the kind of bombing campaign that the British government and its air force commanders had been planning since early in the war', but it was also an end, for my grandfather will not live to bomb Hamburg. The early summer of 1943 marked the start of the moral problem of bombing and the close of my grandfather's war. He was lost, neatly, at just the right time, and so I could tell you here the story of a hero: a pilot of the early bombing, justified and absent from the atrocities of later history. He was not at Hamburg or at Dresden and his death is proof that the bombers had not yet won.

But to excuse him fairly I would have to imagine that had he lived he might have stopped, and nothing I have found about this man indicates to me that this could be true. I think he would have bombed until the end. 'No mortal, either, can escape his fate,' says Hektor, 'coward or brave man, once he comes to be.' Those who come to judge the bombers pause at this moment, and at the heart of their condemnation is the fiction of another possibility. 'They could have resolutely refused to engage in area bombing and firebombing,' says Bess, and for Walzer the air chiefs 'should simply have stopped the bombing campaign'. Grayling reaches the same conclusion in a rhetorical question. 'Should airmen have refused to carry out area-bombing raids?' he asks, and answers: 'Yes.'

This is not to defend the bombers, or to appeal to necessity in explaining away the war, but it is to say that at the end of moral judgement lies a too-clean fiction. This fiction holds that we would choose better than the bombers and so it sets us apart from them; it isolates them from us even as it portions their war into discrete phases. One day in May, it holds, an airman might have said no. In May 1944, as the critics of bombing were gathering, George Orwell reviewed a new pamphlet in his 'As I Please' column for the *Tribune*. Vera Brittain's 'Seed of Chaos', published in both the UK and the US, expressed horror at what she calls 'the policy of "obliteration bombing" now being inflicted by us upon the civilians of enemy and enemy-occupied countries'. 'Owing to our air-raids,' she continues, 'hundreds of thousands of helpless and innocent people in German, Italian, and German-occupied cities are being subjected to agonizing forms of death and injury comparable to the worst tortures of the Middle Ages.'

'Now, no one in his senses regards bombing, or any other operation of war, with anything but disgust,' wrote Orwell in his reply, but continues: 'there is something very distasteful in accepting war as an instrument and at the same time wanting to dodge responsibility for its more obviously barbarous features.' You cannot separate the bomber from the war, or early from late, for all are acts in this one great, terrible story. 'War is by its nature barbarous, it is better to admit that,' wrote Orwell: 'If we see ourselves as the savages we are, some improvement is possible, or at least thinkable.' Condemnation is a kind of distance, for it holds the moral critic above, and at the end it paints the bomber as a blank. Yet simple celebration has at its heart a hollowness that echoes this, for it mourns the ideal in a man, and is blind to his pauses, to that which is his own. If we are to approach the bomber then first we must imagine we are like him.

In the spring of 1943, my grandfather's war was under question. On 11 March, in the House of Commons, the Secretary of State for Air, Sir Archibald Sinclair, stood to report upon the progress of the war. He opens in abstraction, mentioning 'the introduction of new and advanced types of aircraft and scientific equipment', and thanking the Canadian squadrons now joining the Royal Air Force; he notes also the contributions of Maintenance Command and the Air/Sea Rescue Service, and the new Transport Command; and all are platitudes, but as he speaks this wartime caution melts to a counter-tone of urgent defensiveness. 'The past 12 months have been marked by striking changes in the conduct and effectiveness of the bomber offensive,' he says and goes on to detail some strands of 'the pulverising offensive of Bomber Command'. 'The monster raids saturating the enemy's active and passive systems of defence is one example. A second is the success achieved in finding, marking and illuminating targets which has contributed enormously to the recent triumphs of Bomber Command,' he explains, and lists in figures the hundreds of acres of destruction, the thousands of tons of damage, the tens of thousands of homeless. 'Praise the men who are striking these hammer blows at German might,' continues the Secretary of State for Air, 'fearless young men flying through storm and cold and darkness higher than Mont Blanc, through the flak, hunted by the night fighters, but coolly and skilfully identifying and bombing these targets.'

'Praise the men,' he instructs, but as his tone rises there is a nerviness here, for not everyone did. 'They are sustained by the knowledge of duty well done, and of high achievement, and they deserve our thanks and praise,' he insists, but even in the transcript now are the beginnings of another telling of this history, as the listeners shuffle and cough, and then start to disagree. Mr Stokes, the MP for Ipswich, had interrupted Sinclair at the start of his speech, on a small point of order – he questioned whether the Secretary for Air was permitted to read from prepared notes in the House – and as the speech builds to his climax he breaks in again. Next, just as Sinclair is elaborating all the scale of this destruction his rhythm is broken by another question, from Mr Montague, the MP for West Islington. 'When he came to speak of the bombing offensive itself he was full of exultation, justifiably,' he said, 'but he rather suggested or used phrases which might appear to suggest in this country among our own people and among people abroad that he was exulting in the destruction of German cities.' He continues: 'I do not like the idea of wanton destruction.'

This charge has never left the bombers, and in these Commons debates it begins to take its lasting form. Three weeks later, in another session, Mr Stokes returned to query 'whether on any occasion instructions have been given to British airmen to engage in area bombing', and Sinclair could only reply: 'the night bombing of military objectives necessarily involves bombing the area in which they are situated.' They say the bombers were inaccurate; they say their war was unjust; and in the spring of 1943, this was a quietly opening secret, thickening like a bruise from the Commons to the bases, from London out to Bomber County. On 11 May 1943, the pilot J. H. Searby was posted to RAF Wyton as Wing Commander of 83 Squadron, just a week after my grandfather's arrival, and his logbook in the Hendon archives of the RAF preserves his own fears and doubts at precisely this time. On 4 May 1943, after a heavy raid on Dortmund, he noted 'Considerable heavy flak', and added: 'Took ciné (35 mm) film hoping to get pictures to convince the "public" that we do bomb Germany.'

I cannot know if my grandfather heard these troubling questions, this other telling of his history; I cannot know if he felt these doubts. 'Lady, these many things have beset my mind / no less than yours,' says Hektor, but, like my grandfather, he will not tell. The weather turned on 24 May, cold and rain, but the next night he takes his new crew to Düsseldorf. They are home at four the following morning, and in the afternoon there is a brief royal visit to Wyton. King George VI and Queen Elizabeth walk through the base, with Bennett showing them the planes and the men, but my grandfather's attention is elsewhere. It is his son's birthday in two days and he fears he will not be able to get away. He wrote to my grandmother, enclosing a banknote – 'please do not use it to buy food or something with' – for a gift. The next day, he writes again. 'At the moment life is fairly busy & I shall not be able to finish this so will do so tomorrow,' he says, and signs off, 'must leave you now I fear', for he has half an hour of pre-raid training to do in the Lancaster 4904, and then at sixteen minutes past eleven leaves again for Essen. He bombed precisely two hours later, from 21,000 feet, but in clouds could see nothing beneath, and an electrical circuit in the bomb bay failed, catching one 500 lb bomb beneath the plane until it could be jettisoned on the way home. He is back at base by half past three on the morning of 28 May and he said he would write, but he does not need to for this afternoon he drives home, to Honeysuckle Cottage, for the night of his son's birthday.

His escapes are briefer now. There is no time, and in the letters his handwriting pulls right. He drove back to Wyton on the morning of 29 May. 'I had to do a job of work the night after coming home but did not feel at all tired,' he wrote to my grandmother a couple of days later. A. C. Grayling claims that the city of Hamburg at the end of July 1943 suffered 'the first firestorm ever created by bombing', but this is not quite right, for on the night of 29 May 1943, in the blue clear of an early summer night, Bomber Command raised a firestorm at Wuppertal in the Ruhr, and my grandfather was there.

Later, pilots said that the only factor preventing further bombing of Wuppertal was the smoke from the fires they had already started. Wuppertal is formed of two towns on the facing sides of a narrow river valley, and was the home of two great industrial works: the chemical plant of I.G. Farben, and the G. & J. Jaeger factory, which produced ball-bearings. Both are in Elberfeld, but the target tonight was Barmen, on the other side of the river, and the Pathfinders marked in red flares at half past midnight. At forty-seven minutes after the hour, fifty-five Lancasters with the Pathfinder squadrons began dropping 4 lb incendiaries. These are twenty-one inches long, a hexagonal stick, and they are bundled in stacks of twelve, and each burns for eight minutes. At 0048, from 18,000 feet, my grandfather's Lancaster let fall ninety bundles of these, over 1,000 incendiary bombs. The Pathfinders were followed by the main force, which bombed for forty minutes, and there were 611 planes over Wuppertal this night but not one reported anti-aircraft fire. The next day, the reconnaissance brief noted, 'Over 90% of the fully built-up area and more than half of the rest of the town was devastated', and suggested that 2,500 were killed. After the war, the United States Strategic Bombing Survey noted 286,850 4 lb incendiary bombs dropped, as well as sixty 4,000 lb high-explosives, 1,500 smaller explosives, and a further 29,000 phosphorus. 130,000 people lost their homes. It had been raining all of the week before the raid, but this night was dry, and in the fire the asphalt on the roads melted, so no-one could get down to the river. The shelters were at ten times capacity, and at the post-raid briefing at Wyton that dawn, according to the Operations Record Book for 83 Squadron: 'All crews were very enthusiastic about the result of the raid.'

'Fire is a weapon of great antiquity,' notes John Keegan in his *History of Warfare* (1993). In the seventh century the Byzantines used an incendiary agent they called 'Greek fire' which they hosed on to wooden structures. The Chinese invented gunpowder in the eleventh century, and cannons were first made in the fifteenth. On the night of 29 May 1943, my grandfather burned Wuppertal, and this is where the German historian Jörg Friedrich begins his book *The Fire* (*Der Brand*, 2002). In the thin city by the river, he writes, the streets were in flames and 'people often got stuck in the melted asphalt.' They coughed and retched in the smoke, and were scalded in shelters. He quotes a sixteen-year-old trainee driver with the German railway who gathered corpses the next day: 'We recovered them in zinc bathtubs and washtubs. Three fit into one washtub and seven or eight in a bathtub.' Nobody could count the dead, and in London the *Times* reported that 'No industrial city in Germany has ever before been so completely wiped off the map.'

'I had a job of work to do the night after coming home,' wrote my grandfather to my grandmother. 'Unquiet soul, do not be too distressed / by thought of me,' says Hektor to his wife.

What we return to, and it is right that we should do so, is the question of a guilty man. 'Take that sententious poem by Stephen Spender called "On the Poets Who Destroyed Germany in the Spring of 1945",' wrote James Dickey in his collection *Self-Interviews* (1970): 'At the end of the poem the spectator, a civilian who is in no danger because he's not going on the mission, says that, though his life "never paid the price of their wounds," it yet "assumes their guilt, honors, repents and prays for them."' Dickey is slightly misquoting here, and he has jumbled the title, but this may be deliberate for he insists: 'Spender doesn't do anything of the sort! He may pray for them, but he doesn't assume their guilt. That's an easy and cheap poeticism. It's fashionable to talk about guilt in poems.' Dickey, who had flown bombing runs in the Pacific in the closing year of the war and had also served as Consultant in Poetry to the Library of Congress, concludes: 'To have guilt you've got to earn guilt.'

In interviews and at parties, long after the war, Dickey would recount his military service. 'He assumed the role,' his biographer Henry Hart writes, 'of a battle-scarred pilot who had flown one hundred combat missions over the Philippines and Japan', and he stressed often the horror of what he had done. He had dropped, he told an interviewer towards the end of his life, 'three-hundred gallon gasoline tanks full of napalm' on the Japanese, and added: 'We did a lot of bombing, firebombing, napalm, phosphorous.' After the war, he liked to wear a sheepskin flying jacket and he often showed girls a photograph of himself standing by a P-61 'Black Widow' night-fighter. He said that he had crashed in the South China Sea and been rescued by a submarine; he said that he was over Nagasaki when they dropped the atomic bomb. He said that he won a Purple Heart but Dickey's war was a story patchworked up from pieces he had seen, heard, read. It was a quilt of quotations and little lies, repeated over the years, but it was based on something he wanted and that is the sadness of it.

Dickey was a nervous child; he suffered nosebleeds. He wrote his first book, about toothbrushing, when he was five, and as his biographer notes: 'At the age of six he authored *The Life of James Dickey*, in which he characterized himself as a fighter pilot. He illustrated his five-page autobiography with crayon drawing of airplanes.' In January 1943 he enrolled in the Army Air Corps, and he trained at Miami Beach, in North Carolina, and at Maxwell Field in Montgomery, Alabama. In October, in Camden, South Carolina, he crashed on his first solo flight and failed pilot training.

He went to war as a radar observer. He spent the spring of 1944 at gunnery school, and then moved in May to train on P-61s in California. By New Year's Eve he was heading to the Pacific with the 418th Night Fighter Squadron. They arrived in New Guinea in the middle of January 1945, and were posted on with replacement crews to Leyte in the Philippines. In February he was flying local patrols and convoy covers in a plane he named 'The Flying Terrapin' after a poem he liked. 'I'm sorry I can't write you both a letter, but we're flying almost every night,' begins one of his letters to his parents from this time, and another: 'We have been pretty busy the last few days (or nights).' He was doing little combat flying. At the end of June he was posted to Saipan and then Okinawa, the base for Allied air and sea attacks on Japan. On 28 July he flew a bombing and strafing run to Kanoya on the southern coast of Kyushu, and in the last weeks of the war he was on convoy cover and patrols.

This may be lesser combat than he later claimed, but Dickey's stories are nothing so simple as lies. As his biographer notes: 'A memo sent to the commanding general of the eighty-fifth Fighter Wing on May 5 [1945] was full of praise for his integrity and professional ability', and at his discharge in late 1945 his aircrew personnel form listed a total of 119 combat hours and thirty-eight missions. He never took part in the huge firebombing raids of the spring of 1945 – carried out by B-29s stationed at Tinian and other islands in the Marianas, while Dickey was in the Philippines and then Okinawa – but he was nearby. In October 1945 the 418th were relocated to Atsugi Air Base near Yokohama, and from here he visited Tokyo and saw the old burned city.

'The poet is not to be limited by the literal truth,' began Dickey, in a lecture he gave at the Library of Congress in December 1967: 'he is not trying to tell the truth, he is trying to make it.' That poetry is a kind of honest fiction is a claim as old as verse itself but here it has a special richness. For Dickey, who imagined himself a fire-bomber, wrote the finest, strangest poem of this kind of warfare. 'The Firebombing' is not Dickey's best-known work, and perhaps not even his best, for it is a poem of mixed, uncertain tone, and at times melodramatic in the heft of its emotion. But it belongs here, not far from the end of this book, for it lives at the close of the hidden tradition of bombing poets I have tried to uncover.

'The Firebombing' was first published in December 1963, and then collected in *Buckdancer's Choice* (1964), which won the National Book Award, but behind it stands a single guilt of eighteen years before. On 11 August 1945, the poet and his pilot, along with three other P-61 crews, dropped eight 1,000 lb trial firebombs on the port city of Fuchu, and from this moment the poem conjures out a whole compass of war guilt. We are twenty years on, at the opening, and the bomber is now turned suburban homeowner, where 'the palm trees willingly leap / Into the flashlights' on his night walks, and he is old, and he is fat, and he wishes to lose weight. 'The diet exists / For my own good   where I try to drop / Twenty years, eating figs,' he writes and one night he catches himself in the pantry. Perhaps he is raiding the fridge, but as he reaches for the light:

> Snap, a bulb is tricked on in the cockpit
> And some technical-minded stranger with my hands
> Is sitting in a glass treasure-hole of blue light,
> Having potential fire under the undeodorized arms
> Of his wings, on thin bomb-shackles,
> The 'tear-drop-shaped' 300-gallon drop-tanks
> Filled with napalm and gasoline.

In this instant he is back out on a bombing night of two decades before, 'cool and enthralled in the cockpit, / Turned blue by the power of beauty', and now he lets fall the bombs. 'Letting go   letting go,' he writes, and in a Japanese home beneath:

> a reed mat catches fire
> From me, it explodes through field after field
> Bearing its sleeper   another
> Bomb finds a home
> And clings to it like a child.

This is the most devastating metaphor for bombing that I know: for children cling to their parents, and the sticky napalm clings to them; a crime becomes a perfect verse.

'I thought the content of the book repulsive,' wrote the poet Robert Bly in the spring of 1967. He was reviewing *Buckdancer's Choice* for the journal *The Sixties*, and while he does not mention Dickey's military service he insists on the identification of poet and bomber as absolute. 'We must note the unity of the man and his work,' he writes, and finds the poem a failure because it 'makes no real criticism of the American habit of bombing Asians'. In America, the morality of the Allied bombing campaigns of the Second World War became again a knot of controversy during the Vietnam years, but in the same moment those who celebrated Dickey found in 'The Firebombing' a condemnation of this new military adventure in south-east Asia. In *Salmagundi* magazine, in the early summer of 1973, M. L. Rosenthal praised how 'James Dickey's "The Firebombing" discovers and sustains an ambiguous moral awareness deeply true to the situation of having bombed unknown people and their homes in a war.' In the same issue, Norman Silverstein reports that Dickey's 'Air Force experience involved eighty-seven missions rewarded with a silver star and two distinguished flying crosses', and those who came to condemn and those who came to praise all found Dickey's poem remarkable for its presentation of the poet as a bomber.

Dickey, however, was not so sure. In introducing the poem at readings, his son Christopher remembered, he would say:

> The man in the poem has been twenty years ago a bomber pilot and has made firebombing raids on civilian populations over Japan. He is a decent fellow, like most pilots were, and are, and he's thinking now twenty years later in his pleasant suburban home that he is the same person who burned women and children alive with jellied gasoline called napalm.

This could be read as awkward, this wary phrasing of 'a decent fellow' who wonders 'that he is the same person who burned women and children alive', and these could be the traces of a decent horror, but the vagueness here indicates also a theory of poetry at work. In his essay 'The Self as Agent', written in the late sixties, Dickey insisted: 'Every poem written – and particularly those which make use of a figure designated in the poem as "I" – is both an exploration and an invention of identity.' The man in the poem is necessarily apart from the man who wrote it, and 'The Firebombing' poses as a problem the quick identification of poet with bomber, or bomber with homeowner. There are at least two characters here, although as close as twins. It is 'some technical-minded stranger with my hands' who dropped the bombs: he is near in guilt, a neighbour, but not the same.

The quality of napalm is that it sticks and burns, but 'The Fire-bombing' is a poem of the failure of attachment. As the bomber flies he sees beneath him 'Enemy rivers and trees / Sliding off me like snakeskin', and even as he finds himself 'directly over the heart / The *heart* of the fire' he is not quite of it.

> I sail artistically over
> The resort town followed by farms,
> Singing and twisting
> All the handles in heaven

he writes, in a state of 'detachment, / The honored aesthetic evil'. He can imagine far beneath:

> the moment when the roofs will connect
> Their flames, and make a town burning with all
> American fire

but he cannot know the precise quality of his guilt, for even now, so long after, 'Twenty years in the suburbs have not shown me / Which ones were hit and which not'. He was not inside this war. 'My hat should crawl on my head / In streetcars, thinking of it,' he writes: 'The fat on my body should pale', but he is retreating here into the far conditional.

Dickey's is a poetry of the distance: he writes because he is apart. A week before shipping off to the Pacific, in 1944, Dickey had written to his mother asking her to send books by the First World War poets Wilfred Owen and Siegfried Sassoon, and like so many writers of the 1940s he judged his war to be lesser than theirs. In his journals published in the 1971 collection *Sorties* – the title itself promising another bombing story – he asked: 'Why is World War I so fascinating to people these days?', and answered: 'because, in a world continually at war, *that* war is the worst war, as far as the individual soldier is concerned.' He went on:

> I saw some of this in the Pacific, but in comparison to the trench warfare of World War I, even the jungle war of New Guinea and the Philippines – or, for that matter, Vietnam – is comparatively easy. Most of the soldiers now are much better supplied, much better cared for, and much better fed than those poor people floundering around in the slime and the shit and the corpses and rats under the flare lights and enfilades of No Man's Land and of the trenches.

The soldiers of the First World War were so deep inside, he insists here, in the slime and the shit and the corpses and rats, but those fighting now are airmen miles above, sailing artistically over. Where trench poetry comes from an awful closeness, then in the bomber war it is a poetry of separation. 'All this, and I am still hungry,' he writes, near the end of 'The Firebombing', 'still unable / To get down there or see / What really happened'.

My grandfather was never alone those nights. After arriving at Wyton he flew as second pilot on an experienced Lancaster, but by the third week of May he crewed up again. On 19 May and on each of the following four days he flew cross-country runs for two or three hours, and here is when he first flew with his new and final crew. On 22 May, he wrote to my grandmother, and at the end of his letter he promised: 'Next time I write I will tell you all about my crew', but he never wrote that letter, and the men with whom he shared his last raids rest as half-characters in the final pages of this history.

Here is all I can discover. The crew of a Lancaster is seven men: the pilot, flight engineer, navigator and radio operator; the bomb aimer is also the front gunner; and there are two further gunners, mid-upper and rear. On 3 April 1943, a full Lancaster crew, under the pilot, Sergeant Mercer, arrived at RAF Wyton from No. 1660

Conversion Unit at RAF Swinderby. Mercer joined an established 83 Squadron crew as trainee pilot, and flew on operations on 20 April.

The remaining six were Sergeant Norman Greenwood, the flight engineer; Flight Lieutenant Cornelius Geary, the navigator; Flying Officer Christian Miller, the wireless operator; Flying Officer Daniel Thomas, the bomb aimer; and the two gunners, Sergeant James Anderton and Sergeant Charles Nash. Miller and Greenwood are the youngest, each twenty-three, and Anderton is the oldest, at thirty-one. They are not named in the squadron records again in April, but on 15 April all training crews did 'air firing' exercises, and on 17 April there was a lecture by a submarine commander, and that evening the squadron party. On 2 May my grandfather arrived at RAF Wyton, and on 25 May he took off with these six men in a raid on Düsseldorf.

The records are quiet from this time, so I wrote to the Royal Air Force Disclosures Branch. 'Thank you for your letter,' came the reply: 'Unfortunately I am unable to release details from records of service to anyone other than the next of kin.' However, the letter also noted that two of the crew were Canadians, and the Canadian government's 'policy regarding access to records of service may be different from ours'. I wrote to the National Archives of Canada, in Ottawa, and three months later a dirty brown legal envelope, thick as a deck of playing cards, arrived.

Charles Arthur Nash was born ten days after the end of the First World War, and he lived in North Bay, Ontario. He left school at sixteen and worked for six years for the Western Roofing Company, as a labourer then as a salesman, and his service records note also that he once spent two months working as crew on a passenger boat. He enlisted in the Royal Canadian Air Force on 23 June 1941. He was 5 feet 8½ inches, and his left eye was a little weaker than his right. He was, according to the record of his initial interview with the RCAF, 'very keen for W[ireless] AG or Pilot', but he was only recommended as Air Gunner, and sent for training at Mountain View. He reached the UK on 18 July 1942.

Christian Godfrey Miller's parents were English, but they had settled in Montreal. His sister died in 1927, and he had four brothers, all
of whom joined the army when the war broke out. He listed 'motor-
boating & driving and working on cars' as hobbies, and he was a
member of the East Montreal Literary & Dramatic Society. In July
1938, he took a job as 'storeskeeper' in the RCAF depot in Montreal,
and on 16 May 1941 he enlisted 'for the duration of the present war'.
He was 5 feet 10¼ inches, with hazel eyes and perfect eyesight; he
had a scar on his right wrist and his interviewer noted 'a favorable
impression as to character and principles'. But in the photograph
pinned to the file, his brows frown, and at the bottom of the page
the interviewer notes as 'doubtful' whether he is 'suitable for commissioned rank'. He trained as a Wireless Operator/Air Gunner for
the autumn and winter of 1941, and left Canada at the end of April
1942 by boat.

Miller and Nash arrived at No. 1660 Conversion Unit at RAF
Swinderby on 9 February 1943. They had come together from 14
OTU, at RAF Cottesmore, and this is where the crew first met. But
working back from here, their paths fade to blank. Miller came to
Cottesmore on 29 September, from 10 Advanced Flying Unit, while
Nash was posted on from 7 Air Gunnery School at Stormy Down in
Wales on 8 September, after passing final exams. 'Rather slow but
should improve with experience,' runs a note by his name in the
gunnery school log. There is a graduation photograph, too, of Nash
among a tier of men, his legs crossed, his arms folded, his face a little older than the rest. None of the six are mentioned in the Operations Record Book for 14 OTU, while the squadron log for 1660 CU
is missing the pages for the period 28 January to 18 April 1943.

The records thin to air, and now we come to the end of the
archive. Even in my grandfather's letters, these men are phantoms.
The only mention of any of the six comes in a letter he wrote to my
grandmother on 1 June, when he notes: 'am just going out for a short
hard walk. The Welshman (ex parson) of my crew has just started
out on his hike for the nearest pub about 2 miles away & I am going

to meet him there for a pint before closing time.' Later in the letter he adds that at the pub that evening they found 'a notice in the window saying "closed – shortage of beer"'. The Welshman was the bomb aimer Daniel Thomas, and the local archive of war dead in the town of Ammanford in Carmarthenshire lists Daniel Owen Thomas, 'the Son of William Henry and Ruth Thomas', who was lost from 83 Squadron. His name does not appear on the stone memorial in the town.

In the first week of June 2008 my father and I returned to the 57 Squadron reunion at East Kirkby. We probably did not need to, but I wanted to see the bombers together again, and to see who my grandfather might have become, had he grown old, and so once more we got into the car and drove up to Lincolnshire, to the great flat of Bomber County. As before, the women had fixed hair and brooches in the shape of Lancasters, and the men in blue blazers drank more. As before, my father and I looked around the room and thought, no, he wouldn't have been like that at all.

Chapter 7. Bomber Poets

11 June 1943

This is the story of the last days of my grandfather's life, as best I can discover and as best I can tell. The end of the archive is the beginning of poetry, and here at the end of his traces I will once more defer to poets. Their verse stands against all that which is lost.

They were in conversation: they read, and reacted to, and often knew each other. In May 1943, at Chanute Field, Randall Jarrell was reading T. S. Eliot. '*Four Quartets* has good parts but much bad writing,' he told his wife, 'and there never was a poem solemner.' After the war, James Dickey wrote to Jarrell. 'I have learned more about poetry from you than from anyone,' he said, and later he attacked Stephen Spender in print, for his 'sententious', 'easy and cheap' poem about the guilt of bombers. Dickey claimed that he had lunched with Eliot in New York, and Jarrell mocked John Ciardi's war poems. 'It is extremely disappointing that a B-29 gunner shouldn't get more of the feel of what happened to him into what he writes,' he complained, in a review of Ciardi's collection *Other Skies*. Jarrell reviewed Spender, too – 'the poet is a lot smarter man than his style allows him to seem' – and on a night of bombing in London Spender was reminded of Botticelli's illustrations to Dante's *Inferno*. Eliot quoted Dante, in writing of the Blitz, and this is the same book Ciardi translated at the end of the war.

The bomber war came to each of them and weighed upon their writing. From each, bombing forced new verse. Randall Jarrell would have been a lesser poet, had the war never happened; T. S. Eliot's late masterpiece is *Four Quartets*, and without the Blitz this could not have been; James Dickey's 'The Firebombing' requires firebombing. But they were poets before the bombing, and poets after, so each of their works is tainted with survival. My grandfather was outside this conversation of poets.

The only memorial I would care to build would give space also to the forgotten writings of three lost airmen of the bomber war.

Their papers are in the Imperial War Museum in London, letters and logbooks and diaries, and in the grey file boxes are their poems too, unpublished and available. They are forgotten now because they were bombers first and poets second. Theirs is not a great poetry; I have not found a secret genius here. This is a poetry of amateurs, who did not look for prizes or publication, but who saw in verse a way to voice some trouble in what they were daily doing. They did not survive the war. Their story is not a simple corrective to the version offered by conventional literary figures, or set out in the four black volumes of the official British history of the strategic bombing offensive, but it is not quite the same story either. Because their lives were incomplete, their verses are too. Where the others are poets thinking of bombing, these are bombers thinking in poetry.

The first of these bomber poets is Michael Scott, who loved to fly and was impatient with earthly things. 'My attitude to the war is that it is a purely economic one,' he wrote to his father on 30 August 1940, and went on to describe the RAF as 'short of discipline and antiquated in the extreme'. But he also wrote: 'I have always wanted to fly, to cut the umbilical cord which ties me down to the earth', and so he joined the air force. During training, he spent his evenings on base reading the novels of Daphne du Maurier and planning short stories. 'It was beautiful above a sea of clouds at 6500 and the visibility was remarkable,' he noted in his logbook; he liked flying most for its aesthetic possibilities. 'Night flying in, or rather above, the snow,' he recorded in his diary on 3 January 1941: 'White below, black above, and sandwiched in between, an insignificant machine carrying a still more insignificant mortal. Great stuff this flying.'

In flight he saw the limits of mortality, and he loved it for exactly this. 'I have always had a feeling that our stay on earth, that thing which we call "life", is but a transitory stage in our development,' he wrote to his father, in a letter to be sent in case of his loss, and he celebrated here the promise of an airy death. His flying training, he goes on, 'has shown me new realms where man is free from earthly restrictions and conventions; where he can be himself playing hide and seek with the clouds, or watching a strangely silent world beneath, rolling quietly on'. Here at 6,500 feet he found an elegant landscape of a possible next world, and so he was not afraid. In May 1941, Pilot Officer Scott completed training, and was posted to 110 Squadron at RAF Wattisham as a Blenheim pilot.

Scott loved to fly, but he saw in it his death; he was troubled by the war, and in a short typewritten bundle of poems written in the spring of 1941 he wrote out each of the strands of this knot of feeling. 'Why do I weep the follies of my kind?' begins one. 'Why do I weep this man-made frenzied strife?' he asks, as if he wished to celebrate but does not yet know how. 'Death visits hamlet, village, guiltless town,' he writes in another: 'Heaven on earth is made a madman's hell'. These are not quite war poems, but there is a violence in them, a threat of what might come. 'The shrieking wind rides high tonight,' begins one:

> In gusts of shrill despair
> It sways with proud, tempestuous might
> Its kingdom of the air.

The poem does not say this, but a pilot too, in a Blenheim bomber, rides high among the wind, mighty and shrieking.

The poems of Pilot Officer Scott are exercises, stumbling towards a bombing poetry. They are rough and untitled and their energies undirected. This was the spring of 1941, and Scott like many others could not yet see how in the troubles and contradictions of bombing lay a true poetic subject. He unpacked his doubts in nervous lyrics but when he came to write directly of the bombing war this dour and romantic young man took on a new and shallower voice, jangly and war-happy.

> If the Huns start terrorizing you civilians,
> If the bombs begin to rain down thick and fast,

> If you hurry helter-skelter like a rabbit to your air-raid shelter
> If you think that every moment is your last,
> Just forget the raider's trying to destroy you
> Just forget his wrecking havoc overhead.
> Give the boys in Airforce blue the credit for a few
> And when it's over, go quietly to your bed

comforts one, and another promises:

> Each sombre night our bomber squadron hits
> The foe and gets him in his self-dug pits –
> Before the year is out he'll cry us quits.

Conditional, poorly rhymed, and illogical in its neat split of morality – the Huns are terrorizing but the British bombers are valiant – the poetry is awkward, flat.

Scott was a poet of the first bombing campaigns of the war. His poems begin to offer a theory, an idea of apartness, but this could not stand up to combat. On 24 May 1941 he flew his first operation, a sweep out over the East Frisian Islands off the north-west coast of Germany. Ten planes from 110 Squadron took off at half past eleven that morning, and as the Operations Record Book notes:

> 2 aircraft attacked a stationary armed ship about 20 miles N of BORKUM from 200 feet. The results of the bombing by one aircraft were unobserved. This aircraft did not return to base. The bombs of the second aircraft fell 5 yards to starboard, and the ship was machine gunned from the rear turret.

Scott and the other two crew of Blenheim V5426 were listed 'MISSING', later dead. This is a chaotic, pointless end, and the results of the bombing were unobserved; they simply crashed to sea. 'Now I am dead, is all the world still the same?' he asks in one poem, and in another returns to this favoured theme:

> I learned that men who die in peace or war,
> Have reached the death-still hour before the dawn
> When all is quiet but for a lonely lark
> Who gives us hope to greet the rising sun.

Scott is looking beyond a war he did not yet know. He is one aspect of the bomber: marked for mortality, unvoiced, broken between a wish to celebrate and a fear that this war did not bear celebration.

In his last week, my grandfather wrote of food. Dinner was poor on Tuesday, 1 June – 'very bad spam & hard beetroot & then shocking macaroni cheese' – and he asked my grandmother to save him some strawberries. On Friday, he had a cup of tea before going to bed at eleven. 'I shall have an inside like mother's with all this tea,' he wrote, and added that he had found 'the small tin of condensed milk in the back of the car', misplaced from an earlier gift. He wrote again at teatime on Sunday – 'Pardon me I must pop off & get a cuppa' – and there were cherries in the mess. On Tuesday, 8 June, 'there was a grand orange hand out & we each got a dozen.' He ate two, after a squash match that evening, and this week too he was playing games: squash on Thursday evening and Friday morning, followed by 'a run round the sports field', and squash again on Tuesday. On Thursday 'I have put my name down for the 100 yds & throwing the cricket ball in the sports here', and he teases, 'I shall be able to chase you round & throw things at you when I get home', for he was expecting leave within a week. 'I was very near you today but unfortunately was rather high & could not come down to say hello,' he wrote on Monday evening, for his two-hour training flight that afternoon had curved south round London and over Sussex, past Honeysuckle Cottage.

The Operations Record Book for 83 Squadron tells another story of this week: of tense summer weather, high winds and thunder, cancellations. There was hail on 2 June, interrupting the squadron cricket match, and the next day all captains and navigators took a crowded bus into Cambridge, in the rain, for a lecture. The scheduled operation on Oberhausen was cancelled on Friday and again on Saturday. By Sunday evening, as the crews sat down to the briefing at six, the strain is thickening. Again, operations stand down. 'Howls of dismay,' notes the squadron log: 'This is eighth non-operational day.' On Monday, the target changed to Münster. By ten that night six crews were waiting in flight suits for buses to carry them out to the dispersal points, and the Lancasters were fuelled and bombed up, and they were called back. On Tuesday afternoon my grandfather's crew and five others in H2S-ready Lancasters flew out on a night trial and returned to base to find that operations were cancelled. 'This becomes a habit,' runs a note in the squadron log. The next day, he is detailed to the same Lancaster, and flies an hour of training, but as the crew are suiting up the news is the same. 'Disheartened is hardly the word,' records the operations log: 'some crews were so keen they would have gone on their own.' Two pilots, Wellington and Blair, had now been waiting eleven days to fly their final trips. 'S/Ldr Blair, navigation bag between his legs to stop his knees battering themselves to death,' says the Operations Record, and this is the day my grandfather writes about the dozen oranges.

'Between the test and the afternoon briefing is the rumor period,' wrote the American journalist Martha Gellhorn, who visited a bomber base in the autumn of 1943. She described these days as a torment of expectation. 'First you wait for them to go and then you wait for them to get back,' she writes, and soon 'the waiting gets to be a thing you can touch.' On 4 July 1943 the novelist John Steinbeck spent the day on a base in England, and he titled his account simply 'Waiting'. At the end of the month, the RAF psychiatrist Dr E. C. O. Jewkesbury issued a report to the Air Ministry on the particular stresses in his patients. 'Many men find anticipation worse than the event itself and this applies particularly to the interval between briefing and departure for a raid,' he reports: 'Postponement or cancellation of a sortie at the last moment may have resulted in considerable mental stress, particularly in an apprehensive or imaginative type of individual.' Cancellation is double waiting, for you wait to wait once more; the hours are heavy, the nights like knives. Cecil Beaton photographed bomber crews in early 1942, and in the collection *Winged Squadrons* he suggests that 'the cancellation of a trip at the last minute should be counted as half a sortie, for the pilot has been through that amount of strain.' This is not combat but it still can damage, and this week in June the aircrews of 83 Squadron were stranded in the rumour period, in the wait between test and briefing, briefing and raid.

The cruelty of cancellation is that it offers the fiction of safety but marks it also as a fiction. There will be another raid, but in the pause perhaps is space for the kind of alternative thinking that Lord Moran had diagnosed as harmful to soldiers. 'We have to put away any thought of an alternative to the dangerous situation in which we are,' he instructed, in *The Anatomy of Courage*, but each evening this first week of June, as the crews assembled and were again let go, was an alternative to bombing. In time they became accustomed to this; 'it surprised no-one to have it scrubbed at 2200 hours' is a side-note in the squadron log on Monday, 7 June. Because he does not say – because he is not, at least in his letters, what Jewkesbury calls 'an apprehensive or imaginative type of individual' – there is no formal trace of my grandfather's strain this week, but his letters share the thwarted tempo of the squadron log. 'I do not think it will be possible to phone you to-night,' he writes on 6 June, but that night's sortie was cancelled during the briefing. 'Must go & do some work now,' he explains on 9 June, and he found his gloves and pulled on his jacket, boots, and was ready for the plane before they called him back. 'One has <u>odd</u> dreams,' he tells his wife, that same day, but he blamed the oranges he ate before bed. 'A bad thing to do so late,' he writes, 'as it has an unfortunate effect on one's sleep.'

There can be poetry in this double thinking. 'I don't think any of us can be quite happy without some little dream tucked away in his mind,' wrote Flying Officer Frank Blackman, a Canadian navigator on Wellingtons with 429 Squadron. He was based at RCAF Eastmoor, near York, and in April 1943 he met a WAAF called Mary Mileham. 'I know but little of you – as you of me – so that of necessity such a thing is but a dream,' Frank began, in his first letter, but he was sure from the start that she for him could be a dream apart from the daily bombing. As he writes in that same letter:

> I haven't really much to say today – but we are resting in a really beautiful garden this afternoon ready for a possible raid tonight, and I suppose somewhat naturally that in such surroundings on such a lovely day, ones thoughts turn to the sweet things of life. Truly this moment is so peaceful that the prospect of the next few hours seems like an evil dream.

This was 2 May 1943, and he was writing at just after eight in the evening. By late June, he asks her to come to the fence at the edge of Eastmoor airbase one evening, to watch his bomber take off on a raid. 'I cannot go to sleep without telling you how much I love you,' he writes in July, and in September says they should be married. The operations log for 429 Squadron records that he was bombing all this summer – Dortmund on 24 May, Gelsenkirchen two days later, Aachen and then Hamburg – but he never mentions this.

In the archive of the Imperial War Museum are seventeen of Frank's letters to Mary, and none of her replies, so this courtship reads now in shifts and starts; he is desperate then he is grateful. One night, he stays up late and writes that he loves her; the next morning, he writes to apologize for his earlier rush of emotion. He is interrupted; he is tired; he is tormented by his inability to articulate his own clear sense of the rightness of all this, of how for him it fits. 'Words alone are not sufficient,' he tells her, and then later: 'I am trying vainly to explain to you and myself this tangled skein of emotions with which your presence leaves me.' His solution is simple; he turns to poetry.

'I cannot believe there has been much verse written in the air,' Frank wrote to Mary from Eastmoor, and attached to the letter a short poem he had written that morning while on a training flight.

> She lies in sunlight. See – a vision sweet
> I rest – a willing victim – at her feet
> With eyes and hands and lips on fire I kneel
> To take her in my folding arms and feel
> A peace long-sought

it begins, and the imagery takes on density and pathos if we recall that the poet was a navigator on heavy bombers, here imagining himself a victim, at peace, on fire. A couple of weeks later, on another training run, he attempts something a little more ambitious. 'The rhyme I tried was I believe the Italian style that Milton adopted,' he notes in a letter, including a sonnet written inside a Wellington bomber. As perhaps may be excused given the conditions under which it was composed, the sonnet itself is metrically awkward but also seductive and unexpected. 'How like my love, whose gentle form conceals / A brimming heart with love and life and joy,' he writes: 'A paradox of modesty and fire.' However, he added in the letter, she should not expect a whole volume of his works: 'the Air Force do not allow me much time for that sort of thing.'

As he writes, through the summer and autumn, he tells of the stresses of life on base – he shares a hut with another Canadian, who drinks and talks endlessly of 'flak, fighter belts, searchlights', and whose loud nightmares keep Frank awake – and he sends her passages from his favourite poems. He quotes Byron, Shakespeare, translations from the German; 'Tread softly, for you tread on my dreams,' he tells her, after Yeats. On 11 June 1943, he sends a whole letter in verse, sixty-five leaden rhyming couplets:

> But truly Dear this verse I've done
> Has been the most delightful fun

> And now I think I'll go to bed
> Perhaps to dream of you instead.

This night he will dream with relief, for as he narrates in rhyme:

> Tonight I thought I was to go
> Upon a raid with the Wing Co.
> Whose navigator I believe
> Has gone away upon his leave
> This would have been a bind no doubt
> And pleased was I when it came out
> That he was O.C. flying (night)
> Which meant he couldn't go and fight
> So while others eastward fly
> Safe to my bed for once go I.

He was safe this night, but by chance. 'Almost all of us, it is to be hoped, have some such dream which one might try and fulfil but for this wretched stupid war,' Frank told Mary at the end of June, and on 20 February 1944 his bomber crashed in a pine wood not far from Berlin. He is buried there, in the British Military Cemetery on Heerstrasse.

In July, Frank told Mary his recurring nightmare. 'Always the same – and always as disturbing,' he wrote: 'I had the sense of flying by my own volition – but being unable to return to earth.' Here is a second aspect of the bomber poet: quoting old verse in the service of new experience, recording the hours and the hopes of his days, figuring a space apart from the habit of grief. My grandfather does not share so much, but on 9 June 1943 he has a dozen oranges. He eats two, and writes to his wife to promise ten when next he sees her.

The beach where the body washes up is wide and white. He is an RAF pilot, and he is wearing a flight suit, one heavy fur-lined boot;

the other was lost in the fall from his Lancaster, in the sea between Holland and Bomber County. He is a handsome man, dark-haired and English, and he wakes, stands, walks across the beach, unzipping the wet jacket, leaving the boot. He climbs over the dunes, and soon he meets a girl on a bicycle.

This scene occurs near the start of Michael Powell and Emeric Pressburger's 1946 film *A Matter of Life and Death*, which is a fantasy about a bomber who comes back. As the film opens, it is the night of 2 May 1945, and German cities are burning from a thousand-bomber raid. One young pilot, whose crew have all bailed out or been killed, is struggling to bring his Lancaster home through the storm. This is Squadron Leader Peter Carter, played by David Niven in a moustache, and we can see immediately that he is a good and brave man, for although he is a bomber – and we see the mechanics of this war, the thousand raid, the high casualty rate, the fury – he is also a poet. On the wireless, he reaches a young American in a control tower in England. He asks her, 'Are you pretty?', and he quotes poetry to her. 'Give me my scallop-shell of quiet, / My staff of faith to walk upon,' he says, from Sir Walter Ralegh's 'Passionate Man's Pilgrimage', and then:

> But at my back I always hear
> Time's winged chariot hurrying near;
> And yonder all before us lie
> Deserts of vast eternity.

This is from Andrew Marvell, 'To His Coy Mistress'. 'What a marvel,' says Squadron Leader Carter, and although he has no parachute, he jumps.

Peter Carter: his name could be anyone's, but we are given a particular portrait of a bomber, all dates and places. He is twenty-seven, and volunteered in 1941; he trained in Canada, then joined Coastal Command, where he flew a first tour, and went on as instructor. He returned to operations on Lancasters, and is now Master Bomber, with sixty-seven operations, so although he does not say it he must be a Pathfinder. The film in passing tells all of this: it assumes that we know about the bombers, and that we care for them. When Carter finds he has no parachute, he says, 'I'll have my wings soon anyway, big white ones', and he means heaven but the pun is lost unless we know that same phrase was RAF slang for qualifying as an airman.

This movie allows no doubt that the bombers belong in heaven; but perhaps not yet. Heaven here is black and white and there are clean lines and queues. American and English aircrews take the elevator up and collect their wings, and there have been 91,716 invoiced but only 91,715 have arrived. Squadron Leader Carter is supposed to be dead, but the angels lost him in the fog as he fell, and now he isn't. Beneath, in Technicolor, Carter wakes on the beach and falls in love with the girl, and when the heavenly powers send down the Conductor to collect him, he appeals his death sentence, but the plot doubles here. In one story, we are in heaven, and Carter should be dead; but in another, he might only be hallucinating, caught in a fit of religious enthusiasm brought on by injuries from his fall. The film culminates in a parallel set of scenes. On earth, Carter is in surgery, which will decide if he can survive; in heaven, he is on trial for the right to stay alive. And the trial in turn hinges upon poetry. His defence lawyer, arguing for the power of true love, cites a list of English poets as literary witnesses – Donne, Tennyson, Dryden, Shelley – and when the prosecutor counters, 'Is he a poet?', returns: 'He will be, if you give him time.' He wins, for none could argue against John Donne, and Peter Carter is returned to earth.

The greatest fiction of the bombers is that they come back. In training, aircrews heard lectures on how to evade capture after a crash landing; they were given maps of Europe, printed on eighteen-inch squares of silk, and taught phrases, the days of the week in a range of languages, basic greetings. They learned to say, 'I need civilian clothes' in Spanish, and 'Where are the nearest British troops' in French, and to give only name, rank and number. There is a quiet promise here, inside the lesson, and this promise is also a story. You shall come home. Powell and Pressburger's film *One of Our Aircraft is Missing*, released in 1942, opens with the crash of a Wellington bomber over Holland, but the crew jump out, and the plot follows their journey back, helped by the Dutch resistance all the way to a buoy moored off the coast, where they are picked up by the Royal Navy. During the autumn of 1942, and into the new year, Terence Rattigan's *Flare Path* was playing at the Apollo Theatre in London. The play is set in the Falcon Hotel in Milchester, Lincolnshire, as the guests are waiting for the return of bomber crews to the nearby base. There are jokes about WAAFs, and incendiary bombs, and a Polish pilot with an unpronounceable name, and when he is reported missing his wife Doris can only say: 'Of course, they may have force-landed somewhere.' This seems unlikely but just as she says, 'I'm quite ready to face it – Johnny's dead', then he walks in. His Wellington crashed at sea, and he rowed home in the escape dinghy stored in the wing.

The absence and return of the bomber build a powerful narrative arc: this works as a story as it is both nervous and neat. Movies about bombers, made shortly after the war, return to this same moment in scenes of waiting for planes to land. In *Twelve O'Clock High* (1949), an American general played by Gregory Peck has sent out crews for low-level ops on the submarine pens at Saint-Nazaire, and the ground staff play baseball badly to pass the time; when the bombers appear, they count them in, and in *Command Decision* (1948) we are in the control tower with Clark Gable as he numbers his planes down. One, two, three, and then one crashes short. In *A Canterbury Tale* (1944), again directed by Powell and Pressburger, a chirpy Yankee sergeant meets Sheila Sims, and she tells him of her airman beau who never came home. She waits for his letters, she says, and by the end of the film we learn he was trapped in Gibraltar, safe. Like all powerful stories, it is also sometimes true. The cheerfully named Graham Pitchfork has collected two volumes of anecdotes by lost and found airmen. Called *Shot Down and in the Drink* and *Shot*

Down and on the Run, they tell the unlikely scrapes of a Hampden pilot, lost off the Frisian Islands, who was rescued on 14 June 1942 after two weeks floating in a dinghy; the crew of another Hampden, bombing Düsseldorf from RAF Scampton at the end of June 1941, lived for nine days in a dinghy in the North Sea, eating only Horlick's tablets and chocolate. On 8 August 1943 a Canadian pilot from 35 Squadron arrived in Liverpool. He was lost in a raid on Duisburg in May, and crossed Holland, Belgium, France, and Spain by bicycle to make his way home. Appendix 41 of the official British history of the bombing war lists 2,868 Bomber Command aircrew as 'missing now safe' by the end of the war, and a further 9,932 as prisoners of war.

Fiction is life's parasite; it feeds upon the real, and that tearing week at Wyton the bombers of 83 Squadron were not apart from the pull of stories, their hope and resolution. On Wednesday, 9 June, as the operations log is telling a roll of disappointment, of raids cancelled and broken nerves, it pauses for an oddity: 'F/Lt Ogilvie, DFC, who was reported missing 11/3/43 raid on Stuttgart turned up in the mess looking strangely. From the older members he received a voracious welcome and congratulations for his pluck and arduous escape through enemy territory.' Flight Lieutenant A. M. Ogilvie was navigator on a Lancaster shot down by a Messerschmitt near Metz. He jumped at 1,500 feet, was captured and escaped, then walked through France to Spain, with the help of the Resistance, and passed the rest of the war as a navigation instructor at the Pathfinder Training Unit at RAF Warboys. In this week of waiting, here was a perfect ending.

A bombing raid is a simple story. It has a hero, a villain, a journey and a combat; there are two poles, away and safe, and a sequence scored in feet and minutes. It presents a perfect arc and this is why it may hurt, for its start implies its ending and when this fails then sense fails too. The saddest file I ever read, in two years in the archives of war, is bound in blue and holds the letters from parents and wives of missing airmen, sent to the Reverend G. H. Martin,

Chaplain to the Pathfinders at RAF Oakington. They write to thank him for the news that their son or husband is lost, and often, they want one other small thing. 'Would it be any trouble for you to try and find out from the rest of the flight what happened to them,' begins one, and another: 'Perhaps you would be good enough to make further enquiries.' They ask for his cufflinks, his car, his shaving kit, and all are polite and hesitant, and they say: 'I am wondering if you could give me any information.' 'I have heard rumours that the entire crew have been interned in Switzerland,' says one: 'I wondered if you could make some inquiries in that direction for me.'

The purest form of grief seeks only an ending, and the purest of endings are only found in fiction. 'If my husband came down in France and was not captured straight away, I am sure that he has a good chance of escaping, owing to his knowledge of French,' writes one wife; another has 'a great faith though, that my husband & the rest of the crew, will return some day'. In the end we hold on to a story, and in the moment of grief we are hungry for the materials to make this fiction. In the tense mess at Wyton the bombers are cheering, for Flight Lieutenant Ogilvie has walked home.

My grandfather wakes at home, early, fast. He has two children now. The boy is four and the girl is two, and they are softer in the morning, at their best. They scare him as the war does not. Two days ago he wrote: 'I am always going to do things but fear that laziness or middle age is creeping on.' There are three photographs of a morning like this one. He stands in greatcoat by the orchard, tired in his eyes, and by his side is doubled in his son, buttoned in a pale wool duffel. He is in his car, right arm out and around the boy, who is reflected in the polished door. He is raising his left arm as he draws out of the drive. He is gone by twenty minutes after seven.

If my father and I were to do this drive today, our road would flow up and on to the M25, and pull us right round London. By Chingford we would turn on to the M11 and follow it to St Neots, where there was a livestock and poultry market on Thursday, 10 June 1943. But the great loops of England's motorways were started only in the 1970s, and that day my grandfather drove through London. It is rush hour, even after three and a half years of war, and he slows here. 'I was about half an hour later than last time,' he told his wife, and back on base at five minutes past ten. In his room he sees the letter he started two days ago and laid down. He sits to write. 'Tigger, I cannot say how much I enjoyed being home,' he says, and 'Thank the Lord there is only another week to go.' He writes his letters in stages, like a diary of his days, and he tells her too the timing of his drive. This is a pilot's habit, as in a logbook. 'This is the letter I forgot to give you last night,' he says, and then: 'Shall not be able to phone you tonight Tig but will finish this to-morrow. God bless.' Later today he will change his mind and send the letter. It is tempting to read too much into this.

It is Friday, 11 June 1943. He flew one hour on Thursday, but then all ops stood down. 'Complete rest for all armourers and aircrew,' notes the squadron log. There was a bus for Cambridge in the afternoon, but he drove home then for a night, and this morning he is back to find the sky is blue and operations promised again. At lunchtime, he flies a short bombing drill in Lancaster 4904. This is his common plane, from runs on Dortmund and Duisburg in early May, and then Essen at the end of the month. He has flown almost nineteen hours in this plane, first with the older Pathfinders and then with his new crew, and he knows the music of its creaks and scratches, but this afternoon he changes planes. Not long after landing the crew walk across to Lancaster 5686. My grandfather has trained in this plane three times before, but it is new to the crew, new to their bombing.

A Lancaster has many names. First it is 5686, and this is genealogy. In September 1939 the Air Ministry ordered 200 planes from A. V. Roe in Newton Heath, Manchester. Following specification B.19/37, these were to be four-engine bombers, with a maximum weight of 50,000 lb and a cruising speed of 280 mph at 15,000 feet.

During production, the contract was modified. The first 157 planes were delivered as Manchester Mk Is, and the remaining forty-three as Lancaster Mk Is, with Merlin XX engines. 5686 is delivered to 106 Squadron at RAF Coningsby on 21 June 1942, and then straight on to 207 Squadron at RAF Bottesford. In the first week of December it is damaged, and so goes to 38 Maintenance Unit at Llandow in Wales.

Next is OL, and this is a family name. On 12 March 1943, the Lancaster comes to Wyton, to join 83 Squadron, and OL is their call-sign. Now I can follow it through the logbooks of other Path-finder pilots: A. C. Shipway, a Canadian pilot, arrived at Wyton at the start of May and he flies 5686 in operations on Duisburg and Pilsen on 11 and 12 May, just as my grandfather is first training as a Pathfinder.

Finally it is G, and this is a nickname. G for George, the crews might call it, like a pet or uncle. Like all nicknames, this is both par-ticular and common, and my grandfather might not have known it but OL-G had earlier been the call-sign for Lancaster 5913, which flew from Wyton on 28 February 1943 and was lost over Saint-Nazaire. This was bad luck, to be marked by a ghost, and the bombers held their superstitions close. Nash, Greenwood, Miller, Geary, Thomas, Anderton and Swift: seven men beneath the deep green plane. The grass squeaks clean underfoot, for it has rained all week.

Before entering aircraft check pitot head covers removed. Check all cowling and inspection panels, and leading edge secured. Check tyres for creep. These are the instructions as set down in the pilot's and flight engineer's notes for a Mk I Lancaster, and today this is a new plane so the crew do the check a little more firmly than usual. There is a comfort in the form of this; there is surety in a dance step. On entering aircraft check security of emergency escape hatches. Check emergency air bottle pressure. Check hydraulic accumulator pressure, says the manual, so they do.

Some things can only be tested in the air, so in the afternoon they take the Lancaster up for thirty-five minutes and they are home for dinner. Operations stood down for this crew on 5 June and on 6 June and on 8 June. Two days ago, they were in flight suits with the plane bombed up before they were called back, so tonight they might share a disbelief that this was real. 'Thank the Lord there is only another week to go,' writes my grandfather. There were clouds this evening in Bomber County, and at 1800 the meteorological station at Mildenhall, north-east of Cambridge, recorded a temperature of 73 degrees and a firm southerly breeze. The squadron log notes: 'Conditions on take-off anything but ideal', but at twenty-two minutes past eleven Lancaster 5686 lifts up, third in the stream.

Along the runway, the Lancaster leans to port, and my grandfather counters in a push upon the throttle; a last shaking, a shrug of metal upon rubber, rubber upon tarmac, and up at ninety-five miles per hour. At 500 feet he raises the flaps and the nose pulls down. The take-off rhythm rattles out and smoothes now. They are climbing at close to 150 miles per hour, and he clicks off the fuel booster pumps. The cloud is thick with other planes so this must be precise and now the plane is smaller for a moment, one among the crowd. Inside the plane are one 4,000 lb bomb and eight bundles of incendiaries, each a dozen skinny sticks. The big raid tonight is on Düsseldorf, with 783 planes, but they had flown out forty minutes before. My grandfather's Lancaster is one of seventy-two on Münster and they gather just north of Southwold, on the English coast, at half past midnight, and turn south-east.

Over the Channel, Norman Greenwood turns off the IFF machine, and checks that bombs are fused. The skies are clearing by the time they reach the Dutch coast, minutes before one, and they cross into enemy territory at the mouth of the Scheldt. They were warned that flak was heavy here and it is: searchlights and fighters in the black air. South of Turnhout the stream shifts on to a new heading, a smooth north-east, and here at nineteen minutes past one and 15,000 feet a Messerschmitt prowls past a Halifax from my grandfather's bomber group; rear and mid-upper gunners shoot back, and the German plane sheers off. Just to their north, twelve minutes later, another night-fighter is seen and vanishes, and there are red flares about them.

It had been a hot day in Münster, and that evening Dr Franz Weimers heard frogs croaking in the fields around the city. This was the first raid of the year. The alarms began at twenty minutes past one, and howled for over two hours, but the bombing lasted nine minutes. The first Pathfinders marked in yellow at one minute after two, and then confirmed the target in red; at three minutes past, fourteen planes bombed, and a further eight the minute after that. My grandfather was in the main force, but early in the stream, so by eight minutes past the hour he was pulling right then right again to loop around the city and head west. There were night-fighters over Münster, a Messerschmitt seen at 14,000 feet and a Junkers at 20,000. Five planes were lost in the raid: a Stirling, two Halifaxes and two Lancasters. The first Lancaster was caught in searchlights over the target and in evading fell to earth. His was the other.

I have invented much of what came before. In the Pathfinder museum at Wyton, I found a timeline kept by the navigator of another Lancaster. He noted the minutes for crossing the English and Dutch coasts and I borrowed his chronology, fitting it to what I knew. The 'Pilot's and Flight Engineer's Notes for Lancaster Mark I' tell how the plane will pull to port on take-off, and lays down proper speeds; the American journalist Edward R. Murrow rode on a Lancaster late in the war, and spoke in his report of the feeling that a Lancaster shrinks as it reaches the coast. The RAF Wireless Intelligence Survey Air Activity Summary for this night summarizes intercepted enemy radio traffic: 'Between 1146 and 0306 eight hostile aircraft were claimed as shot down or burning,' it records. The Interceptions and Tactics Report is chiefly concerned with the bigger raid on Düsseldorf, and in its closing paragraph counts forty-four British planes as missing. Seventeen were lost to night-fighters, and twenty to flak. 'The remaining 7 A/C must be considered lost due to "causes unknown",' it ends.

The next day, the Air Ministry issued a Summary of Casualties so far in the war. From Bomber Command:

9800 killed (2884 pilots) in operational flying
2913 killed (891 pilots) in non-operational flying
2434 POW (429 pilots)
5078 missing (889 pilots)

At Wyton, like every day, a squadron clerk completed the operations log. He notes the 'decided success' of last night's raid, and adds: 'S/Ldr Swift failed to return. S/Ldr Swift was above average and would have been one of our special crews. His crew were the perfect example and could carry on with crew spirit in ground and in air.' The reconnaissance report on the raid notes that the city is covered with smoke, and 'Severe damage to railway property included hits on platforms and railway tracks in the main passenger station, and the partial destruction of the main building of the goods station, which was still burning at the time of photography.' The next day, the crew are 'posted to war casualties'.

On the morning of 12 June 1943, Dr Weimers went out before six to view the rubble in Münster. On the Aegidiistrasse, shop windows were broken, and an oak door torn like paper. He sent one of his assistants up into the attic of a bombed-out building, to take a photograph through the skeleton of the house and across the rooftops. On Bispinghof, he saw women gossiping, and overheard a watchman on Marienstrasse ask: 'How long is this to go on?' The river was full of rubble, and inside the Aegidiikirche a fine dust waited in stripes of light, for the stained glass was on the floor. In his chronicle, Father Paul Roosen noted 341 heavy bombs and 14,000 incendiary. On Wednesday, 16 June, the citizens of Münster gathered in the gardens of the castle for a funeral ceremony to mark the fifty-two people killed in the air raid. The Infantry Music Corps played Beethoven, and children stood in uniforms; a speaker led a prayer.

> In the face of God and the people shall live for evermore
> What we have created with burning hearts
> Even if we are dead

he said, and 'From death, life is created, / And life leads to death.' The Mayor and the Chief of Police laid wreaths as 'The Good Comrade' played in the background. The next day, 17 June, my grandfather's body washed ashore on a beach in Holland. Two days later, he was buried at Huisduinen Cemetery. On 14 August, the body of Sergeant J. J. Anderton also came to land. His was the only other corpse to be found from my grandfather's final crew.

'This book, I intend to keep in Diary form,' he begins:

> It will be a true account of all my experiences as a Sgt. Radio Operator / Aerial Gunner in the Royal Air Force. I shall endeavour to take the person or person's that read this 'diary' with me on all my flights, studies and school lectures. I hope also to give 'its' reading, the proudness, joy and thrill of being air-crew in the finest Air Force in the world to-day.

This is the opening claim of a book that came to haunt me. The journal of John Riley Byrne is a fat black ledger, swollen with time, and it is listed in the archive catalogue of the Imperial War Museum as 'MS diary and scrapbook (150pp)', but this is not quite all. On that same first page, Byrne calls it also 'SECRET NOTES & Observations'. His true account records the day-to-day of this war, its training and its rituals, but here among the entries are notes upon a secret, something he wished to make known. Byrne sought to take his readers up into the plane and on into what he calls the proudness, the particular sensibility of being a bomber, and so, on the following page, he copies out a poem:

> Speak for the air, your element, you hunters
> Who range across the ribbed and shifting sky:
> Speak for whatever gives you mastery –
> Wings that bear out your purpose, quick-responsive
> Fingers, a fighting heart, a kestrel's eye.
>
> Speak of the rough and tumble in the blue,
> The mast-high sun, the flak, the battering gales:
> You that, until the life you love prevails
> Must follow Death's impersonal vocation –
> Speak from the air and tell your hunter's tales.

He does not note the poet, but this is 'Airmen Broadcast' by Cecil Day Lewis, from *Word Over All* (1943), and perhaps Byrne liked it for the challenge it makes. It asks of airmen that they voice their place. Day Lewis sees that the airmen are separate, wild in a foreign element; and he starts to imagine their landscape for them, the sun high like a mast, the shifting ribs of sky. The poem begins the act of description that it demands but it knows too that the bombers belong with death. They 'follow Death's impersonal vocation' for they are killers and are killed. Below this poem Byrne has pasted a clipping from a newspaper, reporting the loss in combat of Sergeant Air Gunner Denis Stephens. 'My school friend,' he writes. Here on one page are the three strands of his book: a will to record, an attention to death, and a move to poetry.

Byrne began training in Blackpool in October 1942, and by the end of February 1944 had earned his Air Gunner badge, but his scrapbook opens at twenty-five minutes past eight on the morning of Tuesday, 4 April 1944, as he arrives at RAF Millom in Cumberland. 'The first thing "we" had when we got to Camp was breakfast,' he notes: 'Yes real egg on Toast in the Pupils' Sgts' Mess.' He is not yet sure which details to give and so he gives them all: of the mess, he describes 'a Snooker table, Table-tennis table, and a none too good Piano. Which incidentally is covered with beer from long ago.' In these new days his enthusiasm is diffuse, and he clips a small announcement from the local newspaper. 'Wireless Operator Now Commands Bomber Squadron,' runs the headline, and he adds: 'Going places. What?' A week later: 'This is going to be our first night flight. Bags of excitement', but then the next day under the title 'Ordeal by Water' and a quotation from 'The Psalmist' – 'I would hasten my escape / From the windy storm and tempest' – he tells the story of a wireless operator on the same practice run who crashed at sea and was rescued. He pastes in cut-outs of planes, and movie stills of pretty girls, and then on the night of 24 April he reports a '<u>Fatal Accident</u>'. 'One of our Anson Kite's on a navigation detail crashed into Snowdon. 4 of the crew were found dead. And one chappy missing,' he says, and 'It seems hard to know that only the previous day we ate with them in our mess.'

The journal is jumpy – Byrne tells us that his favourite piece of music is the Warsaw Concerto, then pastes in a Cuban sweet wrapper, a postcard from his sister, a saucy cartoon – and its tone is mixed. There can be no simple story of the bombing, no easy hymn to victory for a war where so much was lost. In collage Byrne assembles the pieces of a torn sensibility and his jackdaw rummage finds in poetry a way to voice the strain of this war, its contradictions and its hurt. Because it is incomplete, and because it is in pieces, it is an honest reckoning.

Byrne was a young man, excited. In May 1944, he was posted to 30 OTU, at RAF Hixon, and he was delighted by the food and the clean quarters. His crew fly their first solo in a Wellington, and their first corkscrew, and he sees the 4,000 lb bombs being loaded on to planes on D-Day. He prays to go on ops that day, and by a cut-out of a Lancaster he notes: 'Quiet a novelty going by air to lunch. What?' He lists new phrases he has learned – 'Gen', 'Wizard', 'Dim View' – and under the heading 'The thoughts and feelings of a WOP/AG' he writes: 'I love my flying – always did and always will.' He goes on: 'Nothing is more beautiful to me than to know I am on a flying detail', but this love is desperate. 'If I can't fly Then death is the only way for me,' he notes, and one afternoon in the second week of June, when high-altitude practice is cancelled after lunch, he curses: 'Blast-it!!'

'The foundation of Beauty is surely flight itself,' writes Byrne on one crowded page, which sounds like a quotation, something he heard elsewhere. He writes also of his 'inside-feeling of such joy and proudness' as he watches Lancasters take off, though he knows that not everyone shares his thrill. By the summer of 1944, many had doubted Bomber Command, and so Byrne composes a dog-gerel half-poem. 'If we honour the few,' it begins:

> Is it not fitting
> That we also honour the many
> That gave their lives in smashing
> The heart of the Nazi war machine
> In the Ruhr-valley.

After the Battle of Britain, Winston Churchill famously celebrated the Spitfire and Hurricane pilots of Fighter Command as 'the few' – 'never in the field of human conflict was so much owed by so many to so few,' he said – and the bombers felt and still feel that they deserve the same acclaim. From the opening page of his journal, Byrne tried to give the bombers a kind of glory, but this is a troubling ambition, and even as he attempts to do so he doubles back upon itself. On one full page, Byrne copies out a drinking song called 'The WOP/AG'.

> From far and near you often hear of a pilot's skill and dare
> But little is known of the WOP/AG or why he's really there
> To be exact as a matter of fact he's the backbone of the crew –
> When you take into account the large amount of work he has to do

it begins, with a forced jollity. Byrne was a wireless operator/air gunner, and there are notes upon radio circuits and gunnery technique in the journal, but this song gives his duties as far simpler. There are two roles for this airman. The first, in the chorus, is 'smashing at Huns with Browning guns', and the second is simply dying. 'He meets his fate in a burning crate – somehow – someplace – somewhere,' ends the second verse, and the song builds to a toast: 'So when you see a plane go sailing o'er the blue / Remember there's a WOP aboard – and <u>thank God</u> it isn't you!'

This is less a celebration than a warning, and its tone of resigned horror echoes elsewhere in the journal. On 20 October 1944, Byrne was posted to 550 Squadron at RAF Killingholme, arriving with a full crew, and on 2 November is out on his first operation. 'Now the bombing run over Düsseldorf! I was almost shouting allowed,' he notes in the journal the next day, with a map of the route. Two nights later, he is over Bochum – 'The target was a blazing inferno' – and two days after that on Gelsenkirchen: 'It was a really wonderful experience to see hundreds of kite's attacking the hun.' On 17 December, he bombs Ulm and adds a tourist marvel: 'Ulm incidentally is the town with the largest church-spire in Europe!' But this happy bomber is only one voice. On 2 January, he is over Nuremberg and sees another Lancaster shot down. 'I felt very afraid,' he notes, 'and wondered if these ops were worth while.' Not long after, he copies a poem into his book. It is called 'Bomber Command' by 'Anon':

> Only to fly through cloud, through storm, through night
> Unerring, and to keep their purpose bright,
> Nor turn until their dreadful duty done
> Westward they climb to race the awakened sun.

Bombing can be both bright purpose and dreadful duty, both horror and great joy; tourist and killer, proudness and fear; and all these are parts of the story.

What bombers do is die. In the first week of September, Byrne is reassigned to a new crew, and on 6 December his original crew are lost over Merseburg, near Leipzig. 'The flight I was destined by fate not to go on,' he writes; his teddy-bear mascot was on that plane. 'I know now that I have really something to fly a flight for,' he notes, and throughout the journal he marks the losses of crews in combat and training. 'They died an airman's death,' he had written, of one lost crew in the summer of 1944: 'Like so many of us will die sooner or later – Yes!' This is a fate for all, but even here he is unconvinced. On Thursday, 27 June 1944, late that night, he prays: 'God – it is not your wish that I be killed in this war – But be taken a P.O.W', and in late July he adds: 'I hereby write that I shall during my tour of Ops. be taken a Prisoner-of-War.'

As his war wears on, the journal ticks a roll-call of the lost and poetry takes on the work of mourning. Before the back cover of the black book, Byrne began a list of 'those aircrew who have flown their last flight'. The left side of the page is a poem, borrowed from somewhere, hurt and formal. 'They will no longer see the patches of cloud that dabbled the countryside with shadow,' it begins: 'They will no longer feel the damp coldness of a cloud.' It goes on:

> Their laugh will no longer be heard in the mess
> The click of their glasses in sportive toasts
> The scream of their wives 'neath deadly stress,
> The roar of their motors, their boyish toasts.

Byrne was unmarried, and this shy young man is a strange fit with sportive toasts, but by the spring of 1945 he was well acquainted with loss, and on the right side of the page are nineteen names of friends, fellow trainees, his first crew. On 13 February 1945, according to the Operations Record Book for 550 Squadron, '26 aircraft took off at approximately 2115 hours to attack DRESDEN.' Byrne was WOP/AG on Lancaster NF932, and he lifted at 2129. 'The journey across England was unfortunately marred by a fatal accident in which one of our aircraft was involved,' narrates the squadron log, for at ten minutes past ten Byrne's plane collided with a 300 Squadron Lancaster, and 'the wreckage of both planes was scattered over a wide area as a result of explosions.' The twentieth name on the right side of the final page of the journal is in a different handwriting, a little loopier, an older man. 'Pilot Officer John Riley Byrne. The writer of this diary killed on Feb 13th 1945 on operational duty, Dresden raid, due to a collision in mid-air,' runs the last note, and it is signed, 'J. W. Byrne, his father.'

This is what it means to see a life in history: someone else must finish the work. In the step from memoir to biography, another goes to the archive, and calls up the boxes and books; another drives to Bomber County, in the sadness of an earlier trace. In time, my father and I came to assume roles in our journeys, and we joked that we were bombers too. When he was driving, and I held the map, then I was navigator, and because we live in different time zones there were evenings when I was working and he was up late and then he said he was seeing the bombers out and counting them back in. On a Monday morning we drive to Dover, across golf-course red-brick England, where the houses have names under a high grey haze. On the ferry, there are men in orange overalls with sleeves too short, and at Dunkirk red and black stripes on the square boats in the docks. We cross Belgium, heading north, and there are trucks and tall grass by the sides of the road, under a tall sky.

So much of the war was about this place, about the layout of land. A war has a geography, and in Holland I came to think that the war was so because it was here: the flat, the dunes by the beach making a last barrier, the short sea. Germany is not far, and neither is England, so the bombers thought they could reach home. In Bergen op Zoom people ride bicycles and houses have gables, and all is in its place, but once men fell from the sky. Seven thousand planes crashed in the Netherlands or in Dutch waters during the war. The small parts – the guns, the human remains – stay on the surface, and the heavy parts go deep. By the coast the soil is sandy and the heavy parts will bury themselves as far as four metres down.

The Royal Netherlands Air Force Salvage and Recovery Unit is based at the Logistic Center Woensdrecht, a sprawl of runways and woods where 1,200 people work, and I went to visit Captain Paul Petersen. He is a neat man in a pale-blue uniform and he had prepared a slide show. The first task of his unit is to maintain weapons and communications systems, to give material support to the Dutch air force wherever it may find itself: in Afghanistan and all over the world, he tells me. He has a lot of know-how, he says, and shows me photographs of Chinooks and F-16s, of painting and spraying, and while he talks a girl in a white shirt brings coffee in squat cups, more sugar, a spoon. They are a slapstick bunch, quick to laugh. The second task of his unit is to arrange salvage and recovery when a plane crashes in the Netherlands. It does not happen every day or we would have no planes left, he says.

Not long ago, an F-16 on a training run downed in a nature reserve for sea lions in the Waddenzee so he organized a group of twenty-four people, living on a boat – here is our hotel, he says – to salvage the pieces. He shows me a photograph of the damage, and there is no plane left. Water is like concrete, he says: hit water and it will explode. These are tiny pieces, and he holds up one finger and thumb.

Of the 7,000 planes that crashed on Dutch soil or waters during the war, 80 per cent were recovered by 1945. Captain Petersen tells me that the Germans collected the guns and the ammunition, and then melted down scrap metal to build new bombers. This still leaves close to 1,500 in the mud and waters, and his unit works with these. They started digging in August 1960, and have since then retrieved 150 wrecks. In September 2007, they salvaged a Hampden at Berkhout. Of the four-man crew, two were still posted as missing in action, and the plane was carrying a 4,000 lb bomb load. It took off from RAF Scampton at a quarter past five in the afternoon of 8 November 1941 and when they found the engine it was eight and a half metres down, deep in the grey clay. He shows me photographs of men in green jumpsuits and yellow coats, and a conveyor belt sorting pieces into human remains, ammunition, personal belongings. They found this time a radio set and cable cutters; the ammunition boxes were still full, and the dye markers still worked, and there were name tags and a wedding ring. The Salvage and Recovery Unit work on one or two sites each year. They will go on digging, he says, until all Holland is covered in houses.

A crash site is a grave. You only find a body, he says, if it was thrown from the plane. Inside the wreck there are human remains, explosives and ammunition; there is asbestos from the brake pads and the engine coverings, and radioactive waste from the see-in-the-dark dials in the cockpit, like on your watch, he says, and it is impossible to tell which pieces once were people. Planes and people are not built for impact, but bombs are stronger and so they can still be dangerous. Three years ago, during roadworks on a German autobahn, a digger touched a 500 lb general-purpose bomb and it exploded, killing the driver. Two weeks ago, at Schiphol airport not far from where we sit today, an unexploded bomb surfaced by one of the runways.

For lunch, we have fried eggs with ham, and Gouda cheese in plastic wraps. We drink milk and eat an apple after, and then he takes me to the warehouse and shows me three wooden crates full of jagged silver pieces. They are sharp as a knife, he says, but to me they look like great boxes of salad. There are valves, pistons, the throttle. There are two engines and three propellers of a Lancaster, ED 603, found fifteen metres down in the IJsselmeer. One engine weighs 4,000 lb, and the propellers are twisted and organic. The whole looks once alive, with the barnacles and the propellers like fins and the valves below like gills.

On 7 May 2008, the Salvage and Recovery Unit conducted a funeral. They buried the two airmen from the Hampden found at Berkout – they buried what they thought was the airmen – and unveiled a monument with a brass plaque. The plane's engine was flown back to Bomber County, just across the sea, and then Captain Petersen made four little metal boxes, and painted them the same colour as the plane. Inside each of the boxes, snug like a coffin, he placed a piece of the plane, and then he sent these to the next of kin of the crew. He wanted them to have something they could touch, he tells me.

They bury airmen together, Captain Petersen says, because you cannot tell them apart. The only time you can be sure is when you are dealing with a single operator plane. John Riley Byrne loved his crew, and loved his Lancaster, and near the end of his scrapbook he copied out an old air forces chant called 'The Dying Aviator'. Its chorus is the last words of a pilot who has crashed and lies now in the pieces of his plane:

> Two valve-springs you'll find in my stomach –
> Three spark-plugs are safe in my lungs –
> The 'prop' is in splinters inside me – To my
> Fingers the 'joy-stick' has clung –
> Take the cylinders out of my kidney –
> The connecting-rod out of my brain –
> From the small of my back get the crankshaft
> And assemble the engine again.

It is a merry rhyme of parts, machine and human, but salvage is a messy business and after the funeral, and after the engine has been returned to its base, and after he has made his boxes, Captain Petersen is left with the crates of metal salad. He has warned me that these are sharp but I reach to touch one, and it is warm. I ask him what he will do with all these pieces of old metal, and he tells me he will melt them down as scrap.

You go looking for a bomber but you find a bomb; you go looking for a body but another is there. Before my second trip to Holland I had written to the head of the Dutch Air War Study Group, a club of amateur historians who spend their weekends tracking the Wellingtons and Lancasters lost in the Netherlands, and he forwarded my letter to Hans Nauta. Hans teaches business management at a college in Alkmaar, and his research area for the study group is the thin stripe of Noord-Holland. 'I may have some additional info,' he wrote to me. We agreed to meet at a service station on a roundabout just outside Alkmaar one day in June. When my father and I arrive he is waiting, and we get into his car and drive to the sea.

When Hans was fifteen, his grandfather showed him the serial plate from a Halifax that had fallen on the roof of his bakery during the war. Hans wondered how it came to be there, and so he began his research. A lot of Dutch stories are about the planes overhead, passing this way or that, and as we drive Hans tells me that the bombers crossed into Europe here because the peninsula is easy to recognize from above, and once they were past Noord-Holland then they were over the inland sea, and the IJsselmeer was safe from flak. There were heavy guns at Den Helder and at IJmuiden: 10.5 cm cannons with steel cupolas. But on the coast the heaviest flak was 40 mm, and so the bombers flew the gap. Hans drives us to Egmond aan Zee and parks on the slope of a dune, and we go into a café with a glassed conservatory front. As in an aquarium, the light is still and green, and there is a little sand on the floor. We sit and order coffee, and Hans starts to tell us what happened to my grandfather.

Two Lancasters failed to return from the raid on Münster on the night of 11 June 1943. At 0159, according to the Air Ministry's Interceptions and Tactics Report, a Lancaster dived to starboard to avoid a Junkers 88, and crashed over the target. This leaves one Lancaster, and we know my grandfather downed at sea. That night, Bomber Command also sent close to 800 planes on Düsseldorf, and from both raids four Lancasters were lost over the North Sea. DV 157 of 12 Squadron was hit by flak and crashed into the waters off IJmuiden; one crew member survived. ED 537 of 207

Squadron and ED 304 of 467 Squadron disappeared without trace. One of the two may have been the Lancaster claimed as shot down by Oberfeldwebel Karl-Heinz Scherfling, a night-fighter pilot in Messerschmitt G9+IS, at 0219 fifty kilometres west of where we are sitting.

I began this book because I believe that archives are cathedrals, holy houses where may be answered even the hardest human loss. As he holds his pages now and shows them one by one Hans is certain as a priest, and later when I doubted the story he was telling – it could have been another plane, there were other Lancasters lost that night – he told me: 'It's almost sure', and this is the almost sure of a deeply rational man. Karl-Heinz Scherfling reported downing a second Lancaster, at 0306 forty kilometres west of Alkmaar, and Hans pulls from a thin plastic wallet a photocopy of a map from the Interceptions and Tactics Report. He points to a black flag half an inch off the coast of Holland. Now he unfolds another page, from the Operations Record Book of 605 Squadron, and on this same night at 0308 Mosquito S noted: 'a/c crashed in sea 30 miles off EGMOND/IJMUIDEN.' Last he quotes to me from the summary of shot-down aircraft from the German Supreme Command in the Netherlands. 'At 0305 hours downing of a Lancaster 40 km west of Alkmaar over the sea by a night-fighter,' runs one entry: 'The fate of the crew is unknown.' We know that my grandfather was lost at sea, close enough to shore for bodies to wash in; and we know that the Münster bombers were flying home after those on Düsseldorf: even as I write this a small doubt still holds, but I believe that this was him.

Oberfeldwebel Karl-Heinz Scherfling was a hero of his war. In June 1943 he was flying Messerschmitt 110 night-fighters with 10/NJG 1, a squadron based at Leeuwarden airfield and some nights at Bergen, not far from where we sit today. Hans has a photograph of him too. In portraits of Nazis now it is hard to see beyond the villain, but he is young: thin-lipped, with a parting, and an Iron Cross around his neck. He was twenty-four years old and this was his thirteenth victory, and before he died in July 1944, himself shot down, he claimed thirty-three enemy planes. Later, when Hans sends me his notes on Scherfling, I read that his wife was three months pregnant when he died.

We order second coffees, and Hans describes the radar defences. Along this strip of coast were two ground radar stations, one south of Huisduinen and the other north of Zandvoort, each built in the dunes. At each, a Freya radar tower could see the English bombers from 120 kilometres away and as they rumbled closer two Würz-burg Giant dishes picked up their altitude and location. In time, an officer on the ground guided the night-fighters closer by radio, and once the plane was within two or three kilometres its onboard radar locked on to a single bomber. Then the night-fighter flies beneath the bomber and the pilot pulls the fighter up and throttles down to slow, and fires into the belly of the plane above.

The air is close in the aquarium café, and my father steps away for a moment. In the pause I ask Hans if he knows anything more about the body, and as he answers, yes, he watches me and his move-ments are slow like swimming. He has one more file. He did not want to be confrontational, he says; he did not want to shock or hurt, and he wanted to wait and see how my father might react. I say, I think my father will want to see this, and I hope he cannot hear the desperation in my voice. 'Names are very dangerous,' he says, and in some records he has seen airmen were wearing other men's clothes, and he does not want to get this wrong. We wait, in the stream of late afternoon bright, and my father sits, and Hans begins again.

During the bombing of The Hague in 1944, the Red Cross archive of wartime Dutch burial records was destroyed, Hans says, but a decade ago one of his colleagues in the study group heard that Huisduinen town archive was clearing out old files, and he went to have a look. There among the cemetery folders he found a second set of local burial records, so he kept them, and gave copies to Hans, and now Hans lays upon the table a brief typed pamphlet.

'Wehrmacht Administration for War Losses and Prisoners of War, Berlin' is stamped on the cover, and it is dated 21 June 1943, at Den Helder.

'On 17 June 1943 at 1400 at the coast kilometre marker 13.5 near Callantsoog in North Holland washed ashore,' runs the first column, and:

> Type of airplane and number unknown. Royal Air Force. Probably an officer but unknown. First name unknown. Surname unknown. Name tag not present. In handkerchief and collar of shirt there was the name J. E. Swift inscribed. Date of birth unknown.

I know everything that this file does not know; and this file knows everything that I do not. On the opposite page is a description of the body, signed by a doctor. 'Corpse of a male airman,' it begins: 'Height ca. 170 cm.' According to his Air Ministry file, my grandfather was five feet seven inches, and this is a whisper over 170 centimetres. 'Age of the dead: ca. 30 years,' it says, and my grandfather was two months shy of his thirty-first birthday. 'Teeth: complete,' it says, and I did not know that, nor did I know he was wearing a heavy blue shirt and a grey jumper beneath his uniform on the night he died.

There were scratches on his right hand, and his left leg was broken above the knee. The right side of his skull was crushed, and these were the only visible injuries. He was not wearing a parachute. He was inside the cockpit when the plane hit the water and was killed when his body was thrown through the glass and metal roof on impact. 'On 19 June 1943 at 10 o'clock,' ends the report, 'with military honours buried at the honourable graveyard Huisduinen near Den Helder.'

Later, Hans walks my father and me to the 13.5 kilometre marker on the beach. The bodies of thirty-two airmen washed up here during the war, he says, on this six-kilometre line of sand. Twenty-three were RAF; and three Americans; and six Germans. There is a strong northbound tide along the Dutch coast, and my grandfather had twenty-four miles to come, north by north east, from the grid reference 52.37.30N, 04.15.00E. Out there, the water is twenty-one metres deep at low tide. It is 150 miles to the English coast at Yarmouth. There is an oil rig on the skyline, and beyond it a field of windmills, but the day is old, and we turn our backs to the sea.

Epilogue: Icarus

About suffering they were never wrong,
The Old Masters: how well they understood
Its human position; how it takes place
While someone else is eating or opening a window or just
    walking dully along;
How, when the aged are reverently, passionately waiting
For the miraculous birth, there always must be
Children who did not want it specially to happen, skating
On a pond at the edge of the wood:
They never forgot
That even the dreadful martyrdom must run its course
Anyhow in a corner, some untidy spot
Where the dogs go on with their doggy life and the torturer's
    horse
Scratches its innocent behind on a tree.

In Brueghel's *Icarus*, for instance: how everything turns away
Quite leisurely from the disaster; the ploughman may
Have heard the splash, the forsaken cry,
But for him it was not an important failure; the sun shone
As it had to on the white legs disappearing into the green
Water; and the expensive delicate ship that must have seen
Something amazing, a boy falling out of the sky,
Had somewhere to get to and sailed calmly on.

W. H. Auden, 'Musée des Beaux Arts'

In the winter of 1938, W. H. Auden and Christopher Isherwood
stopped at the Musée des Beaux Arts in Brussels. Two months

earlier, Britain had signed the Munich Agreement, which permitted the German annexation of much of Czechoslovakia, and war was close to inevitable now. At the start of January 1939, these two men will board a boat to New York, to pass the war in the new world. But today the museum is a distraction from the crisis, so Auden wrote a poem about turning away, and about what may be missed in a glimpse.

The poem opens with a curious inversion of syntax, as if language itself were uncertain of what it should look at. It begins with one object – 'suffering' – and only later gives us our subject: the Old Masters, those gold-framed oils waiting on the walls of the slow museum. In the face of suffering, he tells us, we often allow ourselves to look away, and at every scene of pain and history there are always passers-by, 'eating or opening a window or just walking dully along'. There are always those who do not care, who do not mark or mourn, and they are like dogs, going on with their doggy life.

We are looking at a painting, but perhaps we do not notice at first. Even the poet does not mention it until the fourteenth line, and here in the announcement – 'In Brueghel's *Icarus*, for example' – he is almost indifferent. The painting's title and subject are the fall of Icarus, the boy who flew on waxen wings too close to the sun, and so crashed to sea, but instead of this Auden tells how:

> the ploughman may
> Have heard the splash, the forsaken cry,
> But for him it was not an important failure.

The poem has a strange, reluctant time-scheme. We wander along over-running lines which stroll all the way to the edge of the page and by the time we reach Icarus we are an instant too late, and all we catch are 'the white legs disappearing into the green / Water'. This may have been 'something amazing', but all around people are distracted, by business, by their worldly care, and the ship 'Had somewhere to get to and sailed calmly on'.

When Ovid first tells this myth in the *Metamorphoses*, he offers it as a parable of enchantment and desire. Icarus and his father Daedalus are trapped on the island of Crete, longing to return home, so Daedalus builds two pairs of wings of wax and feathers. As they lift off this is a marvel and Ovid imagines how 'Some angler catching a fish with a quivering rod, or shepherd leaning on his crook, or a ploughman resting on the handles of his plough, saw them perhaps, and stood there amazed, believing them to be gods able to travel the sky.' While we hear of the earthly activity of those left behind – for the angler is, even now, catching a fish, and the rod is quick with sudden tension – the flight is an affront to the duty of the day-to-day. The ploughman pauses his work and stands amazed. He cannot look away. Where Auden found distraction Ovid writes of wonder, and since this first telling poets have only rarely turned away. The Neapolitan poet Jacopo Sannazaro, writing at the start of the sixteenth century, ends his sonnet 'Icaro cadde qui' with an insistence upon the resonance of his story:

> His name now echoes loud in every wave,
> Across the sea, throughout an element;
> Who ever in the world gained such a grave?

Later in that century a French translator of the Psalms, Philippe Desportes, extended Sannazaro in describing Icarus as sheer conquest, 'a soul sublime, / That with small loss such great advantage buys'. Four hundred years after that, Anne Sexton's 'To a Friend Whose Work Has Come to Triumph' instructs: 'Consider Icarus.' 'Admire his wings!' she insists, and: 'Think of the difference it made!'

Icarus flies through literary history, and his recurrence is proof of his attraction. His fall is a story about our longing: the Latin *volo*, which means 'I fly', means also 'I wish'. In the house of the priest Amandus at Pompeii from c. AD 50, there is a fresco of the flight of Icarus, and the figures on the ground are each pointing up;

1,500 years later, those figures are still marvelling in the huge painting *The Fall of Icarus* by Maso da San Friano, in the Palazzo Vecchio in Florence, and they linger still fifty years after this in the cycle of paintings by Carlo Saraceni. The outfits change in time – in Pompeii, two regal women in togas, one gold and the other white, are pointing, where in Saraceni's versions of the scene a nobleman in velvet robes and a floppy hat raises his left hand – for the figures on the ground are always us. The clothes may change, but the gesture stays.

Icarus always has an audience. Auden writes himself as looking at a painting – 'In Brueghel's *Icarus*, for instance' – but it is not the one he thought it was. The painting *The Fall of Icarus* in the Musée des Beaux Arts in Brussels is a copy. The less famous original was in December 1938 hanging in a private collection in New York. What Auden saw that day in Brussels is an Icarus by a Brueghel, but the painting before him was executed by Brueghel's son Pieter the Younger. Perhaps he knew, but the story of Icarus is also a story about a son's version of his father's work, and if we hold the two paintings side by side – the original by Brueghel and his son's copy – we see at first what is promised by the title: the fall of Icarus. Both show the boy sinking into the sea while about him the indifferent ploughman and the expensive delicate boat go on. But if we look a moment more then another story shows itself, for in the elder Brueghel's version, Daedalus flies above, but in his son's he has already disappeared from view. The son's version now has supplanted the father's, and we have only Icarus.

Daedalus, Ovid writes in the *Metamorphoses*:

> gave a never to be repeated kiss to his son, and lifting upwards on his wings, flew ahead, anxious for his companion, like a bird, leading her fledglings out of a nest above, into the empty air. He urged the boy to follow, and showed him the dangerous art of flying.

This is a drama of paternal tenderness: at each stage the father's care is stressed as he kisses, urges, teaches. But then, for one long moment, Icarus is distracted by his newfound competence:

> the boy began to delight in his daring flight, and abandoning his guide, drawn by desire for the heavens, soared higher. His nearness to the devouring sun softened the fragrant wax that held the wings: and the wax melted: he flailed with bare arms, but losing his oar-like wings, could not ride the air. Even as his mouth was crying his father's name, it vanished into the dark blue sea, the Icarian Sea, called after him. The unhappy father, no longer a father, shouted 'Icarus, Icarus where are you? Which way should I be looking, to see you?' 'Icarus' he called again. Then he caught sight of the feathers on the waves, and cursed his inventions.

As he rises Ovid emphasizes not the lack of Icarus' attention but the failure of Daedalus' invention: 'and the wax melted.' Even as he begins to fall, the imagery hastens his fate, reminding us that those wings failed not only to keep him in the air but also to move him through the water: they are 'oar-like' but not oars. And Daedalus, left behind, is the first to miss Icarus, and he is the first to long to look: 'Which way should I be looking, to see you?'

The price of forgetting Daedalus, even for an instant, is to forget that our inventions may turn against us. If we only have Icarus, then this is a story about a wayward boy. But if we also tell of Daedalus, we have a parable of technology gone awry. In the *Metamorphoses* Daedalus 'altered the natural order of things' and he was punished; he 'cursed his inventions', and others have done so since, treating the story as a warning. In 1924 Bertrand Russell wrote *Icarus, or the Future of Science* to warn:

> that science will be used to promote the power of dominant groups, rather than to make men happy. Icarus, having been taught to fly by

his father Daedelus, was destroyed by his rashness. I fear that the same may overtake the populations whom modern men of science have taught to fly.

In *Rasselas* (1759), Samuel Johnson's mechanic agrees as he declares: 'If men were all virtuous . . . I should with great alacrity teach them to fly. But what would be the security of the good, if the bad at pleasure could invade them from the sky.' The origins of this moral position – a fear of technology, a wary sense that flight might enable atrocity – lie as far back as Aristotle, who in the fourth century BC offered Icarus as an example of the tragic consequences of human failure to adhere to what he called the golden mean, a gentle moderation between extreme poles. Icarus is a story of extremes, of two claims rubbing against each other: about our time and its time, about machines and men, and flight and falling, and about distraction and the compulsion to look.

'In Brueghel's *Icarus*, for instance,' wrote Auden, but it is no coincidence that he stopped at this painting on this day. In Brussels in December 1938 Auden and Isherwood were finishing the manuscript of their book *Journey to a War*, a gossipy, rambling account of their travels through China that spring while the second Sino-Japanese War escalated. On 29 April they lunched at the British Consulate in Hankow and, as they recount in the strange mixed voice of the book:

> Soon after lunch the sirens began to blare. We put on our smoked glasses and lay down flat on our backs on the Consulate lawn – it is the best way of watching an air-battle if you don't want a stiff neck. Machine-guns and anti-aircraft guns were hammering all around us, but the sky was so brilliant that we seldom caught a glimpse of the planes unless the sun happened to flash on their turning wings. Presently a shell burst close to one of the Japanese bombers; it flared against the blue like a struck match. Down in the road the rickshaw

coolies were delightedly clapping their hands. Then came the roar of another machine, hopelessly out of control; and suddenly, a white parachute mushroomed out over the river while the plane plunged on, down into the lake behind Wuchang.

Auden knew how to look at falling men. This anecdote has the smooth weariness of an accustomed action; you put on your sunglasses, for just as the sun may melt a pair of wax wings, it too can hurt your eyes. Lying on your back on a lawn is 'the best way of watching', he says, for other methods – standing, perhaps, over a plough – have been tried before. There is satisfaction here, in the after-lunch doze, on a sunny spring day, watching an air-show.

The falling boy continues, and so they look. On the night of 15 March 1938, Auden and Isherwood write: 'we climbed to the roof of one of Hankow's tallest buildings.' They are excited; they wait, and then:

> far off, the hollow, approaching roar of bombers, boring their way invisibly through the dark. The dull, punching thud of bombs falling, near the air-field, out in the suburbs. The searchlights crisscrossed, plotting points, like dividers; and suddenly there they were, six of them, flying close together and high up.

'The searchlights followed them right across the sky,' they write, and 'The concussions made you catch your breath; the watchers around us on the roof exclaimed softly, breathlessly: "Look! look! there!"' None could turn away. On 20 April, in the journal: 'I have moved my bed out on to the balcony so as to be able, at any rate, to watch the planes without getting up.'

We are not, quite yet, at the end of Icarus' story. 'Between 1958 and 1962 I produced perhaps three hundred drawings, fifteen bronzes, a group of reliefs in various media and a dozen or so paintings, all centred on that epic flight,' wrote the sculptor Michael Ayrton in a catalogue of his works. Ayrton served with the ground crews at RAF Feltwell during the second half of the war, and, although he never flew, his paintings and drawings return again and again to the falling boy. In 1962, as if simply seeing were not enough, he wrote a novella called *The Testament of Daedalus*, in which the narrating father refuses to close the story. 'I know my own repetitions and many of my names which come and go,' he begins, and 'Icarus, my son, bore different names at the time when men first fought each other in the sky. He has been multiplied and died in squadrons.' He is still with us, he writes, for now is the moment 'when Icarus leaped into the sky again and fought two wars, spilling death on whole cities'. Icarus is a bomber now, a pilot on Lancasters. At RAF Wickenby there is a memorial to the 'one thousand and eighty men of 12 & 126 squadrons who gave their lives on raids from this airfield', and above it a statue of Icarus falling to earth. Of course this should be their myth: the insignia of the RAF is a pair of artificial wings.

I don't know who Icarus is for you, but for me he is Acting Squadron Leader James Eric Swift of 83 Squadron, Bomber Command, who fell to the sea off the coast of Holland on the morning of 12 June 1943. He was returning from bombing Münster. His given name was James, but everybody called him Eric. But that is not quite true: for really, nobody calls him anything. When I was beginning to write this book, my father and I spoke of how we might refer to him, for he did not yet have a name. Names imply a role in the ever-shifting arrangements of a family – Daddy can become Grandpa, and titles like 'your aunt' or 'my brother-in-law' make sense only at certain times – and this man's family role ended on a summer day sixty-five years ago. As Ovid reminds us: Daedalus, 'the unhappy father', was at that moment 'no longer a father'.

I have above my desk two photographs of young men in soft-top sports cars, parked in the drive of my grandparents' house in Sussex. The first photograph was taken in the last year of my grandfather's life, because the man sitting in the car is wearing the shoulder flashes of a Squadron Leader, and my grandfather only reached that rank in July 1942. The car is a smooth and elegant relic of another age: an MG, in that particular shade of muddy resilient green known as British racing green, and its licence plate is XMX 545.

Although the photograph is black-and-white, and the licence plate is not visible, I know these details because my father remembers not only the colour but also, by some strange miracle of recall, the licence plate of a car he has not seen for sixty years. This is not only a photograph of a man in his sports car, for poised on the running board is a small boy in a duffel coat. The boy is my father, and he is three years old.

The boy in the first photograph is the man in the second, and here my father is sitting behind the wheel of a white Alfa Romeo Spider with red leather seats. The licence plate is 131 XPE, and my father is wearing a dark suit and tie. Because it is a sunny day and the roof is down, my father is wearing sunglasses.

If, as with the Brueghel paintings, we hold the two images side by side, they tell the story of a lost father. One figure is common to both, and one goes missing. But this is not what we see first when we look at these two photographs for, as in many families, my father is very like his father: the casual young man, in his suit and sunglasses and his Alfa Romeo, looks much more like the casual young man, in his uniform and his MG, than like the small boy in a duffel coat. Taken literally, it is the son who disappears, and the father remains.

This slight haze, where we can identify the machines but the men who sit in them are collapsing into one another, is not wholly an accident. For although the first photograph is black-and-white, we know the colour of the clothes: because this is an officer in the RAF, he is wearing a uniform the colour of which is blueish-grey, just a shade darker than that colour known as dove-grey. And although we have no whole record of this moment, we know what will happen to him in less than a year: he will fly, and then fall to the sea. As Jacopo Sannazaro wrote, almost 500 years ago:

> With such a fall may well he be content,
> If, soaring to the sky dove-like and brave,
> He with too fierce a flame was burnt and spent.

This dove-like man in his dove-grey suit is also Icarus. His name is Eric. The clothes may change – togas become robes, which are then a uniform, sunglasses – as may the machines – wings become airplanes, and later sports cars – but the gestures remain.

At the start of January 1939, Auden and Isherwood went to Southampton and boarded a boat to New York. Now they were passengers on 'the expensive delicate ship', and now they had 'somewhere to get to and sailed calmly on'. They arrived in America on 26 January, and Auden spent the war there, lecturing, teaching at colleges in the east. But he still wished to look at the war, and in May 1945 Auden joined the United States Strategic Bombing Survey as Research Chief for one of the teams of the Morale Unit. He went to Germany in the middle of May, to travel to six cities in Bavaria, interviewing German civilians on the effects of the bombing. He later joked: 'we asked them if they minded being bombed', but in his letters from this summer in Germany Auden stresses that he had gone to look for himself, and that seeing matters. On 20 May, from 'Somewhere in Germany', he wrote to his old friend Tania Stern, whose apartment he used to stay at in New York. 'The town outside which we live was 92% destroyed in 30 minutes,' he told her, and 'you can't imagine what that looks like unless you see it with your own eyes.' You must see this. At the start of June he wrote to Elizabeth Mayer. He was in Munich now, where she once lived. 'Most of the houses there are still standing, but the city as a whole is gone,' he said, and told her he was researching crime and the black markets during the war. 'Washington is going, I know, to say that the people we've interviewed have pulled the wool over our eyes,' he wrote, 'but it is not so.' He had been there and seen the cities in ruins, the broken places; in August, he returned to England.

Writing in the *Chicago Sun* in March 1942 Auden had discussed war poetry. He was, broadly, dismissive. 'As poetic experiences the incidents of war have nothing special about them,' he claimed, for 'as a rule war experiences are like any others; poets cannot use them until they have become thoroughly digested memories, and when they do finally enter their poetry, their war origin is often barely recognizable.' He waited four years to write his poem of the bombed cities. He had warned that by the time a poet came to treat war experience, the subject might no longer be recognizable, but in 'Memorial for the City', written in June 1949, it is all so clear:

> Across the square,
> Between the burnt-out Law Courts and Police Headquarters,
> Past the Cathedral far too damaged to repair,
> Around the Grand Hotel patched up to hold reporters,
> Near huts of some Emergency Committee,
> The barbed wire runs through the abolished City.

The city is never named, and the poem is reluctant with detail: this is an abstract Cathedral, an archetypal Grand Hotel, and it is, in the end, the only landscape of this war. The bombed city is war poetry.

The scene is rounded with sadness. 'On the right a village is burning, in a market-town to the left / The soldiers fire,' writes Auden in a catalogue of losses: 'The captives are led away, while far in the distance / A tanker sinks into a dedolant sea'. The hurt continues, and where before it was Icarus sinking now it is a tanker; as before, the poet turns from the facts of the moment to the ongoing fall:

> That is the way things happen; for ever and ever
> Plum-blossom falls on the dead, the roar of the waterfall covers

Epilogue: Icarus

> The cries of the whipped and the sighs of the lovers
> And the hard bright light composes
> A meaningless moment into an eternal fact.

In the place of a historical episode, Auden finds a repeated scene; and perhaps eternal patterns can be made to illuminate one man's story. For here, these single hurts – the burning village, the firing soldiers – are not muted by their participation in the ongoing saga of plum-blossom and waterfall, but given resonance. The poem teaches a terrible lesson: 'that is the way things happen', and everything except the gesture fades. In the hard bright light, you put on your sunglasses, and look.

NOTES

My understanding of the bombing war and its relation to poetry has been particularly shaped by three very different books: W. G. Sebald's *On the Natural History of Destruction*, Paul Fussell's *The Great War and Modern Memory* and the four-volume account *The Strategic Air Offensive against Germany, 1939–1945* by Sir Charles Webster and Noble Frankland.

Prologue: A Refusal to Mourn

The title is borrowed from Dylan Thomas's 'A Refusal to Mourn the Death, by Fire, of a Child in London'. For the daily losses of bombers, downed in Holland and the North Sea, I have consulted *The Bomber Command War Diaries: An Operational Reference book, 1939–45* by Martin Middlebrook and Chris Everitt, and the relevant volumes of W. R. Chorley's *Royal Air Force Bomber Command Losses of the Second World War*. The website www.lostbombers.co.uk provides a carefully indexed and searchable version of the information given in Chorley, Middlebrook and Everitt. Sir Frederic Kenyon explains the intentions of the Commonwealth War Graves in *War Graves: How the Cemeteries Abroad will be Designed*, and John Calvin discusses the expectations of mourners in his *Sermons upon the Book of Job*, translated by Arthur Golding.

For Dylan Thomas's movements and reactions during the Blitz I have relied upon Paul Ferris's biography, Gwen Watkins's *Portrait of a Friend* and Thomas's own 'Reminiscences of Childhood' in *On the Air with Dylan Thomas: The Broadcasts*, edited by Ralph Maud. Along with the poems, Thomas's letters – edited by Paul Ferris – give an intimate sense of the poet's heckling, seductive voice and his fantasies of being bombed, his 'burning birdman dreams'. It was in the *Listener* of 11 January 1940 that E. M. Forster advised: '1939 was not a year in which to start a literary career.'

1. Five Minutes after the Air Raid

The title and point of departure for this chapter follow Miroslav Holub's poem 'Five Minutes after the Air Raid', which is collected in *The Faber Book of Modern European Poetry*, edited by A. Alvarez. 'This was the place / the world ended,' writes Holub of one bombed house, but many were struck by that which continued in the moments after bombing.

My very great debt to Virginia Woolf's haunted and articulate diaries and letters should be evident, and I have also relied upon Hermione Lee's exemplary literary biography (for example, for the type of coat Woolf was wearing at her death). Woolf was not alone in finding continuity in the ruins. Like Woolf, the poet Louis MacNeice recorded being hungry in the aftermath of an air raid: in his autobiography *The Strings are False* he writes of eating salami in the Ritz in Barcelona on New Year's Eve 1938 in the minutes after bombs had fallen around him. And like Woolf, Mac-Neice was filled with a curious elation in the rubble of London: in early May 1941 he wrote an essay on 'The Morning after the Blitz' for the American *Picture Post* in which he recalled 'a voice inside me' during an air raid which insisted to him: 'Let her come down. Let them all go. Write them all off.'

For the literary culture of wartime London, I have borrowed details and atmosphere from many studies and memoirs, most notably Robert Hewison's *Under Siege: Literary Life in London, 1939–45* and the reports for the *New Yorker* written by Mollie Panter-Downes and collected in her *London War Notes*. The Mass-Observation archive in the Department of Special Collections at Sussex University is an extravagantly rich source for the social history of mid-century Britain, and I am deeply indebted to the nameless researchers employed by MO whose findings and questionnaires fill the file called 'Poetry 1939–40'.

My readings of the works of Wilfred Owen and of the poetry of the Second World War have been profoundly influenced by Ian Hamilton, whose literary criticism is as subtle as any written in the second half of the twentieth century. Hamilton writes directly of Owen, Sir John Betjeman, and Keith Douglas in *Against Oblivion*; his anthology *The Poetry of War 1939–1945* includes the poems by Donald Bain, Robert Conquest, Richard Eberhart, Sidney Keyes and Stevie Smith. Cecil Day Lewis's 'Where are the War Poets?' was first published in *Word Over All* in 1943; Emanuel Litvinoff's 'See the Wasted Cities!' is included in *Poems of This War by Younger Poets*, edited by Patricia Ledward and Colin Strang; Vernon Scannell's distinction between the poetry of the first and second wars is made in the introduction to his collection of essays *Not Without Glory: Poets of the Second World War*. T. S. Eliot's 'Note on War Poetry' was composed for a collection called *London Calling*, and Emily Dickinson is here quoted from her poem 'Crumbling is Not an Instant's Act'. Robert Graves's misguided radio talk on the absence of war poets was published in the *Listener* on 23 October 1941.

For Cecil Day Lewis, I have used Peter Stanford's thorough biography; for Wilfred Owen, the biography by Jon Stallworthy. As in the case of Dylan Thomas and so many of the poets included in this book, I have for Owen found letters by the poet to be a powerful and subversive supplement to the conventional biographical narrative: letters tell a different story of a life, one defined by wayward loops as much as forward progress, one intrigued by that left unachieved.

For the narrative of my grandfather's raids, I have here and throughout drawn upon the Operations Record Books for various squadrons in Bomber Command. The Operations Record Books are available on microfilm in the National Archives at Kew, and they detail with admirable economy the extraordinary heroisms of the strategic bombing campaigns. They are, like the finest poetry, most moving when most precise, and nothing I have written here would be possible without their record. For the absence of a specific campaign medal, and the larger sense of being left out shared by all the bombers, I have begun with the sensitive discussions in Max Hastings's *Bomber Command* and Patrick Bishop's *Bomber Boys*, but this is only a beginning. It is impossible to spend time with the veterans of Bomber Command without encountering this particular sadness; often, in my interviews, this was our only topic of conversation.

2. It was Not Dying

The title comes from Randall Jarrell's great poem 'Losses'. Jarrell is a moving figure, so captivating in his writing and in the memories of his contemporaries – after his death, Hannah Arendt recalled that when he entered an apartment, 'the household became bewitched' – and yet also sometimes so awkward, so wishful. I have been led, in my sense of him, by a range of writings: his letters, edited by Mary Jarrell, and her tender memoir of him, called *Remembering Randall*; a collection of essays and reminiscences edited by Robert Lowell, Peter Taylor and Robert Penn Warren which was published shortly after his death; Jarrell's own criticism and literary journalism, collected by himself during his life and by Brad Leithauser after his death; his notebooks and rough drafts, in his carefully spaced handwriting, now kept in the Berg Collection at the New York Public Library. The sound recording from Pfeiffer College – 'Randall Jarrell reads and discusses his poems against war' – was a particular help in showing me the humour and deliberate awkwardness of his war poems. Two of Jarrell's lesser-known works clarified for me the imaginative distancing I find so striking in his war poetry. The first is his obituary of the war correspondent Ernie Pyle, which was published in *The Nation* on 19 May 1945, and the second is the children's book *The Bat-Poet*, which is about a bat who cannot sleep during the day so composes verse to explain all that he sees to the other bats. In these two works, Jarrell confronts directly his own desire to write like something else.

The photograph I describe in the first paragraph is from the files of 11 Operational Training Unit at RAF Bassingbourn: National Archives reference AIR 29/644. The syllabi and Operations Record Books for 5 ITW and RAF Kidlington are, like this photograph, in the National Archives at Kew. For further details about flying training I have relied also upon the logbooks and memoirs of other pilots: particularly the pilot's flying log of Squadron Leader Hedley George Hazelden, which is now in the archive of the RAF Museum at Hendon, and the memoirs of Denis Hornsey, DFC, now in the collection of the Imperial War Museum.

3. B is for BOMBERS

For the experience of operational flying I am heavily indebted to the interviews collected in the sound-recording archive of the Imperial War
Museum and the logbooks and letters of airmen kept in the RAF archive
at Hendon. The Interceptions and Tactics Reports for specific raids are
part of the Air Ministry archive now in the National Archives. The Butt
Report of August 1941 and the directives I have quoted here are reprinted
in volume IV of Webster and Frankland's *Strategic Air Offensive against
Germany*. In their letters, airmen rarely give details of raids; they more
often recount their meals and the weather, and often these are quite literally love letters. One letter from an airman at RAF Feltwell to his brother-
in-law in October 1939 struck me particularly for all it did not say. He was
writing to ask advice, for he had met a girl, and taken her to a dance on the
base; he feared, however, that she was too popular among the other pilots
and that his father would disapprove. Although I have not quoted it here,
his particular worry suggests much for me about how the bombers parti-
tioned their lives. Lord Moran's *Anatomy of Courage* greatly helped me to
understand the apartness of the bombers, and Richard Lovell's *Churchill's
Doctor: A Biography of Lord Moran* helped me to understand Lord Moran.

The *Kriegschronik* of Dr Franz Weimers, the local newspapers, the police
reports and the times of air raid warnings are all in the Stadtarchiv Münster. For additional information on the raids, I have used *Bomben auf Münster*, the catalogue of an exhibition at the Stadtmuseum in 1983, Willi
Riegert's *Heimat unter Bomben* (2003) and Karl Reddemann's *Zwischen
Front und Heimat* (1966). The chronicle of the Church of St Aegidius, kept
by Father Paul Roosen and now in the Bistumarchiv in Münster, gave me
an intimate sense of the air raids and their compensations.

The title of this chapter comes from John Ciardi's *Alphabestiary*. In a
review of Ciardi's collection *Other Skies*, Randall Jarrell complained that 'It
is extremely disappointing that a B-29 gunner shouldn't get more of the
feel of what happened to him into what he writes', but I have found Ciardi's war poems, translation of Dante, and the diary published as *Saipan* to

be densely stuffed with the echoes of his bombing career. This chapter has greatly benefited from Edward Cifelli's insightful and precise biography of the poet.

4. England and Nowhere

For my description of RAF Bassingbourn in 1942, I have as elsewhere drawn upon the Operations Record Book and the tower log for 11 OTU. The holiday camp atmosphere suggested by the letters of Sergeant Francis Robert Edwin McCarthy, now in the RAF archive at Hendon, is confirmed in photographs and other diaries in the same archive, and in the Air Ministry reports now held at Kew.

Two particular files have helped me understand both the psychological strain of operational flying and the assumptions behind English psychological analysis in the early 1940s. These are 'Work and Problems of an RAF Neuropsychiatric Centre' by Dr. E. C. O. Jewkesbury, which was submitted to the Air Ministry in July 1943, and *Psychological Disorders in Flying Personnel of the Royal Air Force*, which was published by HMSO in 1947; both are now in the Air Ministry archive at Kew. On the role of science fiction and popular fantasy in the development of bombing strategy and doctrine, I have greatly benefited from the sensitive, insightful readings given in Tami Davis Biddle's *Rhetoric and Reality in Air Warfare*; Azar Gat's *Fascist and Liberal Visions of War*; Lee Kennett's *A History of Strategic Bombing*; and Sven Lindqvist's *A History of Bombing*. Solly Zuckerman's memoir *From Apes to Warlords* describes the formation and work of the Casualty Survey of the Bomb Census, and in an appendix reprints the key report of April 1942, 'Quantitative Study of the Total Effects of Air Raids'. I regret reporting that the Stadt Köln Historisches Archiv, which housed the police reports which were so helpful in my descriptions of wartime Cologne, recently collapsed owing to underground building work in the city.

For the enigmatic figure of T. S. Eliot, I have gratefully followed the descriptions given in the letters of F. V. Morley, Emilio Cecchi and Desmond Mawkins in the Berg Collection at the New York Public Library; in the letters and diaries of Virginia Woolf, particularly her shifting similes; in the reminiscences of William Turner Levy in *Affectionately, T. S. Eliot* and George Seferis in the *Quarterly Review of Literature*, 15 (1967); and in biographies by Ronald Bush, Lyndall Gordon and particularly Peter Ackroyd. Eliot's reading of *Four Quartets* was issued by Angel Records in 1957. I am deeply indebted to Helen Gardner's rich critical study *The Composition of Four Quartets*. The Berg Collection also holds Sylvia Plath's personal copy of *Four Quartets*; although I have not quoted from her extensive annotations here, they clarified for me the poem's struggle between two worlds and two kinds of poetry.

The instructions to fire-watchers are in the Mass-Observation archive at Sussex University. As I have suggested here, war poetry begins with the *Iliad*, and my reading of the *Iliad* – both in this chapter and elsewhere in the book – has been greatly deepened by Simone Weil's charismatic, moving essay 'The Iliad, or the Poem of Force', which is reprinted in *War and the Iliad*.

5. The Most Beautiful City in the World

The title is a quotation from Stephen Spender's *September Journal*, but my sense of the aesthetic appreciation of the bombed city common among artists and writers arises from a range of sources: the reports on London by Ernie Pyle, Janet Flanner and Edward R. Murrow which are now collected in Samuel Hynes's *Reporting World War II*; Rebecca West's journalism for the *New Yorker*, and Alan Moorehead's memoir of the last year of the war, published as *Eclipse*; A. Alvarez's study *Night*, and the sketches of bombed London by Graham Sutherland, Negley Farson, Henry Moore and Edward Ardizzone; the speeches of Winston Churchill; and Cecil Beaton's diaries and his photographs published in *History Under Fire* and *Winged Squadrons*. Although I have not quoted him here, Graham Greene was like all of these captivated by the spectacle of London under the bombs, and his novel *The End of the Affair*, published in 1951, considers deeply the emotional landscape of the ruined city. In Greene's telling, air raid sirens provide the cover which allows the lovers to meet.

London's Natural History by R. S. Fitter transformed my understanding of the impact of bombing. The many volumes of the United States Strategic Bombing Survey have been a very helpful source; in particular, for this chapter, I have drawn upon report #33, 'A Detailed Study of the Effects of Area Bombing on Wuppertal'; #41, 'Cologne Field Report'; #64b, 'The Effects of Strategic Bombing on German Morale'; #65, 'The Effect of Bombing on Health and Medical Care in Germany'; and #154, 'Public Air Raid Shelters in Germany'. I have benefited also from Steven Agoratus's article 'Clark Gable in the Eighth Air Force', published in *Air Power History* in spring 1999, and from Warren G. Harris's biography of Gable.

In addition to Spender's poems, memoirs and criticism, I have relied upon John Sutherland's sympathetic and thorough biography.

6. The Sadness of Soldiers

Leo McKinstry's definitive *Lancaster: The Second World War's Greatest Bomber* was published just as I was finishing this book, and I have consulted it alongside studies by Peter Jacobs and Bill Sweetman. For Don Bennett and the Pathfinder Force, I have relied upon John Maynard's *Bennett and the Pathfinders* and Bennett's memoir *Pathfinder*. My sense of Bennett was greatly helped by the interview with him preserved in the sound archive of the Imperial War Museum.

The debate over the criminality of the strategic bombing offensive has generated many books and studies. I would like here to record my particular debt to Jörg Friedrich's *The Fire*, A. C. Grayling's *Among the Dead Cities*, Richard Overy's *Why the Allies Won*, Adam Tooze's *The Wages of Destruction* and Michael Walzer's *Just and Unjust Wars*, each of which shaped my understanding from a different perspective. Thomas Nagel's 'War and Massacre', published in *Philosophy and Public Affairs* in winter 1972, clarified for me the moral – as distinct from legal – dimensions of the debate. In Finland, at the end of August 1940, Bertolt Brecht noted in his journal that where ancient Greek epigrams often celebrate weapons, 'in our day it is to a great extent moral scruples that prevent the rise of a comparable poetry of objects. The beauty of an aeroplane has something obscene about it.' In this chapter, I wish to answer Brecht by suggesting it is precisely the troubled morals of bombing war – the 'something obscene' about planes – that provoke poetry.

My reading of the poetry and life of James Dickey was inspired by Henry Hart's fine biography *James Dickey: The World as a Lie*. The criticism by Robert Bly, and that published in *Salmagundi*, of 'The Firebombing', sharpened my sense of Dickey's slippery self-presentation. Alongside the poetry, Dickey's journals and essays published in *Sorties* and *Self-Interviews* were particularly helpful. Although I have not discussed it here, Dickey's novel *To the White Sea* reconsiders much of the material of 'The Firebombing', and like the poem imagines the moral consequences of witnessing the bombing.

7. Bomber Poets

The papers of Frank Blackman, John Riley Byrne and Michael Scott are held in the Imperial War Museum; as should be evident from this chapter, the writings of these three bomber poets greatly enriched my thinking on the uses of poetry in wartime, and on the larger issue of the relation between poetry and bombing. Here, as in each chapter, I have relied upon the Operations Record Books for their respective squadrons to complete the picture of their wars.

The ORBs suggest the terrible waiting which dominated life on base, but my understanding of the emotional and psychological impact of delay has been greatly helped by Martha Gellhorn's deceptively simple story 'The Bomber Boys', published in *The Face of War*. In thinking about the return of the bomber and its possibility as a narrative device, I have relied heavily upon Powell and Pressburger's curious and elegant film *A Matter of Life and Death*. The heartbreaking papers of the Reverend G. H. Martin are in the Imperial War Museum.

Epilogue: Icarus

For Auden's visits to Brussels and the United States, I have relied upon biographies of the poet by Humphrey Carpenter, Richard Davenport-Hines and Edward Mendelson. For Auden's reaction to Brueghel's painting,

I have been helped by Alexander Nemerov's essay 'The Flight of Form: Auden, Bruegel, and the Turn to Abstraction in the 1940s', published in *Critical Inquiry* volume 31, number 4, and Arthur F. Kinney's 'Auden, Bruegel, and "Musée des Beaux Arts"', published in *College English* in April 1963. For the transformations of Icarus, I am indebted to Karl Kilinski's *The Flight of Icarus through Western Art*. Auden's letters to Tania Stern and Elizabeth Mayer are in the Berg Collection of the New York Public Library.

This has been a study of the poetry of a particular historical episode: the strategic bombing campaigns of the Second World War. Although my grandfather did not live to know it, the Allies won his war, and they did so in part through bombing. With the bombing of Hiroshima and Nagasaki in August 1945, the war ended, and area bombing of the type practised by Bomber Command and the Eighth Air Force was made anachronistic as a military strategy.

I have argued here, however, for a special kinship between poetry and bombing, and this does not so simply finish. In 1967 James Tate published a collection called *The Lost Pilot*, and the title poem from this volume marks the loss of Tate's own father, a bomber pilot with the Eighth Air Force who was killed in operations over Germany. Tate was five months old when his father was lost, but in the poem he imagines the power to conjure back this lost bomber. 'If I could cajole / you to come back for an evening,/ down from your compulsive / orbiting,' he writes: 'I would touch you.'

Fatherless, Tate finds himself incomplete. 'I feel as if I were / the residue of a stranger's life,' he confesses, 'that I should pursue you.' This is a poem moved by distance, between the orbiting father and the ground-locked son, and it does not entirely wish that distance away. 'I would not try / to fully understand what / it means to you,' Tate promises, for in knowing the bombers we might discover something hard, unwelcome; we might be hurt. The force of this poem lies in this ambivalence. It is strung taut by the poet's haunted desire to keep something hidden, and Tate ends by imagining his father 'passing over again / fast, perfect, and unwilling'. The poet's desire demands the pilot's absence. If all we want is poetry, then it is better for the pilot to circuit at a remove.

ACKNOWLEDGEMENTS

My first debt is to those who remember the war and agreed to speak to me of it, at the squadron reunions or in their homes, in the Netherlands, in England and in Germany. The following people shared with me their stories, made introductions, and helped with translations; without their grace and patience, this book would not have been possible.

In England, I would like to thank A. Alvarez, Sidney Culver, John Holmes, Tom Mackie and Doug Packman. I am deeply grateful to Gordon Lodge of the 57/630 Squadron Association. Chief Technician Johnny Clifford of the Pathfinder Force Museum at RAF Wyton kindly showed my father and me around his base and archive, and Major Geoff Woodcock invited me to spend the day at Bassingbourn and patiently answered my many questions. I owe very particular thanks to Alma Leedham and to Squadron Leader Tony Iveson, DFC, for their exceptional grace and courage. My greataunts Brenda Payne and Dorothy Richardson generously shared with me their memories of a painful family loss.

In the Netherlands, I am grateful to Jaap Wortman of the Dutch Air War Study Group, who introduced me to Hans Nauta. My debt to Hans, as should be evident from the final chapter of the book, goes beyond that which may be settled by a simple thank you. I wish to note here his extraordinary generosity and expertise as a researcher. I am deeply thankful to Captain Paul Petersen and all the members of the Royal Netherlands Air Force Salvage and Recovery Unit, with whom I spent a fascinating day at Woensdrecht Air Base and whose work I enormously admire.

In Germany, Lutz Enders, Hildegard Jacobs, and Gert and Ingrid von Rosenberg were each very generous with their time and assistance. In Cologne, I am particularly grateful to Vera Bening-hoven and Magdalena and Peter Boll. In Münster, Lily Giersiepen, the Reverend Werner Goez, Erika Krabbe and Monica Lüttecke invited me into their homes and shared with me their memories. I am deeply grateful to Annika Merk for her thoroughness and com-mitment.

The records of the bombing war are scattered through many countries, and I owe thanks to archivists and librarians across Europe and North America. I would like to thank specifically the staff and members of the Department of Personnel Records, Library and Archives Canada; the National Meteorological Library and Archive of the Met Office in Exeter; the National Archives in London; the Southampton and Waterside Branch of the WAAF Association; the Department of Research & Information Services at the RAF Museum, Hendon; the Imperial War Museum; the control tower museum at RAF Bassingbourn; the Bomber Command Associ-ation; the Harry Ransom Center at the University of Texas at Austin; the Stadt Köln Historisches Archiv; the Bistumarchiv Münster; and the Stadtarchiv Münster. I owe thanks also to my colleagues in the English Department of Skidmore College, and particularly to Linda Simon and Mason Stokes.

I have been blessed with the support and advice of my agent, David Godwin, and my editors Simon Prosser and Jonathan Galassi. I would like also to thank Sophie Hoult and Charlotte Knight at DGA, Anna Kelly at Hamish Hamilton and Jesse Coleman at FSG, each of whom has made pleasurable the practical business of delivering a book. I am profoundly grateful to the Jerwood Charit-able Foundation, who granted this project one of their Royal Society of Literature Jerwood awards for non-fiction, and to Paula Johnson and Anne Chisholm at the Royal Society of Literature. I would also like to thank Rosie Blau at the *Financial Times* and Mark Amory at the *Spectator* for sending me war-related books to review, and Anne Zahniser for the elegant map.

For their friendship and support in a variety of ways, I am deeply indebted to Turi Munthe and Muzia Sforza, Amanda Branson Gill, Martha Swift and Michael Heath, Katie Roiphe, Joshua van Praag, Camilla Swift, James Shapiro and my mother, Caroline Moorehead. My son, Leo Roiphe, was born a week after I finished the manuscript; it seems not quite right to thank him, yet, but nor would it be proper to leave him out. My father, Jeremy Swift, and I made the journeys described here together; he and I talked over each idea in the book, and it is dedicated to him.

SELECTED BIBLIOGRAPHY

My major sources for the details of operational flying among the squadrons of Bomber Command have been the Air Ministry files (AIR) covering the strategic offensive and the Operations Record Books for each squadron. Both are now kept in the National Archives at Kew.

Ackroyd, Peter. *London: The Biography*. London: Chatto & Windus, 2000

—, *T. S. Eliot: A Life*. New York: Simon & Schuster, 1984

Air Ministry. *Bomber Command*. London: HMSO, 1941

—, *Bomber Command Continues*. London: HMSO, 1942

—, *Duties of Air Raid Wardens*. London: HMSO, 1938

—, *Pilot's and Flight Engineer's Notes: Lancaster Mark I, III, X*. London: HMSO, 1944

—, *Psychological Disorders in Flying Personnel of the Royal Air Force*. London: HMSO, 1947

—, *Target: Germany*. London: HMSO, 1944

Alvarez, A. *The Faber Book of Modern European Poetry*. London: Faber and Faber, 1992

—, *Night*. London: Jonathan Cape, 1994

Auden, W. H. *Journey to a War*. London: Faber and Faber, 1939

—, *Selected Poems*. London: Faber and Faber, 1979

Ayrton, Michael. *Testament of Daedalus*. London: Methuen, 1962

Baedeker Guide. *Germany: A Handbook for Railway Travellers and Motorists*. Leipzig: Karl Baedeker, 1936

Beaton, Cecil. *Air of Glory: A Wartime Scrapbook*. London: HMSO, 1941

—, *History Under Fire*. London: B. T. Batsford, 1941

Beaton, Cecil. *Winged Squadrons*. London: Hutchinson, 1942

—, *The Years Between: Diaries 1939–44*. London: Weidenfeld & Nicolson, 1965

Bell, George. *The Church and Humanity*. London: Longman, 1946

Bennett, D. C. T. *Pathfinder*. London: Sphere, 1972

Bess, Michael. *Choices Under Fire: Moral Dimensions of World War II*. New York: Knopf, 2006

Biddle, Tami Davis. *Rhetoric and Reality in Air Warfare: The Evolution of British and American Ideas about Strategic Bombing, 1914–1945*. Princeton: Princeton University Press, 2004

Bishop, Patrick. *Bomber Boys: Fighting Back 1940–1945*. London: Harper Collins, 2007

Blackman, Frank H. Private papers. Imperial War Museum ref. 80/46/1

Byrne, John Riley. 'MS diary and scrapbook'. IWM 04/24/1

Chorley. W. R. *Royal Air Force Bomber Command Losses of the Second World War*. Hersham, Surrey: Ian Allan, 1995–8

Ciardi, John. *Dante Alighieri: The Inferno*. New Brunswick, NJ: Rutgers University Press, 1954

—, *Saipan*. Fayetteville: University of Arkansas Press, 1988

—, *Selected Poems*. Fayetteville: University of Arkansas Press, 1984

Cifelli, Edward M. *John Ciardi: A Biography*. Fayetteville: University of Arkansas Press, 1997

Crane, Conrad C. *Bombs, Cities, and Civilians: American Airpower Strategy in World War II*. Lawrence: University Press of Kansas, 1993

Day Lewis, Cecil. *A Time to Dance*. London: Hogarth Press, 1935

—, *Georgics of Virgil*. London: Jonathan Cape, 1940

—, *Overtures to Death and Other Poems*. London: Jonathan Cape, 1938

—, *Poems in Wartime*. London: Jonathan Cape, 1940

—, *Word Over All*. London: Jonathan Cape, 1943

Deighton, Len. *Bomber*. New York: Harper & Row, 1970

Dickey, James. *Buckdancer's Choice*. Middletown, Conn.: Wesleyan University Press, 1965

—, *Self-Interviews*. New York: Doubleday, 1970

—, *Sorties*. New York: Doubleday, 1971

—, *The Whole Motion: Collected Poems 1945–1992*. Middletown, Conn.: Wesleyan University Press, 1992

Eliot, T. S. *Collected Poems 1909–1962*. London: Faber and Faber, 1974

—, 'Notes towards a Definition of Culture'. *New English Weekly*, 21 January 1943

—, *Old Possum's Book of Practical Cats*. London: Faber and Faber, 1939

Falconer, Jonathan. *The Bomber Command Handbook, 1939–1945*. Stroud: Sutton, 1998

Farson, Negley. *Bomber's Moon*. New York: Harcourt, Brace and Company, 1941

Ferris, Paul. *Dylan Thomas: The Biography*. Washington, DC: Counterpoint, 2000

Fitter, R. S. *London's Natural History*. London: Collins, 1945

Friedrich, Jörg. *The Fire: The Bombing of Germany, 1940–1945*. New York: Columbia University Press, 2006

Fussell, Paul. *The Great War and Modern Memory*. Oxford: Oxford University Press, 1975

—, *Wartime: Understanding and Behavior in the Second World War*. New York: Oxford University Press, 1989

Gardner, Brian. *The Terrible Rain: The War Poets 1939–1945*. London: Methuen, 1981

Gardner, Helen. *The Composition of Four Quartets*. New York: Oxford University Press, 1978

Gat, Azar. *Fascist and Liberal Visions of War: Fuller, Liddell Hart, Douhet, and Other Modernists*. Oxford: Clarendon Press, 1998

Gellhorn, Martha. *The Face of War*. London: Virago, 1986

Grayling, A. C. *Among the Dead Cities: The History and Moral Legacy of the WWII Bombing of Civilians in Germany and Japan*. New York: Walker & Company, 2006

Hamilton, Ian. *Against Oblivion*. London: Viking, 2002

—, *The Poetry of War 1939–45*. London: Alan Ross, 1965

Hansard. *The Official Report, House of Commons (5th Series)*. London: HMSO, 1909–81

Harrisson, Tom. *Living through the Blitz*. London: Collins, 1976

Hart, Henry. *James Dickey: The World as a Lie*. New York: Picador, 2000

Hastings, Max. *Bomber Command*. New York: The Dial Press, 1979

Hewison, Robert. *Under Siege: Literary Life in London, 1939–45*. London: Weidenfeld & Nicolson, 1977

Homer. *The Iliad*, translated by Robert Fitzgerald. New York: Farrar, Straus and Giroux, 2004

Hubble, Nick. *Mass-Observation and Everyday Life*. New York: Palgrave Macmillan, 2006

Hynes, Samuel. *Reporting World War II: American Journalism 1938–1945*. New York: Library of America, 2001

Jarrell, Randall. *Complete Poems*. New York: Farrar, Straus and Giroux, 1969

—, *Letters*. Boston: Houghton Mifflin Company, 1985

—, *Losses*. New York: Harcourt, Brace and Company, 1948

—, 'Randall Jarrell reads and discusses his poems against war' (sound recording). New York: Caedmon, 1972

Keegan, John. *A History of Warfare*. London: Hutchinson, 1993

Kennett, Lee. *A History of Strategic Bombing*. New York: Scribner, 1982

Kenyon, Sir Frederic. *War Graves: How the Cemeteries Abroad will be Designed*. London: HMSO, 1918

Kilinski, Karl. *The Flight of Icarus through Western Art*. Lewiston, NY; Edwin Mellen Press, 2002

Ledward, Patricia and Colin Strang, *Poems of This War by Younger Poets*. Cambridge: Cambridge University Press, 1943

Levy, William Turner. *Affectionately, T. S. Eliot: The Story of a Friendship: 1947–1965*. Philadelphia: J. B. Lippincott, 1968

Lindqvist, Sven. *A History of Bombing*. New York: The New Press, 2001

Lochner, Louis. *Goebbels' Diaries*. London: Hamish Hamilton, 1948

Longmate, Norman. *The Bombers: The RAF Offensive against Germany, 1939–1945*. London: Hutchinson, 1983

Lowell, Robert, Peter Taylor and Robert Penn Warren. *Randall Jarrell 1914–1965*. New York: Farrar, Straus and Giroux, 1967

MacNeice, Louis. *Collected Poems 1925–1948*. London: Faber and Faber, 1949

—, *The Strings are False: An Unfinished Autobiography*. London: Faber and Faber, 1982

Martin, Reverend G. H. Papers. IWM 93/48/1–2

Mass-Observation. *War Begins at Home by Mass-Observation*. London: Chatto & Windus, 1940

Maud, Ralph. *On the Air with Dylan Thomas: The Broadcasts*. New York: New Directions, 1992

Maynard, John. *Bennett and the Pathfinders*. London: Arms & Armour, 1996

McKinstry, Leo. *Lancaster: The Second World War's Greatest Bomber*. London: John Murray, 2009

Miller, Donald L. *Eighth Air Force*. New York: Simon & Schuster, 2007

Ministry of Economic Works. 'The Bomber's Baedeker'. NA AIR 14/2662

Moorehead, Alan. *Eclipse*. London: Hamish Hamilton, 1945

Moran, Lord Charles. *The Anatomy of Courage*. London: Constable, 1945

Nossack, Hans Erich. *The End: Hamburg 1943*. Chicago: University of Chicago Press, 2004

Nuland, Sherwin. *How We Die*. London: Vintage, 1997

Overy, Richard. *Why the Allies Won*. New York: W. W. Norton & Company, 1995

Owen, Wilfred. *Collected Letters*. Oxford: Oxford University Press, 1967

—, *Collected Poems*. New York: New Directions, 1964

—, *Poems*. London: Faber and Faber, 2004

Owen, Wilfred, *Poems of Wilfred Owen*. New York: Viking Press, 1931

Panter-Downes, Mollie. *London War Notes 1939–1945*. London: Longman, 1972

Pitchfork, Graham. *Shot Down and in the Drink*. London: National Archives, 2007

—, *Shot Down and on the Run*. London: National Archives, 2007

Propp, Vladimir. *Morphology of the Folk Tale*. Austin: University of Texas Press, 1977

Pudney, John and Henry Treece. *Air Force Poetry*. London: Bodley Head, 1944

Richards, J. M. *The Bombed Buildings of Britain*. London: The Architectural Press, 1947

Sebald, W. G. *On the Natural History of Destruction*. New York: Random House, 2003

Shapiro, Harvey. *Poets of World War II*. New York: Library of America, 2003

Sontag, Susan. *Regarding the Pain of Others*. New York: Picador, 2003

Spender, Stephen. *Collected Poems 1928–1953*. London: Faber and Faber, 1960

—, *European Witness*. London: Hamish Hamilton, 1946

—, *World Within World*. London: Hamish Hamilton, 1951

Stallworthy, Jon. *Louis MacNeice*. London: Faber and Faber, 1995

—, *Wilfred Owen*. Oxford: Oxford University Press, 1974

Stanford, Peter. *C. Day Lewis: A Life*. London: Continuum, 2007

Sutherland, John. *Stephen Spender: A Literary Life*. New York: Oxford University Press, 2005

Taylor, Eric. *Operation Millennium: Bomber Harris' Raid on Cologne, May 1942*. London: R. Hale, 1987

Taylor, Fred. *Dresden: Tuesday, 13 February 1945*. London: Bloomsbury, 2004

Terkel, Studs. *The Good War: An Oral History of World War Two*. New York: Pantheon Books, 1984

Terraine, John. *The Right of the Line: The Royal Air Force in the European War, 1939–1945*. London: Hodder & Stoughton, 1985

Thomas, Dylan. *Collected Letters*. London: Dent, 2000

—, *Collected Poems*. London: Dent, 1988

Tooze, Adam. *The Wages of Destruction: The Making and Breaking of the Nazi Economy*. New York: Viking, 2007

United States Strategic Bombing Survey. *The Effects of Strategic Bombing on the German War Economy*. Washington, DC, 1945

—, *Summary Report*. Washington, DC, 1945

Virgil. *The Aeneid*, translated by David West. London: Penguin Classics, 1990

Waller, Maureen. *London 1945: Life in the Debris of War*. London: John Murray, 2004

Walzer, Michael. *Just and Unjust Wars: A Moral Argument with Historical Illustrations*. New York: Basic Books, 1977

Watkins, Gwen. *Portrait of a Friend*. Llandysul, Dyfed: Gomer Press, 1983

Webster, Sir Charles and Noble Frankland. *The Strategic Air Offensive against Germany, 1939–1945*. Uckfield, Sussex: The Naval & Military Press, 2006

Weil, Simone. 'The Iliad, or the Poem of Force'. *War and the Iliad*. New York: New York Review Books, 2005

Weimers, Dr Franz. *Kriegschronik*. Stadtarchiv Münster Amt 43 E 33

Woolf, Virginia. *Between the Acts*. New York: Harcourt, Brace and Company, 1941

—, *The Diary of Virginia Woolf*. London: Hogarth Press, 1977–84

—, *The Letters of Virginia Woolf*. London: Hogarth Press, 1975–80

Zuckerman, Solly. *From Apes to Warlords*. London: Hamish Hamilton, 1978

PERMISSIONS

'Musée des Beaux Arts', from *Collected Poems* by W. H. Auden, reprinted by permission of Faber and Faber Ltd. The papers of Flying Officer Frank Blackman, by kind permission of Mr Philip Mileham. The papers of Sergeant John Riley Byrne, by kind permission of Mr John Johnson. Excerpts from 'The Firebombing', taken from *The Whole Motion: Collected Poems, 1945–92* by James Dickey, copyright © James Dickey, 1992. Reprinted by permission of Wesleyan University Press. Excerpts from 'Little Gidding', from *Collected Poems, 1909–1962* by T. S. Eliot, reprinted by permission of Faber and Faber Ltd. Excerpts from 'Eighth Air Force', 'The Death of the Ball Turret Gunner', 'Losses', 'Second Air Force' and 'The Lines', taken from *The Complete Poems* by Randall Jarrell, copyright © 1969, renewed 1997 by Mary von S. Jarrell. Reprinted by permission of Farrar, Straus and Giroux, LLC. Excerpts from *The Collected Letters of Wilfred Owen*, edited by Harold Owen and John Bell (1967), by permission of Oxford University Press. Excerpt from 'For Johnny' by John Pudney, reprinted by permission of the Estate of John Pudney. Excerpts from 'The Air Raid across the Bay', 'Thoughts during an Air Raid', 'Rejoice in the Abyss' and 'Responsibility: The Pilots Who Destroyed Germany, Spring 1945', taken from *New Collected Poems* by Stephen Spender, copyright © 2004. Reprinted by kind permission of the Estate of Stephen Spender. Excerpts from 'A Refusal to Mourn the Death, By Fire, of a Child in London', 'Among Those Killed in the Dawn Raid was a Man Aged a Hundred' and 'And Death Shall Have No Dominion', from *Collected Poems* by Dylan Thomas; and a letter to Vernon Watkins dated summer 1940, taken from *Collected Letters* by Dylan Thomas. Reprinted by permission of the Estate of Dylan Thomas.